Coursebook

Margaret O'Keeffe
Lewis Lansford
Ros Wright
Evan Frendo
Lizzie Wright

B1

Business
Partner

FT Publishing
FINANCIAL TIMES

GSE
Global Scale of English

Contents

Introduction for learners

Why ... Business Partner?

Our research talking to teachers and learners proved a few very obvious points.

1 People study business English in order to communicate more effectively in their workplace or to find a job in an international environment.

2 To achieve these goals, you need to improve your knowledge of English language as it is used in the workplace, but also develop key skills for the international workplace.

3 People studying business English have different priorities and amounts of study time. You therefore need a flexible course which you can adapt to suit your needs.

Business Partner has been developed to meet these needs by offering a flexible course, focused on delivering a balance of language and skills training that you can immediately use to improve your performance in your workplace, studies or job search.

Why ... skills training?

Language is only one aspect of successful communication. Effective communication also requires an understanding of different business situations and an awareness of different communication styles, especially when working across cultures.

In *Business Partner* we refer to 'Communication skills' and 'Business skills'. Every unit has a lesson on these two areas.

- 'Communication skills' (Lesson 3) means the soft skills you need to work effectively with people whose personality and culture may be different from your own. These include building rapport, responding to consumer concerns or dealing with interruptions.

- 'Business skills' (Lesson 4) means the practical skills you need in different business situations, such as skills for taking part in meetings, presentations and negotiations.

Why ... authentic content?

In order to reflect the real world as closely as possible, *Business Partner* content is based on authentic videos and articles from leading media organisations such as the BBC and the *Financial Times*. These offer a wealth of international business information as well as real examples of British, U.S. and non-native-speaker English.

Why ... video content?

We all use video more and more to communicate and to find out about the world. This is reflected in *Business Partner*, which has two videos in every unit:

- an authentic video package in Lesson 1, based on real-life video clips and interviews suitable for your level of English.

- a dramatised communication skills video in Lesson 3 (see p.6 for more information).

Why ... flexible content?

This course has been developed so that you can adapt it to your own needs. Each unit and lesson works independently, so you can focus on the topics, lessons or skills which are most relevant to you and skip those which don't feel relevant to your needs right now.

You can then use the extra activities and additional materials in MyEnglishLab to work in more depth on the aspects that are important to you.

What's in the units?

Lesson outcome and self-assessment

Each lesson starts with a lesson outcome and ends with a short Self-assessment section. The aim is to encourage you to think about the progress that you have made in relation to the lesson outcome. More detailed self-assessment tasks and suggestions for extra practice are available in MyEnglishLab.

Vocabulary

The main topic vocabulary set is presented and practised in Lesson 1 of each unit, building on vocabulary from the authentic video. You will get lots of opportunities to use the vocabulary in discussions and group tasks.

Functional language

Functional language (such as giving advice, summarising, dealing with objections) gives you the capability to operate in real workplace situations in English. Three functional language sets are presented and practised in every unit: in Lessons 3, 4 and 5. You will practise the language in group speaking and writing tasks.

 In MyEnglishLab you will also find a Functional language bank so that you can quickly refer to lists of useful language when preparing for a business situation, such as a meeting, presentation or interview.

Grammar

The approach to grammar is flexible depending on whether you want to devote a significant amount of time to grammar or to focus on the consolidation of grammar only when you need to.

- There is one main grammar point in each unit, presented and practised in Lesson 2.
- There is a link from Lesson 5 to an optional second grammar point in MyEnglishLab – with short video presentations and interactive practice.

Both grammar points are supported by the Grammar reference section at the back of the coursebook (p.118). This provides a summary of meaning and form, with notes on usage or exceptions, and business English examples.

Listening and video

The course offers a wide variety of listening activities (based on both video and audio recordings) to help you develop your comprehension skills and to hear target language in context. All of the video and audio material is available in MyEnglishLab and includes a range of British, U.S. and non-native-speaker English. Lessons 1 and 3 are based on video (as described above). In four of the eight units, Lesson 2 is based on audio. In all units, you also work with significant audio recordings in Lesson 4 and the Business workshop.

Reading

You will read authentic texts and articles from a variety of sources, particularly the *Financial Times*. Every unit has a main reading text with comprehension tasks. This appears either in Lesson 2 or in the Business workshop.

 In MyEnglishLab, you will also find a Reading bank which offers a longer reading text for every unit with comprehension activities.

Speaking

Collaborative speaking tasks appear at the end of Lessons 1, 3, 4 and the Business workshop in every unit. These tasks encourage you to use the target language and, where relevant, the target skill of the lesson. There are lots of opportunities to personalise these tasks to suit your own situation.

Writing

- Lesson 5 in every unit provides a model text and practice in a business writing skill. The course covers a wide range of genres such as reports, proposals, note-taking and emails, and for different purposes, including formal and informal communication, summarising, invitations, replies and project updates.
- There are also short writing tasks in Lesson 2 which provide controlled practice of the target grammar.
- In MyEnglishLab, you will find a Writing bank which provides models of different types of business writing and useful phrases appropriate to your level of English.

Pronunciation

Two pronunciation points are presented and practised in every unit. Pronunciation points are linked to the content of the unit – usually to a video/audio presentation or to a grammar point. The pronunciation presentations and activities are at the back of the coursebook (p.112), with signposts from the relevant lessons. This section also includes an introduction to pronunciation with British and U.S. phonetic charts.

Reviews

There is a one-page review for each unit at the back of the coursebook (p.104). The review recycles and revises the key vocabulary, grammar and functional language presented in the unit.

Signposts, cross-references and MyEnglishLab

T **Signposts for teachers** in each lesson indicate that there are extra activities in MyEnglishLab which can be printed or displayed on-screen. These activities can be used to extend a lesson or to focus in more depth on a particular section.

L **Signposts for learners** indicate that there are additional interactive activities in MyEnglishLab.

➔ page 000
Cross-references refer to the Pronunciation bank and Grammar reference pages.

MyEnglishLab

Access to *MyEnglishLab* is given through a code printed on the inside front cover of this book. Depending on the version of the course that you are using, you will have access to one of the following options:

Digital Resources powered by MyEnglishLab including: downloadable coursebook resources, all video clips, all audio recordings, Lesson 3 additional interactive video activities, Lesson 5 interactive grammar presentation and practice, Reading bank, Functional language bank, Writing bank and My Self-assessment.

Full content of MyEnglishLab: all of the above plus the full self-study interactive workbook with automatic gradebook. Teachers can assign workbook activities as homework.

The **Global Scale of English (GSE)** is a standardised, granular scale from 10 to 90 which measures English language proficiency. The GSE Learning Objectives for Professional English are aligned with the Common European Framework of Reference (CEFR). Unlike the CEFR, which describes proficiency in terms of broad levels, the Global Scale of English identifies what a learner can do at each point on a more granular scale – and within a CEFR level. The scale is designed to motivate learners by demonstrating incremental progress in their language ability. The Global Scale of English forms the backbone for Pearson English course material and assessment.

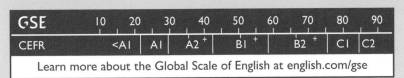

GSE	10	20	30	40	50	60	70	80	90
CEFR		<A1	A1	A2 +	B1 +	B2 +	C1	C2	

Learn more about the Global Scale of English at english.com/gse

COMMUNICATION SKILLS
Video introduction

Introduction

The Communication skills videos (in Lesson 3 of each unit) introduce you to the skills needed to interact successfully in international teams, with people who may have different communication styles due to culture or personality.

In each Communication skills lesson, you will:

1 watch a setup video which introduces the main characters and challenge of the lesson;

2 watch the main character approach the situation in two different ways (Options A and B);

3 answer questions about each approach before watching the conclusion.

There is a storyline running through the eight units, with the main characters appearing in different situations. Each clip, however, can be watched separately and each lesson done independently without the need to watch the preceding video clips.

Communication skills video storyline

Evromed is a small family-owned business with suppliers in China dealing in the pharmaceutical sector. The main market share is in Europe, but the company is expanding to other markets, including Brazil.

The team, headed by Daniel Smith, the Project Manager, is working on launching their latest product: the Diabsensor, which is a device for patients with diabetes.

In addition to the practical project challenges, the people in the team experience challenges as they learn to work with each other.

Characters

Daniel Smith (British), Project Manager (units: 1, 3, 5, 7, 8)

Beata Kowalska (Polish), Account Manager (all units)

Jessica Scott (British), CEO of Evromed (units 1 and 2)

Alex Clarke (British), Account Manager (units 1 and 4)

Mateo Santos (Brazilian), key customer in Brazil (units 4, 6, 7, 8

Clarice Wang (Chinese-British), key supplier from China (units 3 and 5)

 ## Video context by unit

1 **Building rapport**
Video synopsis: *Beata meets her colleagues at Evromed.*

2 **Induction meeting**
Video synopsis: *Beata has an induction meeting with the CEO to learn about the Diabsensor and the company.*

3 **Resolving a problem with a schedule change**
Video synopsis: *Beata and Clarice discuss a change to the schedule.*

4 **Managing conversations**
Video synopsis: *Beata meets Mateo, a key customer in Brazil, to discuss the Diabsensor.*

5 **Managing information**
Video synopsis: *Beata relates her meeting with Mateo to Daniel and Clarice.*

6 **Dealing with disagreement**
Video synopsis: *Beata has a meeting with Mateo about storage requirements for the Diabsensor.*

7 **Solving customer problems**
Video synopsis: *Beata and Daniel discuss Beata's meeting with Mateo. Afterwards they call Mateo to talk about his concerns.*

8 **Closing a deal**
Video synopsis: *Beata presents a possible solution to the storage problem.*

Career choices

> 'Be prepared to develop attributes that work across sectors so you can make the best moves for your career.'
>
> Ashley Hayward,
> Careers Advisor

Unit overview

1.1 >	**Transferable skills** **Lesson outcome:** Learners can use vocabulary related to skills and personal qualities.	**Video:** Transferable skills **Vocabulary:** Transferable skills **Project:** Writing a job description
1.2 >	**Careers advice** **Lesson outcome:** Learners can use a range of phrases for giving advice and making suggestions.	**Listening:** Careers advice programme **Grammar:** Advice and suggestions **Speaking:** Advising how to improve an online profile
1.3 >	**Communication skills:** Building rapport **Lesson outcome:** Learners are aware of simple ways to build rapport at first meetings and can use a range of appropriate questions.	**Video:** Building rapport **Functional language:** Asking questions to build rapport **Task:** Building rapport during a short conversation
1.4 >	**Business skills:** Networking **Lesson outcome:** Learners can use a range of expressions to start, close and show interest in simple, face-to-face conversations on familiar topics.	**Listening:** Advice on networking **Functional language:** Networking at a careers event **Task:** Meeting a recruiter at a careers event
1.5 >	**Writing:** Emails – Introducing yourself **Lesson outcome:** Learners can write an email introducing themselves to work colleagues.	**Model text:** Email introducing yourself **Functional language:** Formal and informal language **Grammar:** Adverbs of degree **Task:** Write an introduction email

Business workshop 1: p.88 | **Review 1:** p.104 | **Pronunciation:** 1.1 Word stress 1.2 Voice range p.114 | **Grammar reference:** p.118

1.1 ▶ Transferable skills

| Lesson outcome | Learners can use vocabulary related to skills and personal qualities. |

Lead-in

Life skills are abilities that are useful in daily tasks at home, work or in education.

1 Tick (✓) the three words or phrases that best describe you.

> calm   good with computers   good with numbers   good with people
> good at problem-solving   organised   reliable   resourceful

2 Work in pairs and compare your answers. Then discuss these questions.

1 Is there an expression in Exercise 1 that definitely *doesn't* describe you?

2 Which is a) the most important b) the least important life skill in the box? Why?

VIDEO

3A Work in pairs or groups. Discuss the question.

According to the video you're going to watch, employers want *skills that can be applied to a range of tasks and roles.* What skills do you think this means? Give examples.

B ▶ 1.1.1   Watch the video. Were any of your ideas mentioned?

4A Watch the video again. Answer the questions.

1 What skills and personal qualities do the speakers talk about? Add them to the list of skills you discussed in Exercise 3.

2 What five ways of communicating are mentioned in the video?

In person, ...

3 What are the three main pieces of advice the video gives?

B Work in pairs and compare your answers. Then think of two or three words to describe *unsuccessful* twenty-first-century workers.

5 Work in pairs or groups. Discuss these questions.

1 Choose one of the transferable skills or personal qualities you listed in Exercise 4A. Think of at least two different situations where it might be useful.

 Teacher's resources: extra activities

2 Which transferable skills are the most important in your current situation, either as a student or a professional? Are there any that aren't important?

Vocabulary

Transferable skills

6 What do these words and phrases from the video mean? Match them with the best situation (a–h).

You ...

1 can **think outside the box**.
2 have **a can-do attitude**.
3 can **set goals**.
4 use **critical thinking**.

You ...

5 have a lot of **determination**.
6 are a **team player**.
7 have **integrity**.
8 have good **communication skills**.

You ...

a decided to save money for a holiday a year in the future.

b did a difficult project without complaining.

c carefully checked information you found on the internet to make sure it was true.

d asked your teacher if you could make a short film instead of handing in an essay.

You ...

e found a wallet with a lot of money in it and returned it to the owner.

f took four tries to pass your driving test, but never gave up, and kept studying and practising.

g worked with a group of friends to start a weekend cycling club.

h spoke clearly when you gave a presentation and really listened to questions from the audience.

7 Complete the tables with the correct words.

Adjective	Noun
1 _____	adaptability
flexible	2 _____
3 _____	motivation
confident	4 _____
5 _____	dependability
resourceful	6 _____

Adjective	Noun
7 _____	independence
ambitious	8 _____
9 _____	passion
enthusiastic	10 _____
11 _____	honesty
authentic	12 _____

8 Work in pairs or small groups.

1 Think of three or four more transferable skills. Use your dictionary if necessary.

2 For each skill, think of a way that a student could develop or demonstrate the skill.

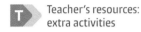

Teacher's resources: extra activities

➡ **page 114** See Pronunciation bank: Word stress

› PROJECT: Writing a job description

9 Look at the jobs below. Discuss how some of the transferable skills from Exercises 6 and 7 are necessary for each job.

> accountant   construction worker   factory worker   journalist   personal trainer
> politician   professional athlete   salesperson   teacher

10A Work in pairs. Think of a job: one from Exercise 9, one you know about or one you would like to do.

- Write down the name of the job, e.g. personal trainer, accountant, salesperson, etc.
- List 3–5 things the person needs to do, e.g. lead classes, take care of company money, meet customers, etc.
- Identify skills that the person needs to have to take care of the responsibilities you've listed. Use skills from Exercises 6 and 7, or your own ideas.

B Write a job description based on your research.

C Work with another pair and read each other's job description. Does your partner's description:

- list 3–5 things the person needs to do?
- identify skills that the person needs to have to take care of the responsibilities you've listed?

D Circle any skills or personal qualities that you think have been used incorrectly. Would you like to apply for the job? Why / Why not?

1.2 〉 Careers advice

Lesson outcome	Learners can use a range of phrases for giving advice and making suggestions.

Lead-in

1 Work in pairs or small groups. Discuss the questions.

1 Can you name three or four different social media platforms?
2 What role does social media play in finding a new job?
3 What information does an online profile on a professional networking site usually have?
4 Is there anything you should avoid putting in an online profile? What? Why?

2 Have you ever received any advice about your career? Talk about:
- who gave it to you.
- what he/she said.
- if the advice was useful in any way.

Listening

3 Work in pairs or small groups. Read the situation and answer the questions.

> A recent graduate has phoned a careers advice programme to ask how he can make his online profile more noticeable to employers.

1 What advice do you think he gets?   2 What advice would you give?

4 🔊 1.01 Listen to the programme. Were any of your ideas from Exercise 3 mentioned? What advice did the host give?

5 Listen to the programme again. Decide if these sentences are *true* (T) or *false* (F).
1 The caller has recently had a job interview.
2 He doesn't know how to make contacts in his industry.
3 The host doesn't recommend using professional networking sites.
4 The caller wants advice about how to improve his online profile.
5 The host asks the caller for specific examples that show his qualities.
6 The caller has experience in web design.
7 He has experience as an outdoor skills instructor.
8 He liked the host's advice.

6 How could you follow the host's advice? What activities do you do that show transferable skills?

I enjoy repairing my car. That show's that I'm good with my hands.

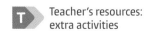
Teacher's resources: extra activities

Grammar **Advice and suggestions**

7A Complete the sentences from the programme using the words and phrases in the box.

could   How   ought   should   Why don't you   Why not try

1 _____ deleting everything you've written about yourself?
2 _____ take your description of yourself ... and for each word, think of an example from your own experience that *shows* who you are?
3 _____ about telling me about something creative that you've done?
4 You really _____ put that on your social media profile – you designed and built a website.
5 You _____ consider putting something about that on your profile.
6 You _____ to think outside the box.

B What three different verb forms are used after the expressions of advice or suggestion?

C **Choose the correct option in italics to complete the sentences.**

1 Why don't you *send / to send* an email to some companies?
2 How about *to set up / setting up* your own website?
3 You should *to research / research* the companies you're interested in.
4 Why not try *make / making* a video for YouTube?
5 You ought *to spend / spending* some time improving your online profile.
6 You could *think / to think* about meeting some people who work in the industry.
7 What about *asking / to ask* your teacher for some help?

➡ page 118 See Grammar reference: Advice and suggestions

8 **Correct the errors in these sentences.**

1 You shouldn't to use words that explain the obvious – like *hard-working*.
2 Why don't you trying giving more details about your IT skills?
3 Should you show your transferable skills rather than explaining them.
4 What about join some online groups to make more contacts?
5 Why not to try writing a blog about your experience?
6 You could doing some volunteer work, then add it to your profile.
7 How about to include more information about your hobbies?
8 You ought give some information about the languages you speak.

T Teacher's resources:
extra activities

Listening **9** ◀) 1.02 **Listen to the second programme. Answer the questions.**

1 Was the expert's advice in the first programme useful or not? How do we know?
2 What problem does the caller have now?

10A **Match the halves of the host's questions. Then listen again and check.**

1	What can I	a	what was your problem?
2	Can you remind me –	b	right?
3	Why don't you tell me	c	help you with today?
4	You're a recent graduate,	d	no kids?
5	And you're single –	e	which is more important: money or excitement?
6	Why not try asking yourself	f	about the two jobs?

B **Match the answers with questions 1–6 in Exercise 10A. Listen again and check.**

a One looks very interesting, but not very well paid. The other is probably a bit boring, but the money is good.
b We spoke a few weeks ago … and I still have a problem.
c That's the problem, Jenny – I really can't decide!
d My professional networking profile – it wasn't working.

e Yep, that's me.
f Yes, that's right.

11A **At the end of the recording, Jenny says *Let me ask you a few more questions*. Work in pairs and think of 3–5 more questions that Jenny might ask the caller.**

B **Work in pairs. Act out a continuation of the dialogue. Then present your dialogue to another group and compare ideas.**

➡ page 114 See Pronunciation bank: Voice range

Speaking **12** **Read the online profile and other information on page 126. With a partner, give advice to the person who wrote the profile, so he/she can improve it.**

13A **You are going to roleplay helping a friend set up a profile on a professional networking website. Student A: Turn to page 126. Student B: Turn to page 128.**

B **When you have finished, change partners and do the roleplay one more time.**

Self-assessment
- How successfully have you achieved the lesson outcome? Give yourself a score from 0 (I need more practice) to 5 (I know this well).
- Go to My Self-assessment in MyEnglishLab to reflect on what you have learnt.

1.3 > COMMUNICATION SKILLS
Building rapport

Lesson outcome	Learners are aware of simple ways to build rapport at first meetings and can use a range of appropriate questions.

Lead-in **1A** Read the definition of building rapport. Discuss how you can build rapport with someone you meet for the first time.

> Building rapport is about developing a shared understanding with another person or group of people that facilitates and improves communication.

B In small groups, think of two examples of spoken and non-verbal (body language) techniques for building rapport with new colleagues or students in your class.

spoken: asking questions, non-verbal: lean forward slightly (if sitting)

VIDEO **2** ▶ 1.3.1 Watch the video as Daniel and Alex prepare for the graduate trainees' induction meeting and answer the questions.

1 How does Daniel describe Beata?
2 What is Jessica looking for in an employee?
3 What do we learn about Alex?
4 What does Alex do to try to build rapport with Beata?

Go to MyEnglishLab for extra video activities.

3A In small groups, discuss which is the best approach (Option A or B) for Beata to take as she meets members of the team for the first time. As a class, decide which video to watch first.

Option A – Beata tries to build rapport by listening to her new colleagues.

Option B – Beata tries to build rapport by demonstrating her knowledge of the product and the company.

B Watch the videos in the sequence the class has decided and answer the same questions for each video.

Option A ▶ 1.3.2 1 How does Beata try to build rapport with Alex/Jessica?
Option B ▶ 1.3.3 2 Is she successful? Why / Why not?
3 What will be the long-term effect of this?

4 In pairs, discuss what you have learnt from the two options about building rapport.

5 ▶ 1.3.4 Watch the Conclusions section of the video and compare what the speaker says with your answers in Exercise 4. Note down the main learning points about building rapport.

Reflection **6** Reflect on how you build rapport when you meet someone for the first time. Then work in pairs and discuss these questions.

1 Which of the verbal techniques mentioned in Exercise 1B do you use in your language?
2 Which of the non-verbal techniques do you use?
3 Which of the techniques you have seen would you like to learn or start using? Which do you consider especially useful?

Functional language

Asking questions to build rapport

7A Complete this extract from the conversation between Alex and Beata using the phrases in the box.

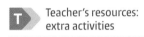

One way of building rapport is to try to find something in common with the other person, then use follow-up questions to continue building rapport.

> do you know   how long   what did you (x 2)   when were   where exactly

Alex: I hear you lived in Tokyo. [1]_____ did you live?

Beata: Suidobashi. [2]_____ it?

Alex: Ah, yes, near the baseball park. I lived there myself for a while. Loved it. [3]_____ were you in Japan for?

Beata: Five years. [4]_____ you in Tokyo?

Alex: 2013 to 2015. About eighteen months.

Beata: [5]_____ do there?

Alex: Teaching English, mainly.

Beata: Teaching. Interesting. [6]_____ like best about it?

Alex: Mainly the food!

B Match a question from Exercise 7A to each category, to ask about:

a duration   **b** likes   **c** location   **d** timing   **e** purpose

C Match the questions to the categories in Exercise 7B.

1 Which places did you visit?

2 What did you like about it?

3 How long did you stay?

4 So when did you go to Berlin?

5 What were you doing there?

6 Did you stay long?

7 What did you and your partner do while you were there?

8A Work in pairs and read the scenario below. Student A: Read the information on page 126. Student B: Read the information on page 128. Note down questions you can ask to build rapport with your partner.

Scenario

You attend a networking/birthday party and you start chatting to another colleague/guest. You introduce yourself. As you chat, you realise you have both been to Barcelona.

T Teacher's resources: extra activities

B Practise asking and answering the questions you noted down in Exercise 8A.

9A Work in small groups. Choose one of the situations below to practise building rapport.

>TASK

1 Your experience of learning English, in your home town or abroad.

2 A meeting, conference or other event that you attended at your place of work or study.

3 A city or country you have visited or lived in.

4 Your last holiday.

B Have a conversation for about two minutes and try to build rapport. Before you start, think about:

• questions you can ask to find out about your partner's experience (location, duration, timing, purpose, likes).

• your own experience and the information you will need to answer your partner's questions.

C At the end, tell the class what you learnt about the members of your group. How successful were you at building rapport?

D In your groups, discuss which questions you used to build rapport and what you found difficult.

Self-assessment

• How successfully have you achieved the lesson outcome? Give yourself a score from 0 (I need more practice) to 5 (I know this well).

• Go to My Self-assessment in MyEnglishLab to reflect on what you have learnt.

> 13 <

Lesson outcome	Learners can use a range of expressions to start, close and show interest in simple, face-to-face conversations on familiar topics.

Lead-in **1A** **In pairs, discuss these questions.**

1 Why do people attend careers events?

2 What are employers looking for at a careers event?

3 Have you ever attended a careers event? What was your experience?

B Work in pairs. Look at these tips on how to prepare for a careers event. Choose the three most important tips for you. Explain your choices to another pair.

1 Look at the list of attending companies and target those that interest you most.

2 Update your CV and bring several copies.

3 Take a file to collect business cards and brochures.

4 Research your target employers and prepare a list of questions you want to ask.

5 Write an online profile.

6 Prepare a short, professional introduction (your experience, strengths, career interests and goals).

7 Dress professionally, as if you were going to an interview.

8 Arrive early, and plan extra time for locating your target employers.

Listening **2A** 🔊 1.03 **Listen and complete the advice on networking at a careers event.**

1	Before the event	*Research, ...*
2	On the day of the event	*Dress professionally, ...*
3	After the event	*Email, ...*

B In small groups, discuss what you think of the advice the recruiter gave.

3A 🔊 1.04 **Ella and Jamie are attending a careers event. They both speak to Ben, a recruiter from a large specialised travel agency. Listen to the two conversations. Who was better prepared, Ella or Jamie?**

B Listen again and answer the questions.

1 How did Ella prepare for the careers event?

2 What relevant skills and qualifications can Ella offer the company?

3 What was the outcome of the conversation with Ben for Ella?

4 What relevant skills can Jamie offer the company?

5 How did Jamie prepare for the careers event?

6 What was the outcome of the conversation with Ben for Jamie?

7 How could Ella and Jamie have been better prepared?

C Work in pairs and discuss the questions.

1 How easy or difficult would it be for you to network at a careers event?

2 What could you do to prepare for this type of event?

Functional language

Networking at a careers event

4A Complete the questions and phrases from the two conversations in Exercise 3 with the words and phrases in the box. Then listen again to check your answers.

> ask you a few questions · been nice talking · could I just ask · for your time
> how are you · in charge of · in touch with · really · see · tell me more · sounds

1 Can you put me _____ the person _____ your marketing projects?
2 Can you _____ about that?
3 I'd like to _____ , if possible.
4 Good morning. _____ enjoying the fair?
5 It's _____ to you.
6 That _____ interesting.
7 I _____ , wonderful.
8 Sorry, _____ you a few questions about Travelogue?
9 Thank you _____ , Ben. I really appreciate it.
10 Oh, _____ ?

B Put the phrases from Exercise 4A into the correct category in the table below.

Starting a conversation	Showing interest	Closing a conversation

C Here are more phrases that you might use during a conversation. Put them into the correct category in the table above.

1 That's interesting.
2 Do you have a few minutes to explain … ?
3 I really appreciate your time, thank you.
4 Could I give you a call next week to discuss this in more detail?
5 Uh-huh.
6 Right.
7 Can I talk to you for a minute?

T Teacher's resources: extra activities

> TASK

5A Work in groups of three. Roleplay a meeting at a careers event between a recruiter for a web design company, Your World, and a candidate for a job. There are three candidate profiles: each person will take the roles of recruiter, candidate and observer once.

Student A (recruiter): Read the information about Your World on page 126.

Student B (candidate): Choose one of the candidates on page 128 and read his/her online profile.

Student C (observer): Look at your instructions on page 130.

B Take a few minutes to prepare, then roleplay your meetings. Remember to show interest and close the conversation when appropriate.

C When you have finished, listen to the observer's feedback. Discuss how easy or difficult it is to participate in a conversation with someone you have just met. Share your group's ideas with the class.

Self-assessment

- How successfully have you achieved the lesson outcome? Give yourself a score from 0 (I need more practice) to 5 (I know this well).
- Go to My Self-assessment in MyEnglishLab to reflect on what you have learnt.

WRITING
Emails – Introducing yourself

Lesson outcome	Learners can write an email introducing themselves to work colleagues.

Lead-in

1A Read the two emails below and choose the correct options in italics.

A

To: Marketing staff
From: Elenor Rinna
Subject: Good morning!

[1]*Dear / Welcome* colleagues,

I would like to introduce [2]*me / myself* as the new Account Executive in your department.

Before I [3]*joined / join* this company, I was working in a similar position in a **very** small company in Sweden. However, I [4]*wanted / am wanting* to work for a larger company so I am **really** excited to be working [5]*by / for* this company.

Please feel free to contact me by email or phone [6]*if / so* you have any questions.

I **very much** look forward to [7]*meet / meeting* you all in person.

[8]*Kind / Truly* regards,

B

To: All staff
From: Alexis Pinar
Subject: Good morning!

Hi everyone,

I'm Alexis Pinar and I want to introduce myself to you. I've just started work here as the new Assistant Designer. I finished [9]*study / studying* business finance at university in June, and I'm excited to be working here. It's **a bit** [10]*scary / afraid* as it's my first job, but I'm sure I'll soon fit in OK.

I'm looking forward to working with you [11]*all / everyone*.

Bye for now,

B Which of these emails do you think is more formal?

Functional language

2A Look at the emails again. Put the phrases in blue from Exercise 1 into the correct place in this table.

	More formal	Less formal
Greeting		
Opening		
New job		
Previous job		
Invitation		
Closing		
Sign off		

B Write these words and phrases in the correct place in the table above. Some phrases may be used in both formal and informal emails.

Best wishes,   Good morning Helen,
I have been appointed as the new Marketing Manager
I hope to meet you all soon
I'm sending this email to introduce myself
I've just got the job of IT Supervisor
I was a Store Manager before
My previous job was as Customer Services Manager
Perhaps we can meet up over lunch today.   Yours,

T Teacher's resources: extra activities

L The email contains examples of adverbs of degree. Go to MyEnglishLab for optional grammar work.

→ page 118 See Grammar reference: Adverbs of degree

›TASK

3A Work in pairs. Turn to page 126 and read an email from a new HR Manager to all company staff. Discuss whether the email needs to be formal or informal and how you could improve it.

B You are the new HR Manager. Write your own introduction email in around 80 words.

C Exchange emails with your partner. Did you both write formal or informal emails? How many phrases from the functional language section did your partner use? What did you like about your partner's email?

Self-assessment	• How successfully have you achieved the lesson outcome? Give yourself a score from 0 (I need more practice) to 5 (I know this well). • Go to My Self-assessment in MyEnglishLab to reflect on what you have learnt.

Business sectors

> 'The rate of change is not going to slow down anytime soon. If anything, competition in most industries will probably speed up even more.'

Dr John P. Kotter,
Kotter International
- Boston, Seattle, London

Unit overview

2.1	**Japan's economy**	**Video:** Japan's economy
	Lesson outcome: Learners can use vocabulary related to different sectors and industries which drive economic activity.	**Vocabulary:** Sectors and industries **Project:** Research sectors and industries

2.2	**The energy industry**	**Reading:** Big oil: From black to green
	Lesson outcome: Learners can use the Past Simple and Past Continuous to talk about past events.	**Grammar:** Past Simple and Past Continuous **Writing:** A short story

2.3	**Communication skills:** Dealing with interruptions	**Video:** Induction meeting
	Lesson outcome: Learners are aware of ways to take turns and can use a range of expressions to interrupt and manage interruptions in a meeting.	**Functional language:** Interrupting and dealing with interruptions **Task:** Discussion during a meeting

2.4	**Business skills:** Voicemail messages	**Listening:** Four voicemail messages
	Lesson outcome: Learners can use a range of expressions to leave a clear and concise voicemail message.	**Functional language:** Leaving a voicemail message **Task:** Leave a voicemail message

2.5	**Writing:** Emails – Action points	**Model text:** Email with action points
	Lesson outcome: Learners can write an email containing action points from a meeting.	**Functional language:** Action points **Grammar:** *will* and *going to* **Task:** Email with action points

2.1 ▸ Japan's economy

Lead-in

1 Look at the photos from Japan. What can you see? What other iconic images represent the country?

2 Discuss these questions.

1 In what ways do you think Japan is very traditional and in what ways is it very modern?

2 How has Japanese popular culture had an impact on the world? Give examples.

3 How has Japanese industry had an impact on the world? Give examples.

4 What do these Japanese companies make or do?

> Canon   Mitsubishi   Nikon   Nintendo   SoftBank   Sony   Toyota

VIDEO

3A Look at the list of industries. Tick (✓) the ones you predict will appear in a video about the development of Japan's economy.

> agriculture   cars   energy   electronics   finance   fishing

B ▶ 2.1.1   Watch the video and check your predictions.

4 Decide if these sentences are *true* (T) or *false* (F). Watch the video again and check. Then correct the incorrect sentences.

1 We think of the USA leading in the internet technology sector.

2 Japan is the second largest industrialised economy in the world.

3 The country's banks and financial market are an important part of the economy.

4 Japan was slow to use robots in car manufacturing.

5 Japanese cars were not popular in other countries in the 1970s.

6 Japan's car manufacturers continue to invent new vehicles in the twenty-first century.

7 The Sony Walkman was a revolutionary product because it was very cheap.

8 Both Nintendo and Sony sell popular video game consoles.

5 Discuss the questions.

1 According to the video, how was Japan able to build a strong car industry?

2 What two examples of more recent innovations in Japan's car industry are mentioned in the video?

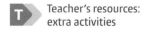

Teacher's resources:
extra activities

3 How did the Sony Walkman change the way we live today?

Vocabulary   Sectors and industries

6 Complete the extracts from the video using the words and phrases in the box.

> automotive   manufacturing   retail   service sector   transportation

Japan's ¹_____ , which includes finance, trade, entertainment, tourism, ²_____ and ³_____ , accounts for a massive three-quarters of Japan's total economic output.

But it has been Japan's ⁴_____ industries that have made the most global impact. The ⁵_____ industry has been particularly successful.

7 Match the three economic sectors (A–C) with the descriptions and the examples (1–3).

Economic sectors

A Primary **→** **B** Secondary **→** **C** Tertiary

Description and examples

1 This involves using raw materials to develop and build products. Examples include the manufacturing and construction industries.

2 Also called the service sector, this includes all the commercial services that connect products and services with consumers. Examples are financial services, retail, the tourism industry as well as transportation. It also includes other public and private services such as education and health care.

3 This involves working with basic materials. For example, extraction of raw materials, agriculture and fishing.

8 Write the correct industry and sector next to each group (1–8).

1 bank, credit card company, insurance agent _____ _____

2 campsite, cruise ship, hotel chain _____ _____

3 furniture maker, steel factory, textile manufacturing _____ _____

4 coal mining, gas extraction, oil drilling _____ _____

5 animal farming, crop growing, wine producing _____ _____

6 airline, courier service, port _____ _____

7 chemical plant, pharmaceutical company, robotics factory _____ _____

8 clothes shop, restaurant, supermarket _____ _____

9 Look at the types of businesses in Exercise 8 and discuss the questions.

1 Which of the sectors and industries were important in the past in your country or region?

2 If any of these industries declined, do you know why?

T ▷ Teacher's resources: extra activities

▷ **PROJECT: Research sectors and industries**

10A **Work in pairs or small groups.**

Research one industry that is active in your country or region. Find out some of the following information:

• a description of the industry.   • the number of employees.

• the size of the industry.   • its economic impact on the country.

Prepare a short presentation with suitable images for some visitors to your region or country. Write 100–120 words. See an example on page 126.

B **Give your presentation to the class.**

C **Watch another group's presentation. Which of the industries has a bigger impact on the economy today?**

Self-assessment

• How successfully have you achieved the lesson outcome? Give yourself a score from 0 (I need more practice) to 5 (I know this well).
• Go to My Self-assessment in MyEnglishLab to reflect on what you have learnt.

❯ 19 ❮

2.2 > The energy industry

Lead-in **1** Match words from each circle to form compound nouns.

climate   fossil
electricity   global   renewable
greenhouse   solar

bill   change
fuel   warming   panels
energies   gases

2A Complete the questions with a compound noun from Exercise 1.
1 Can you name two types of traditional and _____ ?
2 What are some of the advantages of installing _____ on your home?
3 Which of these is not a _____ ? Coal, gas, oil, wood.
4 Do you think _____ is affecting the weather where you live? How?

B Work in groups. Answer the questions above.

→ page 114 See Pronunciation bank: Stress in compound nouns and noun phrases

Reading **3** Look at the social media post on the left. What was the problem and what do you think Mark did about it?

4 Read the first paragraph of the article and check your predictions.

5 Read the whole article and answer the questions.
1 What do you understand by the article headline?
2 In what two ways will Mark save money with his solar panels?
3 What type of company is Total?
4 What was significant about Total buying two-thirds of SunPower?
5 What future risks are there for the oil and gas industry?
6 What two options does the writer say the oil and gas industry has?

6 Discuss the questions.
1 In what ways does it make good or bad business sense for big oil companies to move into renewable energies?
2 Why do you think the transition from fossil fuels to renewable energies will be slow?

Mark Nowicki ✅   ⌄

So, it was snowing all last night, and at about nine o'clock we were just watching TV when suddenly all the electricity went out. These power cuts sometimes happen when there's a big storm. While I was sitting in the dark, I thought we really must do something about this.

T > Teacher's resources: extra activities

FT

Big oil: From black to green

Mark Nowicki put solar panels on the roof of his house last week. He is one of more than one million American homeowners and businesses that now have the panels, motivated by tax deductions and falling costs. He went
5 solar to provide backup power if the electricity failed, and to cut his electricity bills in half. Helping the environment was an extra benefit. 'Green energy compensates for the emissions from my big cars,' he says.

He did not know it, but there was probably another
10 connection between the new panels on his roof and the fuel in his vehicles. The panels came from SunPower, a U.S. solar company controlled by one of the world's largest oil groups, Total of France.

Total bought 66 percent of SunPower five years ago for
15 about $1.4bn, making the biggest investment in renewable energy by any of the large oil and gas companies. The
investment was one answer to the growing threat that many analysts,
20 investors and executives now see facing* the oil and gas industry: the prospect of a long-term transition away from fossil fuels and towards renewable energy.

25 Total, along with the other large international oil companies, is facing a critical choice. Do they diversify into wind and solar power to compete in a world of stricter regulations on greenhouse gas emissions and competition from renewable energy? Or do they stick to oil and gas,
30 knowing the world will continue to need fossil fuels for many years to come? Their decisions will shape the future of the industry, of energy supplies and of the climate.

*If you face a difficult situation, it is going to affect you and you must deal with it.

Grammar   Past Simple and Past Continuous

> … it **was snowing** all last night

> … at about nine o'clock we **were** just **watching** TV when suddenly all the electricity went out.

> While I **was sitting** in the dark, I **thought** we really must do something about this.

7A Look at the phrases from Mark's post. What is the tense of the verbs in bold? How do we form these tenses?

B Complete the sentences with *Past Simple* or *Past Continuous*.

1 We use the _____ to give some background details to the main story, for example, describing the weather at the time.

2 We use the _____ for an action in the past that was interrupted. It also describes actions or events in progress at a specific moment in the past.

3 We use the _____ for shorter, finished actions or events, which can interrupt a longer situation or action in progress. We also use it with a series of short, completed actions.

4 We often use *when* before the _____ and *while* before the _____ .

➜ page 119   See Grammar reference: Past Simple and Past Continuous

8 Choose the correct option in italics to complete the sentences.

1 She *was studying / studied* IT when she *started / was starting* her first business.

2 He *told / was telling* me he wanted to quit his job while we *had / were having* lunch.

3 While I *presented / was presenting* the slides, the electricity *went out / was going out*.

4 We *got / were getting* tired so we *decided / were deciding* to have a break.

5 What *did you do / were you doing* this morning? I *tried / was trying* to phone you twice.

6 I *thought / was thinking* about Carla when she *phoned / was phoning* me.

7 It suddenly *started / was starting* to rain while we *sat / were sitting* in the park.

8 When I *got / was getting* to the office, everyone *already worked / was already working*.

9A Student A: Complete the article using the Past Simple or Past Continuous form of the verbs in brackets. Student B: Turn to page 127.

How it started

Airbnb's co-founders, Joe Gebbia and Brian Chesky, were friends from design school in New York. In 2007, they ¹_____ (share) an apartment in San Francisco. They ²_____ (both / look) for work and having a hard time paying their rent. When they ³_____ (hear) a design conference was coming to San Francisco, and the city's hotels were fully booked, they ⁴_____ (decide) to offer their flat as cheap accommodation to participants. They quickly designed a simple website and soon ⁵_____ (find) three paying guests who slept on airbeds on their living-room floor. They even cooked their guests breakfast and that's where the Airbnb name came from. They charged $80 each a night. As they ⁶_____ (wave) their guests goodbye, they thought they had a new business concept – the idea of a sharing economy.

In the summer of 2008 they had 800 listings but the site ⁷_____ (not make) any money. So they ⁸_____ (fly) to New York, the city where they had the most customers, to find out what problems people ⁹_____ (have) with the service. They found that many of their listing photos were poor quality, so they rented a professional camera and ¹⁰_____ (take) photos of people's apartments. Today, Airbnb has hosted over 35 million guests in 34,000 towns and cities around the world.

 Teacher's resources: extra activities

B Make brief notes about the story in your article and tell your partner the story using your notes.

Writing   **10A** Choose a title from the box and write a short story. Use the example story and notes on page 127 to help you. Write 120–150 words.

> A memorable day at work/university   What a stressful day at work
> That was a nightmare journey/meeting   The holiday of a lifetime

B Work in pairs. Tell each other your story, then ask questions to find out more.

Self-assessment

• How successfully have you achieved the lesson outcome? Give yourself a score from 0 (I need more practice) to 5 (I know this well).
• Go to My Self-assessment in MyEnglishLab to reflect on what you have learnt.

> 21 <

Dealing with interruptions

Lesson outcome	Learners are aware of ways to take turns and can use a range of expressions to interrupt and manage interruptions in a meeting.

Lead-in

1A Think about meetings in your country. Is interrupting a speaker during a meeting considered positively or negatively? Explain your thoughts to a partner.

B Work in pairs and discuss the statements. Do you agree or disagree? Why / Why not?

To participate effectively in a meeting you need to:

1 listen to others.

2 ask questions to be sure you have understood.

3 prepare your contribution in advance.

4 never interrupt someone even if you disagree with him/her.

5 be respectful even if you disagree with someone.

VIDEO

2A ▶ 2.3.1 Watch the video as Beata prepares for an induction meeting with the CEO of Evromed. Choose the correct option in italics to complete the information about Evromed.

1 Evromed is a *multinational / global player / family business*.

2 Evromed currently employs *more than 145 / fewer than 145 / 145* people.

3 Evromed is successful in *Europe / Eastern Europe / China*.

4 Evromed recently won a contract to supply a *hospital / children's home / chain of drugstores* in Brazil with a device for diabetes patients.

B Jessica invites the audience to ask questions 'as we go along'. Work in pairs and discuss the questions.

1 What does she mean?

2 What might happen as a result of this invitation?

3A In small groups, discuss which is the best approach (Option A or B) for Beata to take as she participates in Jessica's induction presentation. As a class, decide which video to watch first.

Option A – Beata should ask lots of questions to show she is motivated and enthusiastic.

Option B – Beata should listen carefully and only ask questions when it is really necessary.

B Watch the videos in the sequence the class has decided and answer the questions for both videos.

Option A ▶ 2.3.2   1 How did Beata show enthusiasm and motivation during the presentation?

Option B ▶ 2.3.3   2 How did the other trainees react to Beata?

3 How did Jessica react to Beata?

4 How does Beata feel at the end of the meeting?

4 In pairs, discuss which approach seems more effective. Why?

5 ▶ 2.3.4 Watch the Conclusions section of the video. Compare what is said with your answers in Exercise 4.

Reflection

6 Think about how you participate in meetings. Then work in pairs and discuss the questions.

1 How comfortable are you interrupting during a meeting or class discussion in your own language?

2 What strategies would you use to interrupt during a meeting or class discussion?

diabsensor

The reliable and pain-free way to manage your diabetes.

The Diabsensor uses a sensor to read the patient's glucose level. It collects the data through a patch on the skin and then sends it to a remote monitor.

 Teacher's resources: extra activities

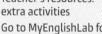 Go to MyEnglishLab for extra video activities.

Functional language

Interrupting and dealing with interruptions

7A Look at this extract from the video. Which phrases in bold are a) accepting an interruption, b) asking permission to interrupt, c) going back to an earlier point?

Beata:	**Sorry to interrupt**, Jessica.
Jessica:	That's OK. **Please go ahead**.
Beata:	When you say 'blood sugar', do you mean 'glucose'?
Jessica:	Glucose. Exactly, yes.
Graduate 2:	Ah, good, thanks. I was wondering about that, too.
Jessica:	**So, as I was saying**, … no more pricking of fingers.

B How does Jessica prevent Beata's final interruption in Option A?

C Match the expressions (1–10) with the correct category (a–d).

1 What did you want to say? __
2 Sure, please continue. __
3 Excuse me for interrupting. __
4 Can I just finish (my point)? __
5 Sorry, I just have one more thing to say. __
6 Can I just say something here? __
7 Before you speak, let me just say … __
8 The point I was making was … __
9 Going back to what I was saying … __
10 If I could just ask you … __

a Asking permission to interrupt
b Accepting an interruption
c Preventing an interruption
d Going back to an earlier point

8 Work in small groups. Choose a situation and roleplay the conversation using phrases from Exercise 7. Students offering advice: interrupt the conversation several times.

1 Student A asks for directions to the nearest restaurant. Students B and C have different directions.
2 Student B wants to know how to make an omelette. Students A and C have different instructions.
3 Student C wants advice on the best way to study English. Students A and B have different pieces of advice.

T Teacher's resources: extra activities

→ page 114 See Pronunciation bank: Stress in phrases for turn taking

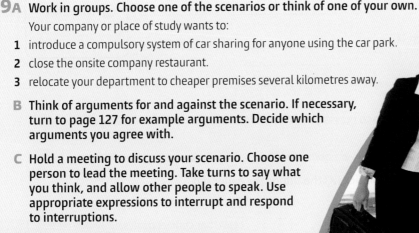

> TASK

9A Work in groups. Choose one of the scenarios or think of one of your own.

Your company or place of study wants to:

1 introduce a compulsory system of car sharing for anyone using the car park.
2 close the onsite company restaurant.
3 relocate your department to cheaper premises several kilometres away.

B Think of arguments for and against the scenario. If necessary, turn to page 127 for example arguments. Decide which arguments you agree with.

C Hold a meeting to discuss your scenario. Choose one person to lead the meeting. Take turns to say what you think, and allow other people to speak. Use appropriate expressions to interrupt and respond to interruptions.

D At the end, discuss how well the group participated in the meeting. How could you improve your approach to turn-taking in future?

Self-assessment

- How successfully have you achieved the lesson outcome? Give yourself a score from 0 (I need more practice) to 5 (I know this well).
- Go to My Self-assessment in MyEnglishLab to reflect on what you have learnt.

Lesson outcome	Learners can use a range of expressions to leave a clear and concise voicemail message.

Lead-in **1A** In pairs, compare how many times you listen to voicemail messages before you understand them. Why?

B In small groups, discuss why it is sometimes difficult to understand a voicemail message.

the caller speaks too fast, the caller doesn't leave his/her full name

C How do you feel about leaving a voicemail message in English on a scale of 1–5 (1 = very comfortable, 5 = totally uncomfortable)? Explain your thoughts in pairs.

Listening **2A** ◀》 2.01 Anya is the assistant to the Human Resources Manager, Emma Newman. It is Monday morning and Anya has four voicemail messages. Listen to the first three messages and tick the correct box.

	is unclear	speaks too fast	sounds annoyed
Caller 1	☐	☐	☐
Caller 2	☐	☐	☐
Caller 3	☐	☐	☐

B ◀》 2.02 Listen to message 1 again and complete the information below. Listen as many times as necessary.

MESSAGE FOR: [1] _____

CALLER: [2] _____ DATE/TIME: *12 March / 9.15*

REASON FOR CALL: [3] *Discuss* _____ *position*

ACTION: [5] _____ TEL: *00* [6] _____

ACTION DEADLINE: [7] _____

COMMENTS: [8] _____ *if can't call*

☐ [4]CALLED

☐ RETURNED YOUR CALL

☐ PLEASE CALL

☐ WILL CALL AGAIN

3A ◀》 2.03 Listen to message 4. What is/are the aim(s) of the message?

The caller is …

1 asking for action.　　**2** asking for information.　　**3** asking for a call back.

B Listen again and tick (✓) the things the caller did.

Leave a greeting	☐	Leave her contact details	☐
Identify herself	☐	Repeat her contact details	☐
State the reason for the call	☐	Offer an alternative communication mode	☐
Request action / information / a call back	☐	Provide a deadline	☐

T Teacher's resources: extra activities

C In pairs, note down the message. Compare your message with the sample on page 128.

Functional language

Leaving a voicemail message

4A Complete the phrases from message 4 below. If necessary, use the audioscript on page 148 to help you.

1	Identify herself	This is _____ .
2	State the reason for the call	Emma asked _____ .
3	Request action	Can she also _____ .
4	Leave her contact details	In case _____ .
5	Offer an alternative communication mode	Maybe she can _____ .
6	Provide a deadline	I'm _____ .
7	Finish the call	I _____ .

B Match the sentences/questions (a–k) with the categories (1–7) in Exercise 4A.

a Please call me back and I'll go over the issue with you in more detail.

b I think my previous message may have been cut off, so I'm calling again.

c It's Thom. I'll spell that for you: that's T for Tango, H for Hotel, O for Oscar, M for Mike.

d My number is 0081 for Japan, then 03-9245-6229. That's 0081-03-9245-6229.

e This is a message for Colleen Baker.

f Could you call me back on my mobile?

g My name's Kaori Akiba from UCI-Tokyo.

h I look forward to hearing from you.

i Could you get back to me by Monday?

j I'd like to discuss … in more detail if possible.

k Can you send me an email or a text message so we can we fix another time to speak?

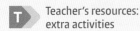
Teacher's resources: extra activities

5A Work in pairs. Student A: Go to page 128. Student B: Go to page 130. Read the information and prepare your message: write notes, review the useful phrases in Exercise 4 and practise leaving your message.

❯TASK

B When you are ready, record your message for your partner. Your partner will listen and write down your message.

C Use the checklist below to review the messages. Reflect on what went well, what didn't go well and how you can improve next time. Then change roles.

1	Identified himself/herself	☐
2	Stated the reason for the call	☐
3	Requested action	☐
4	Left his/her contact details	☐
5	Offered an alternative communication mode	☐
6	Provided a deadline	☐
7	Finished the call	☐

Self-assessment

• How successfully have you achieved the lesson outcome? Give yourself a score from 0 (I need more practice) to 5 (I know this well).
• Go to My Self-assessment in MyEnglishLab to reflect on what you have learnt.

❯ 25 ❮

Lesson outcome	Learners can write an email containing action points from a meeting.

Lead-in **1A** 🔊 2.04 **Listen to the meeting between Alice, Matthew and Stanley and complete the key action points below.**

To: Project team
Subject: Factory in Indonesia

As you know, we **are going to** build a factory in Indonesia next year. The project **will involve** a lot of organisation and planning, so we had a meeting with Stanley Dongoran, our Indonesian partner, yesterday to discuss the next stages. Here are the key action points which resulted from the meeting.

KEY ACTION POINTS

- get licence from Indonesian ¹_____ Board
- visit Indonesia next ²_____
- ³_____ bank account
- choose good ⁴_____ for factory
- ⁵_____ the business premises
- organise other necessary ⁶_____
- interview candidates for ⁷_____ position
- book ⁸_____ and accommodation – Matthew by tomorrow

Please note that there **will be** a full team meeting next Monday. We expect everyone to attend.

B **Check your answers with the audioscript on page 148.**

Functional language **2** **Look at the tips for writing an email that includes action points. Complete the table with examples of each tip from the email above.**

Tips	Examples
1 Give brief background about the meeting which led to the actions points.	
2 List the points in the order in which you must do them.	
3 Use the same grammatical structure at the beginning of every action point.	
4 Add the name of the person who is going to do the task if possible.	
5 Put the date you want the task finished if possible.	

T Teacher's resources: extra activities

L The email contains examples of *will* and *going to* for the future. Go to MyEnglishLab for optional grammar work.

➔ **page 119** See Grammar reference: *will* and *going to*

TASK

3A 🔊 2.05 **Turn to page 128 and look at the points. Then listen to the meeting and put the points in the order they are going to do them. Delete any which are not mentioned. Check your answers with a partner.**

B **Write an email to the CEO with the action points for informing people about the takeover in around 100 words.**

C **Exchange emails with your partner. Did you both write formal or informal emails? How many phrases from the functional language box did your partner use? What ideas from your partner's email can you use to improve your email?**

Self-assessment	• How successfully have you achieved the lesson outcome? Give yourself a score from 0 (I need more practice) to 5 (I know this well). • Go to My Self-assessment in MyEnglishLab to reflect on what you have learnt.

Projects

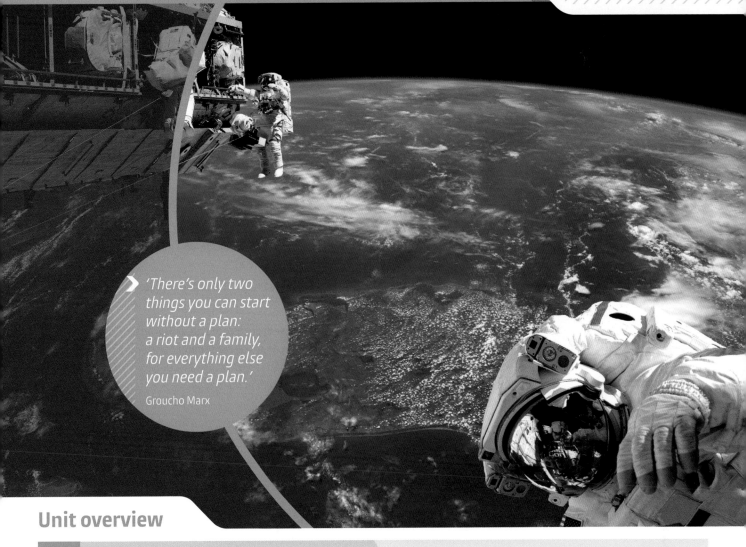

> 'There's only two things you can start without a plan: a riot and a family, for everything else you need a plan.'
>
> Groucho Marx

Unit overview

3.1 **Project management**

Lesson outcome: Learners can use vocabulary related to project management.

Video: Project management
Vocabulary: Managing projects; Word building – verbs and nouns
Project: A project debriefing and lessons learnt

3.2 **Large-scale projects**

Lesson outcome: Learners can understand and practise making comparisons.

Listening: Three canals
Grammar: Comparatives and superlatives
Speaking: Choosing the winning bid

3.3 **Communication skills:** Giving instructions

Lesson outcome: Learners are aware of different ways of telling people what to do, and can use a range of phrases for giving and responding to instructions, and standing their ground.

Video: Resolving a problem with a schedule change
Functional language: Giving and responding to instructions, standing your ground
Task: Giving and responding to instructions

3.4 **Business skills:** Meetings: Updates and action

Lesson outcome: Learners can use a range of expressions to give and receive updates, and to discuss follow-up action items.

Listening: A stand-up meeting
Functional language: Asking for and giving updates
Task: An update meeting

3.5 **Writing:** Email requesting an update

Lesson outcome: Learners can write an internal email requesting updates on a project.

Model text: Email requesting an update
Functional language: Asking for information
Grammar: (not) enough
Task: Email requesting an update

| **Business workshop 3:** p.92 | **Review 3:** p.106 | **Pronunciation:** 3.1 Stress in derived words 3.2 Weak forms in comparisons p.115 | **Grammar reference:** p.120 |

3.1 ▶ Project management

Lesson outcome Learners can use vocabulary related to project management.

Lead-in 1 **Discuss your views on these comments. Which view do you most agree with in each pair?**

1 **a** Having a detailed schedule increases stress. It's better to have a more relaxed approach to work.

b The only way to do everything you need to do is to organise your life and have a detailed schedule – and follow it.

2 **a** Everyone should have a personal budget. Controlling your money is the key to financial happiness.

b It's important to enjoy life and not to worry too much about how you spend your money.

VIDEO 2**A** **You're going to watch a video about London's Millennium Bridge, which opened on 10 June 2000 but was closed two days later. Do you know or can you guess why the bridge was closed?**

B ▶ 3.1.1 **Watch the video and check your ideas. Did the engineers solve the problem? How?**

3 **Watch the video again and decide if these sentences are *true* (T) or *false* (F).**

1 The problems with the bridge were a nightmare because many people were hurt.

2 Some people crossing the bridge felt ill.

3 The designers expected there to be some movement in the bridge.

4 The project managers did not try to reduce risk.

5 After closing the bridge, one of the most important jobs was to identify the problem and find a solution.

6 The problem was caused by people reacting to the slight movement of the bridge.

7 Fixing the bridge required a lot of extra time and money.

8 Now, Londoners don't like using the bridge because they feel afraid of it.

4 **Work in pairs or small groups. Discuss these questions.**

1 Think of another example of a project or product failing and becoming big news. What happened?

2 Some people still call the Millennium Bridge 'the Wobbly Bridge'. Do you think this means the bridge will always be seen as a failure? Why / Why not?

Teacher's resources: extra activities

Vocabulary **Managing projects**

5 **Complete the sentences from the video using the words and phrases in the box.**

> anticipating   budget   milestones   predict   project managers
> risk management   risk register   setback

1 The Millennium Bridge opened in the year 2000, on the millennium, but that was actually slightly behind schedule and slightly over-_____ .

2 One of the central parts of a project manager's job is _____ .

3 ... so that's _____ all the things that could possibly go wrong.

4 After a _____ like this, the project manager's highest priority is to manage all the different specialist teams who are working on the bridge.

5 Together, they're going to have to come up with a new plan of what to do, which is going to involve setting new budgets, coming up with new schedules, and agreeing new _____ .

6 I don't think it's fair to blame the _____ on the Millennium Bridge for the wobble.

7 It's not the kind of risk you can just _____ easily.

8 From now on, you can be sure that at the top of every project manager's _____ , 'bridge wobble' will appear.

Teacher's resources: extra activities

Word building – verbs and nouns

6 Complete the table with the correct word forms.

verb	noun
manage	management
construct	1 _____
suspend	2 _____
3 _____	movement
4 _____	investigation
communicate	5 _____
identify	6 _____
7 _____	solution
add	8 _____
9 _____	attachment
decide	10 _____

7A Choose the correct option in italics to complete the sentences.

1 In large public *construct / construction* projects like the Millennium Bridge, why is risk *manage / management* so important?

2 It took engineers two years to *investigate / investigation* and *identify / identification* the problem and find a *solve / solution*. Was this a reasonable amount of time? Why / Why not?

3 After the engineers *attached / attachment* additional parts, the *move / movement* of the bridge stopped. Imagine that they were unable to stop the wobble. What do you think they could have done?

B Work in pairs or small groups. Discuss the questions above.

➔ **page 115** See Pronunciation bank: Stress in derived words

PROJECT: A project debriefing and lessons learnt

8A Think of a project you have worked on – in education, your job, as a volunteer or as a hobby. Answer the questions and make notes.

1 What was the project? (Possible ideas: a presentation, a performance, a drawing or painting, a paper or other piece of writing, building or making something, painting or decorating, organising an event, etc.)

2 Who did you work with on the project?

3 What went well with the project?

4 What was the project's biggest challenge: the schedule, the budget, working with a team, getting the content right, something else?

5 What would you do differently next time?

B Work in pairs. Ask your partner questions 1–5 above and complete the form opposite with his/her answers.

9A Work as a class. Based on your debriefing documents, make a list of dos and don'ts for project managers.

Don't
- *wait until the last minute to start work.*

Do
- *meet with team members regularly.*

B As a class, choose the best five dos and don'ts for project managers.

PROJECT DEBRIEFING

Project description:

Team members:

Successes:

Challenges:

Lessons learnt / Improvements for next time:

Self-assessment
- How successfully have you achieved the lesson outcome? Give yourself a score from 0 (I need more practice) to 5 (I know this well).
- Go to My Self-assessment in MyEnglishLab to reflect on what you have learnt.

| Lesson outcome | Learners can understand and practise making comparisons. |

Lead-in **1A** **Work in pairs or small groups. Look at the map and photos and answer the questions.**

1 Why do governments decide to build shipping canals? What are the benefits?
2 What kinds of jobs does this sort of building project create? Who works on a big canal-building project?
3 Can you name any other shipping canals?

The Panama Canal

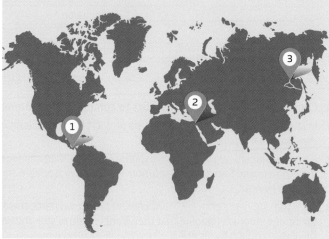

The Suez Canal

The Grand Canal

B **Match each description with a canal on the map.**

a goes through the desert in Egypt, connecting the Mediterranean Sea with the Red Sea
b connects the Atlantic and Pacific Oceans by crossing Central America
c connects the Chinese capital city of Beijing with several rivers and other cities

Listening **2** ◀) 3.01 **Listen. Match each canal with two facts.**

1 The Grand Canal   a took the longest to build.
2 The Suez Canal   b was more expensive than expected.
3 The Panama Canal   c was cheaper than expected.
    d is the oldest.
    e took ten years to build.
    f opened in 1914.

3 **Listen again. Complete the information about each project.**

Grand Canal, China

Length: [1]_____ km
The budget: none
The schedule: none – took about [2]_____ years to complete
The team: [3]_____ million men and women – mostly labourers and engineers
Minimum width: 100 m
Minimum depth: less than 1 m

Suez Canal, Egypt

The schedule: late by [4]_____ years
The team: [5]_____ million people in total, [6]_____ at any given time – labourers, engineers, accountants, project managers
The cost: $100 million, over budget by [7]_____ percent
Length: [8]_____ km
Minimum depth: 12 m
Minimum width: [9]_____ m

Panama Canal, Panama

Length: [10]_____ km
The schedule: the American project was late by [11]_____ years
The team: 75,000 engineers, specialised machine operators, labourers
The cost: $[12]_____ million – $23 million under budget
Minimum width: [13]_____ m
Minimum depth: [14]_____ m

 Teacher's resources: extra activities

Grammar   Comparatives and superlatives

4A 🔊 3.02   **Listen and complete the extracts.**

1 It's the _____ artificial waterway in the world.

2 But what's _____ than the length of the canal is its age.

3 When they were working the _____ on the project, five million men and women were involved in the construction.

4 They finished _____ than planned.

5 It is still one of the _____ shipping routes in the world.

6 The canal makes the journey between the North Atlantic and the Indian Ocean much _____ than going around Africa.

7 It reduces the trip by 7,000 km, making the journey _____ and time-consuming.

8 The Panama team had to work a lot _____ than the Suez team.

9 Construction in the jungles of Panama wasn't _____ digging in Egypt's dry, sandy desert.

10 In fact the digging itself was the _____ part of the job.

B **Choose the correct option in italics to complete the sentences.**

1 We use the *comparative / superlative* form to say how two things are similar or different.

2 We use the *comparative / superlative* form to show that one thing has got more or less of a quality than all the others in the same group.

➡ **page 120** See Grammar reference: Comparatives and superlatives

5 **Look at the information in Exercises 2 and 3. Complete the sentences with the correct form of the words in brackets. Add *than* or *as … as* where necessary.**

1 The Suez Canal is _____ the Grand Canal. (long)

2 The Suez Canal was _____ project of the three. (profitable)

3 The Grand Canal is _____ of the three canals. (modern)

4 The Suez Canal was _____ the Panama Canal. (expensive)

5 The workforce on the Panama Canal was _____ the workforce on the Grand Canal. (large)

6 Work on the Panama Canal finished _____ work on the Suez Canal. (late)

T Teacher's resources: extra activities

➡ **page 115** See Pronunciation bank: Weak forms in comparisons

Listening   **6A** 🔊 3.03   **Listen to three bids to provide a new computer network for a shipping company. Answer the questions.**

1 Which supplier can start the soonest?   2 Which supplier is the cheapest?

B **Listen again and complete the notes.**

	Bid A	Bid B	Bid C
When they can start			
How long it will take			
Can we continue using the office?			
Product support			
Guarantee			
Price			

Speaking   **7A** **You are going to choose a company to install the new computer network. Look at the notes in Exercise 6B. Compare the bids using the comparative and superlative forms of the words in the box.**

> bad   cheap   convenient   expensive   fast   good   inconvenient   slow

B **Hold a meeting to discuss the choices. As a group, decide which bid to choose.**

Self-assessment

- How successfully have you achieved the lesson outcome? Give yourself a score from 0 (I need more practice) to 5 (I know this well).
- Go to My Self-assessment in MyEnglishLab to reflect on what you have learnt.

Lesson outcome	Learners are aware of different ways of telling people what to do, and can use a range of phrases for giving and responding to instructions, and standing their ground.

Lead-in 1A **Work in pairs and discuss the statements. Which one do you agree with more?**

1 As a leader, you should insist on having your way.

2 As a leader, you should be prepared to listen and change your mind.

B **What are the advantages and disadvantages of each approach?**

VIDEO 2A ▶ 3.3.1 **Watch the video from the beginning to 01:15. Match the names with the roles.**

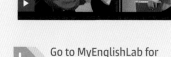

1 Daniel   **a** sub-supplier

2 Beata   **b** project manager

3 Clarice   **c** main contact

B **How do you think Beata feels about her new responsibilities? How do you think the meeting with Clarice will go?**

C **Watch the next part of the video.**

1 What is the problem?

2 Match the dates on the timeline with the events (a–d).

Go to MyEnglishLab for extra video activites.

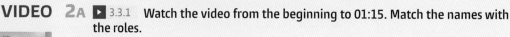

17 April: ___   9 May: _d_   28 May: ___

APRIL   **MAY**   10 May: ___   **JUNE**

a The container arrives in the UK.

b Beata's new deadline for some components.

c The delivery leaves the factory in Shenzhen.

d The original date for the shipment to arrive in the UK.

3A **In small groups, discuss which is the best approach (Option A or B) for Beata to take in this discussion with Clarice. As a class, decide which video to watch first.**

Option A – Beata should be polite and friendly to Clarice, but at the same time needs to show her authority. She should stand her ground.

Option B – Beata should be polite and friendly to Clarice, but at the same time show Clarice that she is willing to help. They need to work well together.

B **Watch the two videos in the sequence the class has decided and answer the same questions for each video.**

Option A ▶ 3.3.2   1 Is there a solution? If so, what is it?

Option B ▶ 3.3.3   2 How do they arrive at the solution?

3 How does Clarice feel? Why?

4 How will this affect their future working relationship?

4 **In pairs, discuss these questions.**

1 How did the discussions go? Was one approach better than the other? Give reasons for your answer.

2 Can you think of any other ways Beata might have handled the situation?

5 ▶ 3.3.4 **Watch the Conclusions section of the video. What do you need to think about when telling people what to do? Do you agree? Why / Why not?**

Reflection 6 **Think about the following questions. Then discuss your answers with a partner.**

1 Is it always important for leaders to build good relationships with the people they work with? Give examples when it might not be important.

2 How do you think you would deal with such a situation?

Functional language

Giving and responding to instructions, standing your ground

7A Match 1–7 with a–h to make sentences from the video. There is one ending you don't need.

1	Can you bring Clarice	a new deadline.
2	No problem, leave it	b on this.
3	I have no room for	c with me.
4	You need to meet this	d can do it.
5	I can't compromise	e able to do it.
6	I think we	f manoeuvre on this.
7	I'm afraid I'm just	g not that flexible.
		h up to speed?

B Match the sentences in Exercise 7A with the categories (a–c) below.

a telling someone what to do

b responding to an instruction

c standing your ground

C Match the phrases (1–7) below with the categories in Exercise 7B.

1 I'm sorry, there's no flexibility on this deadline.

2 Yes, I can certainly do that.

3 We need you to [lower your costs / get more resources].

4 I'd like you to change the [delivery date / deadline / supplier].

5 I would like to help you, but I can't.

6 Sure, no problem.

7 My hands are tied.

8 Work in pairs. Your classroom is going to be painted. Choose your roles and roleplay the conversation using phrases from Exercise 7. Try to stand your ground.

Student A: You are in charge. You want to make sure the room is empty of all furniture and fittings by tomorrow evening. Your partner is your helper.

Student B: You are a helper. Your partner is in charge. You think it is more efficient to leave some things in the room, and cover them with a large sheet of plastic.

 Teacher's resources: extra activities

9A Work in small groups. Read the scenarios below and decide who will take the role of the leader for each scenario.

Scenario 1
There has been a small earthquake. No one in your room is hurt. You hear a fire alarm in the distance. All the others in your group are looking at you to lead. Tell them what to do.

Scenario 2
You are looking after some foreign visitors. As a group, you have just decided to go and do some sightseeing in your area. Think about the tasks that need to be done, decide who will do them, and then tell the others in the group what they have to do.

Scenario 3
You need to move to new accommodation next month, but you have not yet started the process. The others in your group have offered to help. Tell them what to do.

>TASK

B If you are the leader, think about how to deal with the situation. If you are not the leader, turn to page 129 and read the information.

C Take turns to roleplay the scenarios. Try to use phrases from Exercise 7.

D At the end, discuss what went well, what didn't go well, and how you can improve next time.

Self-assessment

• How successfully have you achieved the lesson outcome? Give yourself a score from 0 (I need more practice) to 5 (I know this well).

• Go to My Self-assessment in MyEnglishLab to reflect on what you have learnt.

Lesson outcome	Learners can use a range of expressions to give and receive updates, and to discuss follow-up action items.

Lead-in **1A** Work in pairs. Read the definitions and discuss the questions.

to update someone (verb) – to tell someone the most recent information about a situation	**an update** (noun) – the most recent information about a situation	**to action something** (verb) – to do a specific thing that needs to be done, especially after discussing it	**an action item** (noun) – the thing that needs to be done

1 What kinds of updates do you give and receive in a typical week?
2 What action items do you have at the moment?

B Meetings are very common in the workplace. With your partner, discuss what kinds of meetings you attend, or have attended.

Listening **2A** ◀) 3.04 Listen to a team leader explaining a new procedure for meetings. What type of meeting is it?

B Listen again and answer the questions.

1 How long does she expect the meeting to take?
2 What is the aim of the meeting?
3 How often will the meetings take place?
4 What time will the meetings start?
5 What is the ball for?
6 What information will each person give?
7 What will happen after the meeting?

3A ◀) 3.05 Listen to the next part of the meeting as three participants give their information. Complete the table below.

	Yesterday	Today	Problems/Impediments
Jack			
Sal			
Tom			

B Listen again and check your answers. Which of the three speakers was the most difficult to understand? Why?

4 Work in pairs. Use your notes in Exercise 3 to rewrite what the third speaker said. If necessary, look at the audioscript on page 149. Practise reading your version out loud. Compare your version with others in the class.

5 Listen to the meeting again. Think about who the team leader will speak to after the meeting and what follow-up action items they will discuss. Make notes, then discuss your ideas in pairs.

6 ◀) 3.06 Listen to a conversation after the meeting. The team leader's boss is asking her some questions. Try to answer each question yourself before you listen to the team leader's answer.

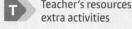
Teacher's resources: extra activities

Functional language

Asking for and giving updates

7 Match the beginnings (1–7) with the endings (a–g) to make questions from the audio which are used to ask for an update.

1 How are we doing with the
2 What's happening with
3 And where are
4 Can you bring me up
5 What's the latest
6 Can you give
7 When will you be able to bring me up to

a me an update on the plans?
b redrafting of the China contract?
c to date on the programme for today?
d the deadlines?
e speed on the factory shutdown?
f on the new schedule?
g we with the logo?

8A Complete the sentences from the audio using the words in the box.

agreed   finish   followed up   impediment   progress   see   spent   worked   work on

1 Yesterday I _____ on the new contract for the China project.

2 So the draft contract is in _____ , and I expect to complete it today.

3 The only _____ I see is time.

4 I had a meeting with a sub-supplier in the morning, where we _____ some new deadlines.

5 We _____ the meeting with a nice lunch.

6 Today my plan is to _____ writing a summary of yesterday's meeting.

7 I don't _____ any impediments at the moment.

8 I'm planning to _____ the designs for the new logo.

9 Yesterday I _____ most of the day discussing ideas for the new logo.

B Which sentences in Exercise 8A a) give an update on a past action b) talk about planned actions c) refer to an impediment (problem)?

9A Work in pairs. Note down possible answers to the questions in Exercise 7. Then listen again to track 3.06 to check your answers.

T Teacher's resources: extra activities

B Practise asking and answering the questions.

10A Work in small groups. Read the notes on the three scenarios. Think about how you would use the format from the audio (giving an update on a past action, talking about planned actions, referring to any problems) to give updates on these three issues.

❯TASK

1 TH37 PROJECT

The project team has now been agreed.

The first project meeting is planned for next week. We are working on the agenda at the moment.

The final budget is expected by Friday this week, but it may not be sufficient.

2 HOLIDAY PLANS

The agreed dates for the factory shutdown will be 16 Dec–4 Jan.

Discussions with department heads are happening today.

We still need to find volunteers to answer the telephones during the shutdown.

3 DELIVERY OF NEW OFFICE FURNITURE

The delivery dates were changed yesterday. The new date is Wednesday next week.

We need to inform all departments and make sure this date is OK with everyone.

We need to find someone to deal with the delivery company. (Normally Jonathan, but he is away on a course.)

B When you are ready, take turns to ask for and give updates to the group on the scenarios and answer any questions (maximum five minutes per person). Follow the updates by discussing possible action items and noting these down.

C When you have finished, discuss what went well and what was difficult about the discussion. In particular, who gave the clearest update? What phrases did he/she use?

Self-assessment

• How successfully have you achieved the lesson outcome? Give yourself a score from 0 (I need more practice) to 5 (I know this well).

• Go to My Self-assessment in MyEnglishLab to reflect on what you have learnt.

WRITING
Email requesting an update

Lesson outcome — Learners can write an internal email requesting updates on a project.

Lead-in 1A Read the email below. What is Wilhelm asking John to do?

To: John Carver, Project Manager
From: Wilhelm Haas, Finance Manager
Subject: Building project update

Dear John,

I'd like to know if the first stage of the building project is moving **fast enough** and will meet the orignal deadlines, so could you let me know what the curent position is? If you are not going to meet the deadlines, would you check when we can get together to go over the shedule?

Also the CFO is now worried that there aren't **enough funds** to complete the project on time, especially as there have been sevral problems. I'd therefore be grateful if you could send me cost details for last month, particularly any aditional purchases you made.

I understand that whether conditions were **not good enough to** start the second stage of the project last week. I'd appreciate it if you could meet me tomorrow afternoon to discuss the rescheduled dates. Could you also ask your asistant to join us, please?

Reguards

Wilhelm

B Underline eight spelling mistakes and correct them.

C Check your answers with a partner. Then check the spellings in a dictionary.

Functional language 2 Complete the table below with words from the box.

appreciate   grateful   help   if   mind   possible   possibly   request   to   what

Statement	Question
I'd like to know ¹_____ the first stage of the building is moving fast enough.	Could you let me know ⁶_____ the current position is?
I'd therefore be ²_____ if you could send me cost details for last month.	Could you ask your assistant ⁷_____ join us, please?
I'd ³_____ it if you could meet me tomorrow afternoon.	Would you ⁸_____ sending me the details?
I need your ⁴_____ with the monthly report.	Would it be ⁹_____ to have a meeting next week?
I'd like to ⁵_____ a meeting with the manager.	Could you ¹⁰_____ meet me tomorrow?

Teacher's resources: extra activities

The email contains examples of adjective/ adverb + *enough* and *enough* + noun/*to*. Go to MyEnglishLab for optional grammar work.

→ **page 120** See Grammar reference: *(not) enough*

TASK

3A Turn to page 129 and read the situation. In pairs, discuss the exact information you want to find out about the different points.

B Write an email to the project leader requesting an update on the refurbishment in around 150 words.

C Exchange emails with your partner. In what ways are your emails the same? How many phrases from the functional language box did your partner use? Did your partner use different phrases from you?

Self-assessment

- How successfully have you achieved the lesson outcome? Give yourself a score from 0 (I need more practice) to 5 (I know this well).
- Go to My Self-assessment in MyEnglishLab to reflect on what you have learnt.

Global markets

> 'We have yet to see the full impact of the open, global marketplace.'
>
> Lou Pritchett, former Vice-President, Procter & Gamble

Unit overview

4.1 One size fits all

Lesson outcome: Learners can use vocabulary related to global markets.

Video: A food company's strategy for growth
Vocabulary: Global markets: adjective and noun collocations; word building
Project: Adapt to a new market

4.2 Online markets

Lesson outcome: Learners can use past and present passive forms when speaking and writing.

Reading: Who wants to be a sofapreneur?
Grammar: Present Simple and Past Simple passive
Writing: A product description

4.3 Communication skills: Managing conversations

Lesson outcome: Learners are aware of different approaches to managing a conversation and can use a range of expressions to signal and respond to a change of topic.

Video: Managing conversations
Functional language: Changing the subject and staying on track
Task: A conversation between a client and a supplier

4.4 Business skills: Building consensus

Lesson outcome: Learners can use a range of expressions to build consensus in a discussion on a familiar topic.

Listening: A meeting to build consensus
Functional language: Reaching agreement
Task: A discussion to reach agreement

4.5 Writing: Letter confirming an order

Lesson outcome: Learners can write an order confirmation letter.

Model text: Letter confirming an order
Functional language: Confirming order details
Grammar: Verbs + prepositions
Task: Write an order confirmation letter

4.1 > One size fits all

Lead-in

1 Discuss the questions.

1 What do you understand by the expression 'one size fits all'? To what extent is that true in global markets? Think about some of the items in the box.

> cars   clothes   coffee   fast food   ice cream   soft drinks

2 Will everyone in the world want the same food, clothes and other products in the future? Why / Why not?

VIDEO

2 How do you think Volvo cars and Starbucks coffee adapted their products for the Chinese market?

3 ▶ 4.1.1 **Watch the video and check your predictions.**

4 Watch the video again and choose the correct option in italics.

1 China has the world's largest *rich elite / middle class*.
2 Customising products for the mass market *is / is not* an important consideration.
3 There is no front passenger seat in *Volvo's / Jaguar's* luxury car for China.
4 Volvo's and Jaguar's new cars are for people *with a chauffeur / who like big vehicles*.
5 Global brands have made *slight / major* changes to products for China's middle class.
6 Starbucks didn't include its *name / logo* in the first shop it opened in China.
7 The company introduced some special *coffees / teas* for Chinese consumers.
8 Starbucks *doesn't think / thinks* the demand for coffee will grow in China.

5 Work in pairs and discuss the questions.

1 Why did Volvo and Starbucks make changes for the Chinese market?
2 What special features would you most like to have in a car?
3 How could Starbucks grow their coffee market in China?
4 How could a Chinese tea brand grow their global market?

> T > Teacher's resources:
> extra activities

Vocabulary **Global markets: adjective and noun collocations; word building**

6A Check you know the meaning of the words in the two boxes.

> consumer   local   luxury   marketing   target   product

> brands   customisation   goods   preferences   strategy   territories

B Choose a word from each box above to complete the phrases from the video.

Multinationals need to analyse their [1]_____ , adjust their [2]_____ and adapt their products to meet [3]_____ .

Therefore, [4]_____ is an important consideration for selling into China. This can affect both high-end [5]_____ as well as mass-market [6]_____ .

7 Complete the table with words from the video.

Verb	Noun	Adjective
1 _____	adaptation/adaptability	adaptable
2 _____	appeal	appealing
consume	consumer/3 _____	consumable
customise	4 _____	5 _____/customisable
6 _____	7 _____	grown
prefer	8 _____	preferable
produce	9 _____/production	productive
10 _____	specialist/specialisation	special
standardise	11 _____/standardisation	standard
target	12 _____	

8A Complete the text with the correct form of the words in brackets.

IKEA stores in China invite customers to try out furniture

IKEA opened its first store in Shanghai 20 years ago. In Chinese cities families typically live in small apartments, so the furniture retailer ¹_____ (custom) its products based on local needs and ²_____ (prefer). When it opened, IKEA's low-price strategy was confusing for many Chinese ³_____ (consume) because Western products are seen as aspirational in Asian markets. So the company ⁴_____ (target) young middle-class professionals, customers with a relatively higher income who were more aware of Western styles. IKEA also ⁵_____ (adapt) its marketing strategy, using Chinese social media and micro-blogging website Weibo to help make the brand ⁶_____ (appeal) to the urban youth. Today, the company continues to reduce prices thanks to mass ⁷_____ (produce) in its local factories and its market is ⁸_____ (grow) fast in China.

T Teacher's resources: extra activities

B Work in pairs. Say what surprised you most about IKEA's customisation for China.

▶ PROJECT: Adapt to a new market

9A Work in pairs or small groups. As members of a company's marketing team, you want to introduce a store or product to a new international market.
- Make notes to describe a store or product from your country. Use one of these ideas or your own.

> a national or local fast-food chain   a regional drink or dish   a clothes store

- Decide where you want to place this new store or product. Choose a country you know about, or use an imaginary country. Create a profile for the country, including information about what customers want.

B In your groups, discuss the following points.
- Do you think the standard store or product would do well in the new market? Why / Why not?
- Would you recommend customisation for your new market? If so, what would you customise?
- What would make a good promotion and marketing strategy? (e.g. TV adverts with a local celebrity)

C Present the product or store and your recommendations to the class. Then listen to the other groups and, as a class, decide which would be the a) easiest and b) hardest to adapt for a different market.

Self-assessment
- How successfully have you achieved the lesson outcome? Give yourself a score from 0 (I need more practice) to 5 (I know this well).
- Go to My Self-assessment in MyEnglishLab to reflect on what you have learnt.

4.2 > Online markets

Lead-in

1 Work in pairs. Look at the logos and discuss the questions.

1 What type of sites are they? Match each site with a description.

a _____ is a global online auction and shopping site for individuals and small businesses.

b _____ is China's biggest e-commerce and shopping website.

c _____ is an online food delivery service.

d _____ started as an online , it's now the largest online retailer in the USA.

2 How can an individual earn money using e-commerce websites and apps?

Reading

2 Read the article quickly. How many internet sites are mentioned?

3 Read the headline and the article again and answer the questions.

1 What is a 'sofapreneur'? Someone who …
  a earns money online while working from home.
  b spends a lot of time sitting on his/her sofa.
  c runs an online business which sells furniture.

2 What two employment statistics are mentioned from the USA?

3 Which two groups have difficulties doing traditional jobs?

4 What is the risk to other small businesses from sofapreneurs?

5 What does the writer think governments must do? Why?

6 How does Einar Parker feel about his full-time job?

7 Why does he enjoy his jewellery business?

8 Is the writer in general positive or negative about sofapreneurs?

4 Work in pairs and discuss the questions.

1 Can you think of one more benefit and disadvantage of online marketplaces?

2 Do you think that websites like PeoplePerHour are changing the way companies employ people?

Teacher's resources: extra activities

3 Do you know anyone who sells products or gets freelance work via online marketplaces?

FT

Who wants to be a sofapreneur?

By Sarah O'Connor

Alibaba is used by hundreds of millions of people around the world. Thanks to e-commerce sites like this anyone can be an import–export magnate* without leaving the sofa. Thanks to Airbnb, anyone can be a hotel manager. Today there is a growing number of 'sofapreneurs' making money from websites like Alibaba, eBay and Airbnb, and many of them are not even doing it full time. Freelancer sites like PeoplePerHour say many of their users are office staff who log on after work.

It is estimated that one percent of U.S. adults earn money from these websites. JPMorgan Chase says of this group that most of them rely on the sites for less than a quarter of their income. Still, that is valuable in a world of weak economic growth, low wages and insecure employment. In some cases, these sites are giving people who might have difficulties doing a traditional job a way to earn money, for instance because of health reasons or caring responsibilities. They can also offer lower prices to consumers. However, governments will have to make sure sofapreneurs cannot compete unfairly with other small businesses by simply avoiding tax.

One of the biggest benefits is the hardest to measure. Many of the people I've interviewed who sell products on these sites say that it gives them a sense of satisfaction they do not have in their day jobs. Last year I spoke to Einar Parker, who spent his days working on the production line at a car seat factory. He began making jewellery in his spare time and set up his own shop on Etsy. The site was started twelve years ago to sell homemade goods. 'You don't think a lot when you're on an assembly line, but I've got something to think of, coming up with ideas,' he explained. 'That is my escape.' Sofapreneurship seems to be making people a little richer and a little happier, and that is no bad thing.

*rich and powerful person in business

Grammar Present Simple and Past Simple passive

5A Look at these extracts from the article. What verb forms are the words in bold? What tense are they?

> **1**
> Alibaba **is used** by hundreds of millions of people around the world.

> **2**
> The site **was started** twelve years ago to sell homemade goods.

B Look at sentence 1 again. Which preposition do we use to show who does the action?

→ **page 121** See Grammar reference: Present Simple and Past Simple passive

6 Complete the listings on an e-commerce site with the active or present passive form of the verbs in brackets.

These personalised necklaces ¹_____ (make) of wood. Orders ²_____ (deliver) within 72 hours in the EU.

Each handmade ceramic bowl ³_____ (paint) by hand. It ⁴_____ (not recommend) to put them in the microwave, oven or dishwasher. We ⁵_____ (ship) worldwide.

Our high-quality cotton T-shirts ⁶_____ (print) specially to order and ⁷_____ (dispatch) within two days. Just ⁸_____ (select) your size and colour and the words you ⁹_____ (require).

These coffee cups and mugs ¹⁰_____ (design) by me and ¹¹_____ (pack) in a gift box. If your items ¹²_____ (need) by a certain date, please contact me.

7A Complete the passive sentences with the past or present passive form of the verbs in brackets.

1 Alibaba _____ (set up) by Jack Ma, who is said to be one of China's richest men today.

2 Sellers using Alibaba's and eBay's sites _____ (not charge) a commission on goods sold.

3 Airbnb's headquarters _____ (base) in San Francisco, California.

4 Hotels _____ (not allow) to advertise rooms on the Airbnb site.

5 Some homes/offices on the website _____ (own) by Airbnb.

6 When eBay _____ (create) in 1995 it _____ (call) AuctionWeb.

7 eBay _____ (buy) by Google in 2016.

8 Very little money _____ (need) to start an Etsy shop online.

B Decide if the sentences in Exercise 7A are *true* (T) or *false* (F). Check your answers on page 129.

T Teacher's resources: extra activities

Writing **8** Work in pairs. Imagine you want to be a sofapreneur. Look at the examples in Exercise 6 again. Think about what products you could make and sell online or what services you could offer. Write a short description of your products or services for an e-commerce site. Write 60 to 80 words.

Self-assessment
- How successfully have you achieved the lesson outcome? Give yourself a score from 0 (I need more practice) to 5 (I know this well).
- Go to My Self-assessment in MyEnglishLab to reflect on what you have learnt.

Lesson outcome	Learners are aware of different approaches to managing a conversation and can use a range of expressions to signal and respond to a change of topic.

Lead-in **1A** Work in small groups. Give examples of your own experiences of meeting people who are different from you. Here are some possible differences to think about.

1 their national culture
2 their age
3 their education

4 the culture of their organisation
5 their work/profession

B Discuss the questions.

1 What is easy or difficult about such encounters?
2 How is it different from meeting friends, colleagues and members of your family? Why?

VIDEO **2A** ▶ 4.3.1 Watch the video of Alex and Beata talking about Beata's forthcoming trip to Rio de Janeiro. Answer the questions.

1 Has Alex ever been to Rio de Janeiro?
2 How well does he know Mateo?
3 What does Alex mean when he says, 'It's difficult to stay on track sometimes'?
4 What preparation has Beata done for the trip?
5 What advice does Alex give Beata? Do you think it is useful advice? Why?

B Watch the video again. Why is Beata worried about the trip?

L Go to MyEnglishLab for extra video activities.

3A Based on what you have seen so far, how should Beata behave in the meeting with Mateo? As a class, decide which option to watch first.

Option A – Listen to Mateo, but politely try to stay on the topic of the Diabsensor and not be distracted. Stay focused on why she is in Rio.

Option B – Listen to Mateo, show interest in what he is saying and not worry about the Diabsensor. Go with the flow – he is the client, after all.

B Watch the video in the sequence the class has decided and answer the questions for each video.

Option A ▶ 4.3.2
1 What topics do Beata and Mateo talk about?
2 How does Beata try to turn the discussion towards the Diabsensor?
3 How does Mateo react to these attempts?
4 Alex warned Beata that Mateo likes to multitask (do different tasks at the same time). What example of this do we see?
5 Overall, how well does Beata manage the conversation?

Option B ▶ 4.3.3
1 What topics do Beata and Mateo talk about?
2 How does Beata show an interest in what Mateo is saying?
3 Does Beata try to turn the discussion towards the Diabsensor?
4 Alex warned Beata that Mateo likes to multitask (do different tasks at the same time). What example of this do we see?
5 Overall, how well does Beata manage the conversation?

4 In pairs, discuss what you have learnt from Beata's experience about adapting your communication style.

1 What is the effect of going with the flow?
2 What is the effect of focusing on the task in hand?

5 ▶ 4.3.4 Watch the Conclusions section of the video and note down the main learning point. How far do you agree with this? Why?

Reflection **6** Think about the following questions. Then discuss your answers with a partner.

1 Compare yourself to Beata in a similar situation. How do you think you would manage?
2 Is 'go with the flow' a useful tip for you when you meet new people? Why / Why not?

Functional language

Changing the subject and staying on track

7 Look at these phrases from the video. Decide which are for changing the subject (C) and which are for staying on track (S).

1 There will be plenty of time for that later.
2 I really think we should get to the ...
3 Is this a good moment to start talking about the ... ?
4 We'll come to that later.

5 That reminds me.
6 We'll get to the ... in a moment.
7 Can we move to ... ?
8 Before I forget, ...

8 Use words from the phrases in Exercise 7 to complete the dialogue. In pairs, practise reading the dialogue.

A: So, ¹_____ item 3 on the agenda, the new minibus?

B: Yes, of course. It will be delivered next Monday morning. So we can use it for the trip to the factory on Tuesday.

A: Is ²_____ factory visit? What's the plan?

B: We'll ³_____ details of the factory visit ⁴_____ .

A: Actually, that ⁵_____ , I need to check if my children are being picked up from school today. The bus company is on strike.

B: I'm sure there ⁶_____ . Could we first finish discussing the minibus? Then we'll have a break and you can sort out your children's bus.

9A Work in pairs and discuss one of these topics using phrases from Exercise 7. One person tries to talk about the topic, the other tries to change the subject. After a few minutes, change partners and choose a new topic.

- Plans for next week
- Organising a surprise birthday party for a friend
- A new smartphone on the market
- A trip abroad

B Write short dialogues based on your discussions.

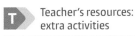 Teacher's resources: extra activities

→ page 115 See Pronunciation bank: Pronunciation of -(e)s endings

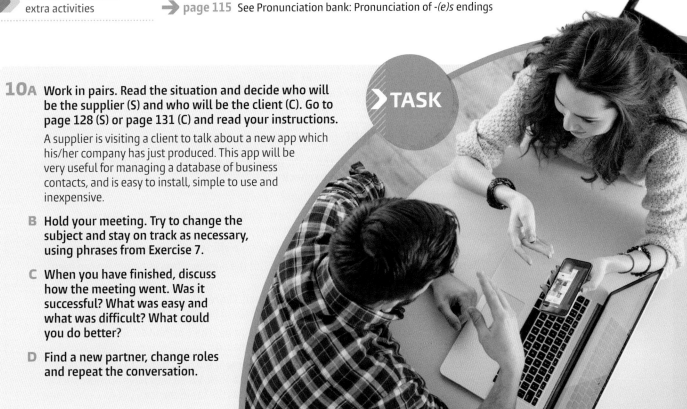

> TASK

10A Work in pairs. Read the situation and decide who will be the supplier (S) and who will be the client (C). Go to page 128 (S) or page 131 (C) and read your instructions.

A supplier is visiting a client to talk about a new app which his/her company has just produced. This app will be very useful for managing a database of business contacts, and is easy to install, simple to use and inexpensive.

B Hold your meeting. Try to change the subject and stay on track as necessary, using phrases from Exercise 7.

C When you have finished, discuss how the meeting went. Was it successful? What was easy and what was difficult? What could you do better?

D Find a new partner, change roles and repeat the conversation.

Self-assessment

- How successfully have you achieved the lesson outcome? Give yourself a score from 0 (I need more practice) to 5 (I know this well).
- Go to My Self-assessment in MyEnglishLab to reflect on what you have learnt.

4.4 ▶ BUSINESS SKILLS
Building consensus

Lesson outcome	Learners can use a range of expressions to build consensus in a discussion on a familiar topic.

Lead-in

1 Work in small groups and discuss the questions. Then share your ideas with the class.

1 Building consensus (reaching agreement) in a group can be difficult. Why is this?

2 How do we decide what *consensus* means? Does everyone have to agree, or is a majority enough?

3 Can anyone say no to a decision, or is it a manager's job to decide?

4 Some people think that different cultures find consensus in different ways. Do you agree? Think of examples from your own experience to support your arguments.

Listening

2 ◀) 4.01 Listen to the beginning of a meeting.

1 What does the speaker want to do?

2 According to the speaker, what is building consensus about?

3 Complete the sentences using the words in the box. Then listen again to check.

> chance   important   involved   respected

1 If we want to build consensus, we must make sure that everybody is _____ in the conversation. Everybody must have the _____ to speak.

2 And second, everybody's opinion is of equal weight and is to be _____ . No one in the group is more _____ than anyone else.

4 ◀) 4.02 Listen to the next part of the meeting. Has this group reached a consensus? Explain your answer.

5 Listen again and answer the questions.

1 What are the three options the manager mentions?

2 What are 'talking sticks'?

3 What does the manager mean by 'process'?

4 What does the manager mean by 'narrowing down'?

 Teacher's resources: extra activities

Functional language

Reaching agreement

6 Put this conversation in the right order so that it makes sense. The first two are done for you. Then listen to check.

Manager: Yes, Jose? What do you think? — `1`

Tanya: **I'm afraid I disagree.** It will be much better in smaller groups. That way everyone gets much more talking time. — ☐

Dorothy: **Yes, I agree, too.** We can be much more efficient if we work in small groups. — ☐

Dorothy: **So we need to** find consensus about the number of sticks before we can even start a real discussion? — ☐

Jose: Well, **I don't think** my idea is that bad. **I agree that** in a big group one or two people could dominate, but that is easy to fix. We use talking sticks. — ☐

Jose: So **I think we should** stay as one big group. There are not so many of us, and it will be easy for everyone to be heard. — `2`

Jose: Each person has two sticks. This gives them the right to talk twice. Each time they say something they must give up a stick. When they have no more sticks they cannot talk. That way everyone has the same chance. — ☐

Jose: That was just an example. Of course we need to decide how many sticks to use. — ☐

Sam: **I agree with** Tanya. Much better. With a big group one or two people always dominate. — ☐

Sam: What are talking sticks? — ☐

Sam: Actually **that's not a bad idea**. But we will need more than two sticks. — ☐

7A Put the phrases in bold from Exercise 6 into the correct category in the table below.

Expressing agreement	*Yes, I agree, too.*
Expressing disagreement	
Making a suggestion	
Reacting to a suggestion	

B Match the phrases in bold (1–6) with the categories in Exercise 7A.

1 **Yes, I think you're right.**
2 **Sorry, I don't agree with you**.
3 **Why don't we** work as one big group?
4 **Good idea!** Let's think about that.
5 **I'm not sure I agree with you** on that.
6 **How about if** we break into small groups after ten minutes?

T Teacher's resources:
extra activities

→ **page 115** See Pronunciation bank: Consonant–vowel linking between words

8A **Work in small groups. Choose one of the following topics to discuss, or suggest a different topic. Individually, take a few minutes to note down your ideas.**

1 The maximum and minimum number of working hours in a week.
2 The ideal number of public holidays in a year.
3 What makes a good language learner.

B **Follow the four steps to discuss your ideas and try to reach agreement.**

1 Take turns to explain your ideas. When you are not speaking, listen and make notes.
2 Read your notes and decide which idea(s) you prefer.
3 Take turns to state your preferences and list them on the board.
4 As a group, discuss the preferences list using phrases from Exercises 6 and 7. Try to reach agreement on the best idea.

▶TASK

C **When you have finished, discuss how well the group participated in the meeting. Share your answers with the class.**

1 Did you find it useful to write down your ideas?
2 Did the discussion follow the structure in Exercise 8B?
3 Did the group succeed in reaching agreement?
4 Which phrases in Exercises 6 and 7 did you use?

Self-assessment

• How successfully have you achieved the lesson outcome? Give yourself a score from 0 (I need more practice) to 5 (I know this well).
• Go to My Self-assessment in MyEnglishLab to reflect on what you have learnt.

Lesson outcome — Learners can write an order confirmation letter.

Lead-in **1** **Read the order confirmation letter and complete it with the words in the box.**

agreed enclose hesitate order payment received sincerely thank

Dear Mr Chahal,

ORDER CONFIRMATION

We **are writing to** you to confirm your ¹_____ number 674190 for 1,000 123/XC units a week for 12 weeks, which we ²_____ this morning.

As ³_____ at the meeting last week when we **talked about** your order, I confirm that we will deliver the goods to your factory in Mumbai every week for a twelve-week period at a price of $4.40 per unit. Last week we discussed a discount of 10 percent providing you **pay for** the goods on time. You will be pleased to know that this is included in the final price of $4,000 per month. We also confirm that the first delivery will be on 05/11.

⁴_____ terms are $4,000 monthly, 30 days after the date of the invoice and we ⁵_____ full terms and conditions for your records.

We ⁶_____ you for your business and look forward to working with you. If you have any queries, please do not ⁷_____ to contact us.

Yours ⁸_____ .

Functional language **2** **Complete the table with phrases or sentences from the letter, then add the phrases in the box to the table.**

cash on delivery Dear Sir/Madam, order number 01 for five chairs Yours faithfully, this is to confirm your order we are pleased to confirm your order we look forward to supplying you again in the future payment in advance details of our new range are enclosed we will deliver the goods to your head office

Function	Examples
Greeting	*Dear Mr Chahal,*
Opening	
Order details	
Delivery details	
Payment terms	
Enclosures	
Ending	
Closing	

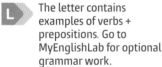

T Teacher's resources: extra activities

L The letter contains examples of verbs + prepositions. Go to MyEnglishLab for optional grammar work.

➤ **page 121** See Grammar reference: Verbs + prepositions

➤TASK

3A **Turn to page 129 and read the letter. In pairs, discuss how you could improve it.**

B **Look at the order form and handwritten notes on page 130. Write an order confirmation letter to Ms Liang in around 150 words.**

C **Exchange letters with your partner. Did your partner use different language from you? How many phrases from the functional language box did your partner use?**

Self-assessment
- How successfully have you achieved the lesson outcome? Give yourself a score from 0 (I need more practice) to 5 (I know this well).
- Go to My Self-assessment in MyEnglishLab to reflect on what you have learnt.

Design and innovation

> 'There's a way to do it better – find it.'
> Thomas Edison

Unit overview

5.1 ▶ Innovative product design

Lesson outcome	Learners can use vocabulary related to innovative product design.

Lead-in **1A** Tick (✓) the sentence(s) that best describe(s) your attitude to your lunch break during the week.

1 It's an opportunity to relax and talk with friends.
2 I eat only because it's necessary – food is fuel.
3 I enjoy choosing food and eating it.
4 I usually do something else while I eat – reading, studying, texting.
5 A long lunch break is a waste of time.
6 In a cafeteria, I don't like ordering food and waiting for it.
7 I don't usually eat lunch.
8 I prefer to eat without talking to anyone.

B Compare your answers with a partner.

 VIDEO **2A** Look at the photos of Eatsa, a new restaurant in San Francisco. How do you think customers order and receive their food?

B ▶ 5.1.1 Watch the video and check your ideas. How is Eatsa different from a traditional restaurant or cafeteria?

3 Watch the video again. Decide if these sentences are *true* (T) or *false* (F). Correct the incorrect sentences.

1 According to Scott Drummond, customers mostly want fast and accurate service.
2 Customers choose meals that are already prepared.
3 The reporter waits about three minutes for his lunch to arrive.
4 The customer in the leather jacket says he has 30–45 minutes for lunch.
5 The customer in the red tie feels happy that he didn't have to speak to anyone.
6 In general, restaurants are using more technology and fewer workers.
7 According to Scott Drummond, though his restaurant doesn't have cashiers, it does offer workers other jobs.
8 According to Mike Peng, there are a lot of restaurants exactly like Eatsa in Japan.

4 Number the sentences and phrases in the correct order. Then watch the video again from 00:14 to 00:41 and check your answers.

a the patience for the old ways of going out and buying food, interacting with
b We've addressed that by creating a process that's incredibly fast, incredibly precise
c Technology is allowing us to provide a product at an unprecedented speed,
d so the time-pressed consumer in the financial district really doesn't have
e and ultimately gives the customer much more control about what they want for lunch.
f somebody who might not hear your order correctly.

5A The video mentions several positive and negative things about this type of restaurant. List the ones you can remember and any others you can think of.

Positive	Negative
Fast, …	*No human contact, …*

 Teacher's resources: extra activities

B Would you like to eat at Eatsa? Why / Why not?

Vocabulary   Technological innovation

6 Complete the summary with the words and phrases from the video.

> automated   choice   customise   disrupt   innovation   interact   magical   place   swipe

A new way to eat

Eatsa is using technological ¹_____ to ²_____ the cafeteria business.
Eatsa customers don't ³_____ with staff, but instead use a more ⁴_____
approach to ordering food. First, they ⁵_____ their credit card in a touch-screen
device. Then they ⁶_____ their meal. Next, they ⁷_____ their order, and
it's ready in under two minutes. Customers love the ⁸_____ , the speed and the
⁹_____ moments along the way.

Describing innovative products

7A Match the words (1–9) with the best definition (a–i). Use your dictionary if necessary.

1	advanced	**a**	new, different and better than the things that came before
2	stylish	**b**	attractive in a fashionable way
3	innovative	**c**	can be trusted to do what you need or expect
4	dependable	**d**	easy to use or operate
5	user-friendly	**e**	using the most modern ideas, equipment and methods
6	unique	**f**	the best
7	top-of the-range	**g**	carefully planned and made for a certain purpose
8	classic	**h**	the only one of its kind
9	well-designed	**i**	attractive in a traditional way

B Work in pairs. For each adjective above, think of a product that you own or know about that fits the description.

My sister's car is a classic design.
Ballpoint pens are very well designed.

C Compare your ideas with another pair.

Teacher's resources:
extra activities

➤ **page 116** See Pronunciation bank: Numbers of syllables in words

---

➤ PROJECT: Innovation in business

8A Work in pairs. Think of a business you visit often – a supermarket, clothing shop, car mechanic's, etc. Make a list of three to six things that happen when you go there.

Car mechanic's: I phone to make an appointment. I drive the car there. I speak with the mechanic and explain the problem. The mechanic repairs the car. I use my credit card and pay for the work.

B Look at your list. Could any of the steps be done in a different way, perhaps using different technology?

Instead of phoning, I could book my appointment on the internet. At that time, I could add a note about the problem with the car. The mechanic could pick up the car at my house. Instead of paying with my credit card, I could pay by bank transfer.

C Work with another pair and explain your ideas to each other. Then, for each one, make a suggestion for an action to take.

We should set up an online appointment system.

Self-assessment

- How successfully have you achieved the lesson outcome? Give yourself a score from 0 (I need more practice) to 5 (I know this well).
- Go to My Self-assessment in MyEnglishLab to reflect on what you have learnt.

| **Lesson outcome** | Learners can use the Present Perfect with *just, already* and *yet*. |

Lead-in

1A When companies develop new products, they use Quality Assurance Testers. Which of these products would you enjoy testing? Which ones would you not want to evaluate? Why?

> cars   cleaning products   computer games   make-up   motorcycles
> musical instruments   snack foods   sports clothes

I'd love to test cars. I love driving!

I wouldn't enjoy testing musical instruments because I can't play one.

B Think of three or four products to add to the list.

2 What do you think is a) the worst and b) the best part of being a product tester? Why? Think about testing similar products over and over, testing products you don't like, whether or not you would have to pay for the products.

Reading

3 Read the article and answer the questions.

1 What type of product testing is it about?

2 What good and bad points of the job does the article mention?

a dream job
in product development

'People think I play video games all day, but that isn't what I do,' says the video games tester who gives us only his online nickname – TestPilot. 'As a tester, I've never really played the games – not in a normal way. I try to find problems with them.
5 For example, I've done a lot of 'matrix testing' where you make every character in a fighting game go against every other character, looking for issues with the game's function, or with the art and design. It's fun, but it's also hard work.' TestPilot adds that he also does a lot of administrative work. 'Today, I've
10 already spent two hours in meetings. And I've just spent an hour writing emails. I haven't even looked at a video game yet today.'

TestPilot has worked as a Quality Assurance Tester in the video games industry for about six years. Before that, he studied economics and politics at university. 'I've always enjoyed
15 gaming, but I never expected to get a job in the industry.' After finishing his degree, TestPilot looked for office jobs. Then a friend mentioned the games-testing job. 'For a laugh, I attended a group job interview, and they selected me. It was a total surprise!' At first, his parents often asked, 'Have you found a real
20 job yet?' But when they realised he was happy and could afford to pay his bills, they stopped asking.

TestPilot has worked for three companies. 'After three years in my first job, I left that company for a position with better pay.' But then two years later, that firm went out of business and
25 TestPilot moved on. 'I've been with my current company for a year. They've just made me Quality Assurance Manager, so I feel happy about that. To be honest, the money isn't great, but it's enough. I've already had two pay increases, and I haven't become bored with it yet, and I don't expect to. So I guess this is
30 my career, now!'

The biggest problem, says TestPilot, is that he doesn't often play games for fun these days. 'It's too much like work.'

4 **Read the article again. The statements below are incorrect. Underline the information in the article that shows the correct information.**
1 TestPilot spends most of his time playing video games.
2 Being a video game Quality Assurance Tester is the easiest job in the world.
3 TestPilot has just started working as a video games tester.
4 As a child, he dreamt of working as a games tester.
5 TestPilot's employer has never promoted him.
6 After work, he relaxes by playing video games.

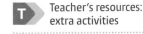
Teacher's resources: extra activities

5A **In your opinion, what are the pros and cons of TestPilot's job? Write a list. Then decide if you would like to do the job or not.**

B **Work in pairs and compare your answers. Did you list the same pros and cons?**

Grammar

Present Perfect Simple with *just, already* and *yet*

6 **Read the sentences from the article and answer the questions.**
a Today, I've **already** spent two hours in meetings.
b I've **just** spent an hour writing emails.
c I haven't even looked at a video game **yet** today.
d They've **just** made me Quality Assurance Manager, so I feel happy about that.
e I've **already** had two pay increases.
f I haven't become bored with it **yet**, and I don't expect to.

Which two sentences
1 describe things that have happened very recently?
2 describe things that have not been done or have not happened?
3 describe things that happened some time in the past, without saying specifically when?

7 **Choose the correct option in italics to complete the sentences.**
1 I've *tested already / already tested* three types of cleaning product today.
2 We can ignore this bill because we've *just paid it / paid it yet*.
3 I need to talk to Jim today, but I haven't seen him *yet / already*.
4 She's *just / yet* finished writing her test report.
5 I've been here for six months, and I haven't had a pay increase *already / yet*.
6 *Has he started his new job already? / Already has he started his new job?*

8 **Complete these sentences so they're true for you.**
1 Today, I haven't _____ yet.
2 This week, I've already _____ .
3 I've just _____ .

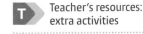
Teacher's resources: extra activities

→ **page 122** See Grammar reference: Present Perfect Simple with *just, already* and *yet*
→ **page 116** See Pronunciation bank: Contrastive stress

Speaking

9A **Look at the list of activities that people do in a typical day at work. Add three or four ideas of your own.**
make phone calls, write emails, go to meetings

B **Write five questions using your ideas to find out what your partner has done today. Use the Present Perfect Simple.**
Have you made a phone call yet? Have you written any emails yet?

C **Take turns to ask and answer questions.**
A: Have you made a phone call yet? B: No, not yet. But I've had three meetings already.

Self-assessment

- How successfully have you achieved the lesson outcome? Give yourself a score from 0 (I need more practice) to 5 (I know this well).
- Go to My Self-assessment in MyEnglishLab to reflect on what you have learnt.

Lesson outcome	Learners are aware of different approaches to giving information, and can use a range of questions to ask for different kinds of information.

Lead-in

1A **Read this comment. In pairs, discuss whether you agree with it and why.**

'Questions are the key to success in business.'

B **Think about meetings or discussions you have in your work or course of study and discuss these questions.**

1 Do you ask lots of questions or do you simply listen and take notes? Why?

2 Why is it important to ask questions?

VIDEO

2A ▶ 5.3.1 **Watch as Beata prepares for her conference call with Daniel and Clarice. Note down what Beata says about:**

1 Mateo.

2 the conference call with Daniel and Clarice.

Go to MyEnglishLab for extra video activities.

B **What do you think will happen during the conference call?**

3A **In small groups, discuss which is the best approach (Option A or B) for Beata to take as she participates in her conference call with Daniel and Clarice. As a class, decide which video to watch first.**

Option A – Beata tells Daniel and Clarice everything that has happened, including minor and unimportant details.

Option B – Beata gives Daniel and Clarice an overview.

B **Watch the videos in the sequence the class has decided and answer the same questions for each video.**

Option A ▶ 5.3.2

Option B ▶ 5.3.3

1 What information did Beata give Daniel and Clarice about the meeting with Mateo?

2 How did Daniel try to get more information / the right information from Beata?

3 Did Daniel get the information he needed?

4 How did Beata feel at the end of the conference call?

4 **In pairs, discuss the pros and cons of Beata's approach in each option.**

5 ▶ 5.3.4 **Watch the Conclusions section of the video and note down the points the speaker makes about managing information and asking questions.**

Reflection

6 **Think about the following questions. Then work in pairs and discuss your answers.**

1 What kind of questions do you typically ask in discussion at work or in your studies?

2 How can you make sure you take part in discussions in English successfully?

Functional language

Asking open and closed questions

7A Match the beginnings (1–5) with the endings (a–e) to form sentences from the video.

1	Tell us about	a	want us to change, exactly?
2	Why did they	b	the colour?
3	Can we change	c	ever met him?
4	What does Mateo	d	your meeting with Mateo.
5	Have you	e	spend so much time on this?

a 'Can we change the colour of the product?'

b 'What do you think about changing the colour of the product?'

B Read the questions on the left. Which question:

1 can be answered with *Yes* or *No*?

2 invites the other person to give his/her opinion and provide more details?

3 is an open question?

4 is a closed question?

8A Match the questions from Exercise 7A to the categories in the table.

Encouraging someone to speak	Asking for confirmation	Asking for information
Clarice, what do you think? Tell us about the rest of the discussion. _____	Is it possible to change the packaging design? Can you get back to us by Monday? _____ _____	What do you mean, a problem with the design of the packaging ? What's wrong with the colour? How long will it take you to confirm this? _____ _____

 Teacher's resources: extra activities

B Work in pairs. Write a response for each question in Exercise 7A. Then practise asking and answering the questions.

9A Work in pairs. You have both been practising a presentation for an important meeting or assignment. You have agreed to give each other feedback on your presentation skills. You have watched the presentation and made some notes. Read your notes. Student A: Turn to page 136. Student B: Turn to page 133.

> **TASK**

B Prepare questions to ask about your own presentation skills. Use the questions in Exercises 7 and 8 to help you. Ask about:

1 the content of the presentation.

2 the length of the presentation.

3 the slides.

4 your delivery (how clearly you spoke, if you spoke slowly or quickly, your pronunciation).

5 your body language.

C Take turns to ask your partner questions about your presentation skills. Ask for clarification if you don't understand your partner's feedback.

D Think about the questions you used to ask for feedback. Discuss what went well, what didn't go well and how you can improve next time.

Self-assessment

- How successfully have you achieved the lesson outcome? Give yourself a score from 0 (I need more practice) to 5 (I know this well).
- Go to My Self-assessment in MyEnglishLab to reflect on what you have learnt.

Lesson outcome Learners are able to use a range of expressions to describe the features and benefits of a product.

Lead-in **1A** Think about a product you bought recently, e.g. a mobile phone, a games console. Work in small groups and discuss the questions.

1 Why did you want to buy this product?
2 Did you research similar products first? Why / Why not?
3 Why did you finally choose this product?

B Read these comments from marketing experts. Then complete the definitions below using the words in the box

'People don't buy oranges because they are round.'

'People buy benefits, not features.'

> benefits   features

1 _____ are general information about a product, e.g. what it does, its dimensions, etc.
2 _____ are what a product can do for the buyer, e.g. solve a problem.

Listening **2A** ◀⏺ 5.01 Listen to two Sales Representatives, Kendra and Paolo, describing the new ZX3 Hot-Seat during a product launch. Which speaker talks mainly about *features* and which speaker talks mainly about *benefits*?

B Work in pairs and discuss the questions.
1 What type of chair is the ZX3 Hot-Seat?
2 Who do you think might buy the ZX3 Hot-Seat, and why?

3A ◀⏺ 5.02 Listen to Kendra's presentation again and complete the product specifications for the ZX3 Hot-Seat.

ZX3 Hot-Seat	Product Specifications
Dimensions:	[1]_____ mm x 480 mm
Weight:	[2]_____ g
Colour(s):	red, [3]_____ and _____
Materials:	[4]_____ : memory foam
	[5]_____ : water-resistant nylon mesh
	[6]_____ : heavy-duty rubber

B ◀⏺ 5.03 Listen to Paolo's presentation again and tick (✓) the benefits you hear.

1 comfortable ☐   3 easy to clean ☐   5 lightweight ☐   7 easy to carry ☐
2 stylish ☐   4 practical ☐   6 cheap ☐   8 mobile-compatible ☐

Functional language | **Describing features and benefits**

4A Complete Kendra's description of the retractable arm feature using the verbs in the box.

> comes in   comes with   made of   measures   weighs

As you can see, [the ZX3 Hot-Seat] [1]_____ retractable arms to provide maximum comfort. Each arm [2]_____ 300 by 125 mm, [3]_____ 45 g, is [4]_____ lightweight plastic and [5]_____ black or grey.

B Complete Paolo's description of the product's benefits using the phrases in the box.

> allow you to   lets you   make it easier to   means that you can   so it's easier to

Well, the ZX3 Hot-Seat is the solution. For example, its heated seat [1]_____ combine the excitement of the stadium with the comfort of home. For added comfort, there are optional arm-rests which [2]_____ sit back and relax as you watch the game, while the plastic cup-holder [3]_____ enjoy your favourite drink at the same time. The Hot-Seat has a washable cover [4]_____ clean, plus the lightweight seat with handles and straps [5]_____ carry.

Tip

To describe how products are used, we can say: *It's (used) for holding* hot and cold drinks. *It's designed for sitting* outside.

5A Work in pairs. Match the products/services (A–C) with the features (1–6) and benefits (a–f).

Product	Features	Benefits
A military-style rucksack	**1** additional side pockets	**a** place for your student/work ID or keys
B smart phone	**2** free home-delivery service	**b** ability to post photos on social media at any time
C newly opened supermarket	**3** 5G internet connection	**c** save money
	4 washable fabric	**d** no need to interrupt your busy schedule (to go shopping)
	5 weekly discounts on fresh products	**e** no need to carry two phones
	6 dual SIM	**f** easy to keep clean

It's for … ; It has … , which means you can … ; It comes with … , which allows you to …

B Practise describing the usage, features and benefits of these products/services. Use the phrases in Exercise 4.

T Teacher's resources: extra activities

6A Work in pairs. Your team at your place of work or college wants to buy a new printer. You have been asked to research the new printer and report back informally to the rest of the team. Follow these steps.

1 Turn to page 131 and choose a printer.

2 Read about the printer's features and decide on the benefits.

3 Prepare your presentation. Decide who will talk about the features and who will talk about the benefits. (You can include a presentation slide if you wish.)

B Work with another pair. Take turns to give your presentations using phrases from Exercise 4 to describe the features and benefits. When you are listening, note down one or two questions to ask at the end of the presentation. Decide which printer you will buy.

C As a group, discuss what went well and what didn't go so well and how you could improve in the future.

❯**TASK**

Self-assessment

- How successfully have you achieved the lesson outcome? Give yourself a score from 0 (I need more practice) to 5 (I know this well).
- Go to My Self-assessment in MyEnglishLab to reflect on what you have learnt.

| Lesson outcome | Learners can write a product review. |

Lead-in **1A** Read the product review and complete it with one word in each gap.

GKKFONE 2 | Rating: ★★★☆☆ | RRP: £72.00

I chose this phone because the adverts said it performed ¹_____ well as its more expensive competitors. For the price, it is **pretty** good value for money. ²_____ **practical strong** packaging the phone came in also included a screen protector and cover, ³_____ saved me having to buy them. The **extremely attractive silver** phone has a **large clear** screen, making it very easy ⁴_____ use. It's not quite as fast as some major competitors, but it offers a **fairly good** performance. I was impressed ⁵_____ the **long-lasting lightweight** battery and, although other reviewers said the battery stopped charging after a month, mine charges perfectly.

The main downside ⁶_____ the **new** fingerprint ID system, which doesn't always work first time. Another problem is the camera, which sometimes freezes, so I have to turn the phone ⁷_____ and on to get it to work. However, the picture quality is great.

⁸_____ you want a phone to rival the more expensive brands, I recommend the GKKFONE 2.

B Work in pairs and check your answers.

Functional language **2** Complete the table with the words in the box.

> another   chose   decided   downside   impressed   included
> most   particularly   problem   said   thing   worst

Introduction	Good points	Bad points
I ¹_____ this phone because …	The packaging also ⁴_____ a screen protector and cover.	The main ⁹_____ is the new fingerprint ID system.
We bought the phone …	⁵_____ good thing is that the phone has a fairly large clear screen.	Another ¹⁰_____ is the camera.
The adverts ²_____ it performed as well as more expensive ones.	I was ⁶_____ by …	One ¹¹_____ I didn't like was …
I ³_____ to buy this phone because …	I ⁷_____ liked the …	The ¹²_____ thing about the phone is …
	What I liked ⁸_____ was …	

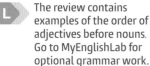
Teacher's resources: extra activities

The review contains examples of the order of adjectives before nouns. Go to MyEnglishLab for optional grammar work.

➡ **page 122** See Grammar reference: Order of adjectives before nouns

TASK

3A Work in pairs. Turn to page 129 and read the online product review. Discuss how you could improve it, then write your improved review.

B Write a review of a product you have recently bought. Say what it does, what you think is good about it and what is not so good and give any recommendations. Write around 150 words.

C Exchange reviews with a partner. In what ways are your reviews the same? How many phrases from the functional language box did your partner use? Did your partner use different phrases from you?

Self-assessment
- How successfully have you achieved the lesson outcome? Give yourself a score from 0 (I need more practice) to 5 (I know this well).
- Go to My Self-assessment in MyEnglishLab to reflect on what you have learnt.

Safety and security

> 'We don't see investment in safety as a cost to our business; we see it more as an asset.'

Paul Neal, O'Donovan Waste Disposal (from the video)

Unit overview

6.1	**Safety at work** **Lesson outcome:** Learners can use vocabulary related to health and safety at work.	**Video:** Health and safety at a company **Vocabulary:** Health and safety **Project:** Accident questionnaire
6.2	**Being security-conscious** **Lesson outcome:** Learners can use a range of modal verbs to talk about prohibition, obligation and no obligation in the past and present.	**Listening:** Security measures in the workplace **Grammar:** Modal verbs of prohibition, obligation and no obligation **Writing:** Email about new security measures
6.3	**Communication skills:** Dealing with disagreement **Lesson outcome:** Learners can use a range of expressions to discuss rules and requirements and explain their position.	**Video:** Dealing with disagreement **Functional language:** Explaining rules and requirements **Task:** Convincing someone of your arguments
6.4	**Business skills:** Dealing with conflict **Lesson outcome:** Learners can suggest a resolution to a conflict in a simple negotiation using a range of expressions.	**Listening:** Discussion about a problem at work **Functional language:** Resolving a conflict **Task:** Resolving a conflict
6.5	**Writing:** Instructions and warnings **Lesson outcome:** Learners can write simple guidelines about what to do in different situations.	**Model text:** Instructions on using equipment **Functional language:** Instructions and warnings **Grammar:** Linking words for time **Task:** Guidelines for company staff

6.1 > Safety at work

Lead-in **1A** Work in groups. Do this quick quiz to find out how much you know about international safety symbols. Match 1–5 with a–e.

International safety symbols

1 Square or rectangular red signs indicate
2 Square or rectangular green signs typically indicate
3 Circular red signs with a diagonal line indicate
4 Circular blue signs typically indicate
5 Triangular yellow signs indicate

a that certain actions are prohibited.
b that wearing a certain type of protective equipment is obligatory.
c there is a possible risk and you should be careful.
d where to find firefighting equipment.
e emergency procedures or an emergency location.

B Which safety symbols have you noticed in the place where you work or study?

VIDEO **2A** You are going to watch a video about health and safety at a company. Look at the two images from the video. Can you predict what the company does?

B ▶ 6.1.1 Watch the video and check your predictions.

3 Watch the video again and correct the factual error in each sentence.
1 O'Donovan Waste Disposal is based in Manchester.
2 Paul Neal is the company's Factory Supervisor.
3 The company collects waste and burns it.
4 Protecting the environment is a priority for the company.
5 In order to protect cyclists, vehicles are smaller so the driver can see more.
6 The company has also put alarms and electronic sensors on vehicles.
7 The police can view the images from truck cameras if there are problems.
8 Senior staff at the recycling centre are given protective clothing and training.
9 Whenever there is an accident, it is recorded in a database and investigated.

4 Work in pairs or groups. Discuss these questions.
1 How do you think being safer would benefit a company?
2 Who is responsible for health and safety where you work or study? What does their role involve?
3 What health and safety training do people receive in your organisation? How satisfied with the training are you?

 Teacher's resources: extra activities

Vocabulary   **Health and safety**

5 Work in pairs. Match the verb and noun collocations from the video. What does each verb mean in the context?

1	fit	**a**	a risk of injury
2	handle	**b**	side guards / cameras and sensors
3	pose	**c**	training programmes
4	issue (someone with)	**d**	an accident / incident
5	hold	**e**	clothing / personal safety equipment
6	record	**f**	waste materials / sharp debris

6A Label items 1–7 in the photo with the words for personal safety clothing and equipment.

cut-resistant gloves   ear defenders   face mask   goggles   hard hat
high-visibility clothing   steel toe-cap boots

B Have you ever had to wear any personal safety clothing and equipment?

7A Check the meaning of these verbs related to accidents.

bleed   break   cut   damage   drop   fall   hit   hurt   injure   slip

B Choose the correct option in italics to complete these sentences from a company's accident book.

1 The cleaner *dropped / fell* a heavy box on his foot and *bled / broke* three toes.
2 The kitchen assistant *broke / cut* his finger with a sharp knife and it *bled / injured* a lot.
3 When the technician *dropped / slipped* and *fell / hit* on the wet floor, she *hurt / slipped* her knees.
4 He badly *hit / damaged* his back when moving heavy waste in the warehouse.
5 The admin assistant *fell / hit* her head on the open cupboard door.
6 He *injured / slipped* his neck when he crashed his car into the wall.

8 Have you ever had any first aid training? Would you like to be a first aider? Why / Why not?

T Teacher's resources: extra activities

PROJECT: Accident questionnaire

9A Work in groups of four or more. Look at the results of a survey and check the vocabulary.

B Ask each other questions based on the survey. Make notes about the group's accidents and injuries.

Have you ever broken a bone? How did it happen? Where did it happen? When was it?

C Prepare the results of your group's accident survey. Use the survey in Exercise 9A to help you.

D Present your findings to another group. Which group has had most accidents? What are the most common accidents and injuries people mentioned?

SURVEY RESULTS

None of us has ever broken a bone.
One of us has had first aid training.
Two of us have had an accident recently.
Three of us have a scar from a cut.
All of us have had sports injuries.

Self-assessment
• How successfully have you achieved the lesson outcome? Give yourself a score from 0 (I need more practice) to 5 (I know this well).
• Go to My Self-assessment in MyEnglishLab to reflect on what you have learnt.

6.2 ❯ Being security-conscious

Lesson outcome	Learners can use a range of modal verbs to talk about prohibition, obligation and no obligation in the past and present.

Lead-in

1A **What do you know about these typical security measures? Match some of them with the photos.**

> card-operated lift   CCTV   fingerprint scanner   ID badge   metal detector
> security doors   security guard   security tags   x-ray machine

B **What examples of security measures do you see in your everyday life? Where? How do you feel about these measures? Why?**

Listening

2 🔊 6.01 **Listen to three people talking about security measures in the workplace. Which speaker has the most security measures at work? Which one has the least?**

Jenn   Paul   Aisha

3 **Listen to the three speakers again and choose the correct option.**

1 Jenn says that the guests use their room key card to
   a get in and out of the hotel lifts.
   b go up and down in the lift.
   c get access to the stairs.

2 She mentions that guests sometimes complain because
   a the system to operate the lifts is complicated.
   b they have problems opening their room doors.
   c they have restricted access to other floors.

3 Paul feels that the receptionist
   a can't control access very well.
   b is not responsible for answering the phones.
   c does not have enough work to keep her busy.

4 He says that
   a staff and students don't take precautions.
   b the security cameras are not very useful.
   c there have been some problems with crime.

5 Aisha feels that the office regulations
   a were stricter in the past.
   b have become much stricter.
   c haven't changed much over the years.

6 Which use of her ID badge doesn't she mention?
   a recording her work time
   b getting through doors
   c operating office equipment

4 **Discuss the questions.**

1 Which of the workplace(s) mentioned do you think needs to improve security? Why? How?

2 What low-tech and hi-tech security measures were mentioned? Can you think of any others?

3 How could companies use radio frequency ID cards to follow their staff's movements? What do you think about companies checking on employees in this way?

 Teacher's resources: extra activities

Grammar Modal verbs of prohibition, obligation and no obligation

5A 🔊 6.02 **Complete these phrases from the recording. Listen and check.**

1 Guests _____ use their room key card in the lifts.

2 You _____ take the lift.

3 She _____ answer the phones.

4 You _____ bring in any pen drives.

5 In the past you _____ wear your photo ID.

6 Your badge _____ be visible on you at all times.

B Which word or words above express the idea that:

a this isn't allowed or permitted? _____

b it is necessary to do this? _____ , _____ , _____

c it is not necessary to do this? _____

d it was not necessary to do this in the past? _____

➤ **page 123** See Grammar reference: Modal verbs of prohibition, obligation and no obligation

6 Look at the groups of sentences. Do all three in each group mean the same or do they have different meanings? Write *S* (same) or *D* (different).

1 a You must switch off your mobile.

  b You have to switch off your mobile.

  c You need to switch off your mobile.

2 a We mustn't use personal email accounts for work.

  b We don't have to use personal email accounts for work.

  c We don't need to use personal email accounts for work.

3 a Do we need to wear these visitor ID badges?

  b Do we have to wear these visitor ID badges?

  c Must we wear these visitor ID badges?

4 a They didn't have to use CCTV here.

  b They mustn't use CCTV here.

  c They didn't need to use CCTV here.

7 Complete the article about shop security measures with the correct positive or negative modal verb form. More than one modal verb may be possible.

Shop security past and present

Retail theft, also known as shoplifting, is a major problem for shops. In the past, prevention measures were more personal and low-tech. Shopkeepers and employees [1]_____ watch customers closely and the security system [2]_____ be any more sophisticated than that.

In today's competitive retail industry, security systems [3]_____ be more subtle and cost effective. However, they [4]_____ be so aggressive that it makes potential customers feel uncomfortable and loses the shop sales. Theft-prevention [5]_____ stop thieves but [6]_____ frighten real shoppers.

With radio frequency ID chips it is now possible to follow items and send instant alerts to security guards when these are moving towards the door. The retailer also [7]_____ accept that theft is sometimes committed by staff. The solution [8]_____ be expensive or frightening for employees. Staff lockers with glass doors is one simple option.

 Teacher's resources: extra activities

➤ **page 116** See Pronunciation bank: Phrasing and pausing

Writing

8A Imagine you are responsible for security in your organisation and want to introduce a new security measure. Write an email to everyone in the organisation. Write around 80 words. Include the following:

- Say what the security measure is (e.g. ID badges, security guards, etc.).
- Say why the measure is being introduced.
- Tell them about any prohibitions and obligations. Use modal verbs from this lesson.

B Read each other's emails and find out who introduced the strictest measures.

Lesson outcome — Learners can use a range of expressions to discuss rules and requirements and explain their position.

Lead-in **1A** Work in pairs and discuss the statement about speaking with confidence. Do you agree or disagree?

'You're either confident or you're not. It's not something you can learn.'

B How can you seem more confident in your own language? Think about how you speak, and about your body language.

VIDEO **2** ▶ 6.3.1 Watch the video as Beata reflects on her upcoming meeting with Mateo. Answer the questions.

1 How does Beata feel about the meeting with Mateo?
2 Why does she feel like this?
3 What outcome for the meeting does Beata want?
4 What do you think will happen during the meeting? Why?

3A In small groups, discuss which is the best approach (Option A or B) for Beata to take in the meeting with Mateo. As a class, decide which video to watch first.

Option A – Beata decides to focus on maintaining a good business relationship with Mateo.

Option B – Beata decides to focus on achieving her business objective.

Go to MyEnglishLab for extra video activities.

B Watch the videos in the sequence the class has decided and answer the same questions for each video.

Option A ▶ 6.3.2 | 1 How should the Diabsensor be stored?
Option B ▶ 6.3.3 | 2 How does Mateo suggest storing the product?
3 How does Beata respond to Mateo's objections?
4 What is the outcome of the meeting?
5 How does Beata feel at the end of the meeting?

4 Which option has the most positive outcome for Evromed? Discuss in pairs and agree what you can learn from Beata's experience.

5 ▶ 6.3.4 Watch the Conclusions section of the video and note down the points the speaker makes about explaining rules and requirements.

Reflection **6** Think about the following questions. Then discuss your answers with a partner.

1 In general, how confident do you feel speaking English?
2 How confident would you feel participating in a difficult conversation in English?
3 Have you ever had a difficult conversation in English? How confident did you feel?

Functional language

Explaining rules and requirements

7A Use the phrases (a–i) to complete the sentences from the video in the table.

a it's a question of	**d** My position is	**g** needs storing at
b I understand that	**e** It's great that you	**h** don't need to worry about
c We can't ... unless	**f** We really appreciate all	**i** must be refrigerated

A Explaining rules	Let me get this straight. The Diabsensor [1]_____ around 5°C? [The product] [2]_____ , otherwise it's unsafe. You [3]_____ [all those EU rules].
B Stating your position	As I explained, [4]_____ safety. [5]_____ clear. [6]_____ go ahead with the delivery _____ the necessary storage measures are in place.
C Maintaining a positive relationship	[7]_____ the work you're doing. [8]_____ have already done so much [to promote the product]. [9]_____ this is difficult for you.

B Match the sentences to the correct category (A–C) in Exercise 7A.

1 Either you [find a compromise / review the production costs] or I can't [approve the delivery / sign off on the budget]. ____

2 The Diabsensor has to be stored at around 5°C. ____

3 I'm sure we want [the same outcome / to reach a compromise]. ____

4 I'm not comfortable agreeing to [the delivery] without the [correct storage / safety] measures in place. ____

5 I can see you've already done a lot [to help promote the product / establish an efficient workflow]. ____

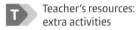

Communication tip

When you give a strong opinion, try to maintain a positive relationship by showing empathy.

T Teacher's resources: extra activities

8 In pairs, practise responding to these colleagues, using the prompts.

Student A: Go to page 134 and respond to a colleague saying:

'You said the report needed to be finished by the end of this week. However, it's more complex than I thought. I really need another two days to complete it, if possible.'

Student B: Go to page 138 and respond to a colleague saying:

'Could you confirm my holiday request, please? I'd like to buy my tickets to Sydney.'

> **TASK**

9A Work in groups of three. Choose one of the scenarios below and decide who will take the roles of employee/student, supervisor/tutor, and observer.

B Turn to page 133 and read the pros and cons of each scenario. Student A (employee/student) and Student B (supervisor/tutor): Write 1–2 more pros and cons for your role, then prepare your arguments. Student C (observer): Look at your instructions on page 131.

Scenarios

1 An employee wants to work from home one day a week.

2 An employee has asked for time off to take an advanced course in computer skills.

C Roleplay your meetings and try to convince your partner of your arguments. Maintain a good relationship with your partner.

D When you have finished, listen to the observer's feedback. Discuss what went well, what didn't go well and how you can improve next time.

Self-assessment

- How successfully have you achieved the lesson outcome? Give yourself a score from 0 (I need more practice) to 5 (I know this well).
- Go to My Self-assessment in MyEnglishLab to reflect on what you have learnt.

Lesson outcome — Learners can suggest a resolution to a conflict in a simple negotiation using a range of expressions.

Lead-in 1A Work in pairs. Look at some of the reasons for possible conflict in a team. Have you experienced any of these at your work or place of study?

WORK, WORK, WORK!

LOVE THIS SPACE & WASH UP

SLIPS, TRIPS & FALLS

B Tick (✔) the statement(s) you agree with and explain your choices to your partner.

1 I avoid conflict where possible.
2 I am very bad at dealing with conflict.
3 I am usually able to remain calm during a conflict.
4 I believe conflict can sometimes be positive.

C In small groups, think of 3–4 pieces of advice for two people trying to resolve a conflict.

Don't use an aggressive tone of voice.

Listening 2A ◀》6.03 Tony and Alex are discussing a problem at work. Listen to Part 1. Which situation in Exercise 1A is the cause of the conflict?

B Correct the false statements. Then listen again and check.

1 The ZX390 is faulty.
2 Tony's apprentices are responsible for cleaning the workshop.
3 The cleaner is currently on holiday.
4 Tony and Alex are worried about completing the Japanese order on time.
5 Alex understands Tony's concerns *and* those of the management team.

C In pairs, discuss how Alex and Tony could resolve this conflict. Compare your ideas with the rest of the group.

D ◀》6.04 Listen to Part 2 and answer the questions.

1 What practical solution does Alex suggest to help resolve the problem?
2 How does Tony react to the suggestion?
3 Are Alex and Tony able to resolve the conflict?
4 What three things does Alex say will happen next?

Functional language

Resolving a conflict

3A Complete the sentences from the conversation with the words in the box.

> appreciate both check come difficult happy proceed saying
> see suggestion understand

1 I _____ it's _____ for you, Tony.
2 I _____ what you're _____ , Alex, but what's the solution?
3 I totally agree. I can _____ it from _____ sides.
4 So how do we _____ ?
5 I think we need to _____ to a compromise.
6 My _____ is to supply your team with slip-resistant footwear.
7 Can I just _____ you're _____ with this idea before I speak to the management team?

B Match the sentences in Exercise 3A with the correct category (a–d). One sentence falls into two categories.

a Empathising (showing understanding)
b Asking for suggestions
c Making suggestions
d Checking someone agrees

C Here are more phrases to resolve a conflict. Match them with the correct category in Exercise 3B (a–d).

1 I can see how annoying it is for you.
2 Why don't you try discussing it with him first?
3 Can we come to an agreement on this?
4 It might be a good idea to think about all the details.
5 I know how you feel.
6 Do you agree?
7 What do you suggest?
8 How would you deal with the problem?

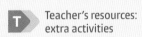 Teacher's resources: extra activities

➔ **page 116** See Pronunciation bank: Stress in phrases

❯**TASK**

4A Work in pairs and read the scenario. You are going to practise resolving the conflict.

Scenario

Several colleagues have complained about a new intern using his/her mobile phone in the office. The intern's supervisor has agreed to meet the intern and one of the colleagues to resolve the situation.

B Decide who will be the supervisor and who will be the intern. Read your role cards. Supervisors: Turn to page 132. Interns: Turn to page 134. Review the phrases in Exercise 3. Prepare your arguments and plan how you could resolve the conflict.

C When you are ready, roleplay the conversation between the supervisor and the intern. Make sure you show understanding, and ask for and make suggestions. At the end, check that your partner agrees, and review the situation.

D Reflect on what went well, what didn't go well and how you could improve next time. Change roles and start again or choose another scenario from Exercise 1A.

Self-assessment

• How successfully have you achieved the lesson outcome? Give yourself a score from 0 (I need more practice) to 5 (I know this well).
• Go to My Self-assessment in MyEnglishLab to reflect on what you have learnt.

WRITING
Instructions and warnings

Lesson outcome	Learners can write simple guidelines about what to do in different situations.

Lead-in **1A Complete the guidelines with the verbs in the box.**

be   follow   make   put   remove   report   touch   watch

USING EQUIPMENT – general instructions & warnings

DOs
- ✔ ¹_____ on protective clothing supplied **before** entering the room.
- ✔ ²_____ the manufacturer's instructions and guides for the equipment.
- ✔ ³_____ sure you put everything away in its correct place **after** using it.
- ✔ ⁴_____ any problems with equipment **as soon as** you notice them.

DON'Ts
- ✘ Don't ⁵_____ faulty or damaged equipment.
- ✘ Don't ⁶_____ protective guards from the equipment.

WARNINGS
- ⚠ ⁷_____ out for clothes or jewellery that can get caught in the equipment.
- ⚠ ⁸_____ careful not to distract people **while** they are working on the equipment.

B Work in pairs and compare your answers.

Functional language

2 Label the instructions *Do* (D), *Don't* (DT) or *Warning* (W).
1 No one is permitted to enter without protective clothing.
2 You must wear your ID badge at all times.
3 Beware of trip hazards.
4 Make sure you switch the machine off.
5 Don't forget to clean the machine every day.
6 Put signs out when the floor is wet.
7 You are not allowed to eat or drink near the machines.
8 Be careful of forklift trucks.

T Teacher's resources: extra activities

L The guidelines contain examples of linking words for time. Go to MyEnglishLab for optional grammar work.

➔ **page 123** See Grammar reference: Linking words for time

▶TASK

3A Work in pairs, A and B.
Student A: Turn to page 132 and look at the information about lifting heavy loads.
Student B: Turn to page 134 and look at the information about what to do in a fire.
In your pairs, create guidelines for staff under the following headings:
A: Before lifting, Lifting, Putting down, Never
B: You must, If you find a fire, How to escape, If you cannot leave office, Never

B Write the guidelines giving company staff instructions in around 120 words.

C In new pairs, one A and one B, exchange guidelines. Decide how clear the instructions are and give each other feedback on the strong points and suggest changes where necessary.

Self-assessment	• How successfully have you achieved the lesson outcome? Give yourself a score from 0 (I need more practice) to 5 (I know this well). • Go to My Self-assessment in MyEnglishLab to reflect on what you have learnt.

Customer service

> 'Customer service is not a department, it's everyone's job.'
> Anonymous

Unit overview

7.1 > Airline customer service
Lesson outcome: Learners can use vocabulary related to customer service.

Video: Customer service in the airline industry
Vocabulary: Customer service
Project: Design a premium service

7.2 > Hanging on the telephone
Lesson outcome: Learners can use a range of verbs taking *to*-infinitive or *-ing*.

Listening: Complaint about a service
Grammar: Verb + *to*-infinitive or *-ing*
Writing: A complaint on a company forum

7.3 > Communication skills: Responding to customer concerns
Lesson outcome: Learners can use a range of expressions to manage customer relationships and support a colleague.

Video: Solving customer problems
Functional language: Responding to customer concerns
Task: Deal with customer complaints

7.4 > Business skills: Generating and presenting ideas
Lesson outcome: Learners can use a range of expressions to generate and present ideas.

Listening: Training day on customer service
Functional language: Discussing and presenting ideas
Task: Generate and present ideas

7.5 > Writing: External 'thank you' email
Lesson outcome: Learners can write an email expressing thanks.

Model text: A 'thank you' email
Functional language: Opening, giving details and closing a 'thank you' email
Grammar: *some (of), any, all (of), most (of), no, none (of)*
Task: A 'thank you' email

Business workshop 7: p.100 | **Review 7:** p.110 | **Pronunciation:** 7.2 Unstressed syllables at the end of a sentence | **Grammar reference:** p.124
7.4 Introducing a topic p.117

7.1 ▶ Airline customer service

Lesson outcome	Learners can use vocabulary related to customer service.

Lead-in

1 Work in groups. Discuss what represents good customer service for you. Think about these businesses and other services you know. Use some of the phrases in the box below.

> airline   bank   hotel   internet provider   online retailer   restaurant   shop

> it's easy to find what I want   I trust them   it's easy to get solutions to problems
> the staff are competent/efficient/friendly/experienced/polite/well-trained
> the quality is high   the service is fast   the payment system is clear and easy

VIDEO

2 ▶ 7.1.1 Watch the video and put these items in the order they are mentioned.

a training airline ground staff

b a special meal offered by one airline

c air travel in the past

d research into customer needs

e the philosophy of one low-cost airline

3 Watch the first part of the video again (00:00 to 02:23). Complete the summary notes about low-cost airlines with one or two words you hear.

Today the airline industry gives passengers a choice of different levels of customer service. Ryanair is a pioneer of low-cost flight. If you don't want to [1]_____ , you'll pay for priority boarding and any other [2]_____ . Journalist Siobhán Creaton says that you get a cheap flight and they get you there safely and usually [3]_____ , but the airline is not going to put you in [4]_____ if your flight is delayed. Low-cost airline Easyjet gives staff [5]_____ in which they roleplay typical [6]_____ with dissatisfied passengers.

4 Watch the second part of the video (02:24 to 04:12) again. Underline and correct the six factual errors in the summary notes about the premium service.

In the premium service segment, airlines remove little extras that passengers ask least for. For example, United Airlines attracts business-class and first-class passengers with its faster queue to check in. The company's CEO says that their research showed that a good food service was most important for passengers. British Airways distinguishes its first-class service through an elaborate ritual on board: the British breakfast. For airlines, things like a big lunch and comfortable bed are ways to make passengers feel more important and better cared for.

5 Work in pairs or groups. Discuss these questions.

1 What pros and cons of the two types of airline did the video mention?

2 Which of these would you be prepared to pay more for? Can you add to the list?

- extra luggage allowance
- more comfortable seat
- quality food service
- no queuing to board
- hotel room if your flight is delayed

T Teacher's resources: extra activities

Vocabulary Customer service

A

> body   business-/first-
> exclusive   premium
> 'no-frills'   personal
> priority   VIP

B

> attention   boarding   class
> features   flight   language
> service   treatment

6A Match words from boxes A and B to make common adjective and noun collocations from the video.

B Write a collocation from Exercise 6A next to each meaning.

1 very high-quality service _____

2 things only available to particular people _____

3 higher standard of seats, food, etc. available on a train, aircraft, etc. _____

4 given special care and respect _____

5 getting on the plane earlier than other passengers _____

6 giving an individual person special care _____

7 Complete the table with the correct word forms.

Verb	Noun	Adjective
	anxiety	1 _____
apologise	2 _____	apologetic/unapologetic
3 _____	assistance	
complain	4 _____	
	confidence	5 _____
6 _____	demand	demanding/undemanding
empathise	7 _____	empathetic
8 _____	handling	
help	help	9 _____ 10 _____
request	11 _____	
satisfy	satisfaction	12 _____ 13 _____
14 _____	upset	upset

8 Complete the sentences with the correct prepositions.

1 The passengers were getting anxious _____ long queues at check-in.
2 The airline apologised _____ passengers _____ the delay.
3 The cabin crew are available to offer assistance _____ passengers.
4 I complained _____ the airline _____ the slow service.
5 The training session helped staff feel confident _____ handling upset passengers.
6 We are not satisfied _____ the compensation we received for the delay.

9 Discuss the questions.

1 Do you ever get anxious about flying? What do you do to calm down?
2 Have you recently been dissatisfied with a product or service? What and why?

T Teacher's resources: extra activities

➤ PROJECT: Design a premium service

10A Work in groups. Discuss the questions.

1 Look at the businesses in Exercise 1 again. What are some things each one might offer as a premium service?
2 Can you think of any other types of businesses that offer a premium service? Do you use any of these services?
3 When would you consider paying more to be a premium customer?

B Choose one type of business and design a premium service. Think about some of the items in the box or use your own ideas.

> exclusive goods or services loyalty cards
> personalisation priority services

C Present your ideas for a premium service to another group. What is the best idea each group has?

Self-assessment

- How successfully have you achieved the lesson outcome? Give yourself a score from 0 (I need more practice) to 5 (I know this well).
- Go to My Self-assessment in MyEnglishLab to reflect on what you have learnt.

7.2 > Hanging on the telephone

Lesson outcome

Learners can use a range of verbs taking *to*-infinitive or *-ing*.

Lead-in

1 Discuss the questions.

1 Look at the five typical ways to communicate with a customer service department on the left: email, chatbot, live chat, social media forum, telephone. As a customer, which do you prefer? Why?

2 Have you ever experienced any of the following when phoning a customer service call centre? Tick (✓) any you have.

  a an automated message gives you a list of options

  b you listen to music or advertising while waiting

  c an automated message says all the agents are busy

  d you are transferred between departments

  e you have to call several times about the same issue

  f you get bored waiting and hang up

3 Which experiences in question 2 do you find most annoying or frustrating?

Listening

2A ◀) 7.01 Listen to two phone conversations in which a customer calls her internet and phone provider. What was each call about?

B In which conversation do you think the agent used a script? Why?

3 ◀) 7.02 Listen to the first phone call again and complete the useful phrases with a word or short phrase.

1 All our agents are _____ right now, please hold.

2 Good afternoon, my name is David. _____ your name, please?

3 _____ I help you, Angela?

4 Is the _____ in your name?

5 Can I _____ for some further identification?

6 Can you _____ the phone number for this account, Angela?

7 I'll _____ to our customer service agents.

8 I'm sorry, I can't hear you very well. Could you _____ , please?

9 This will take a few seconds. I'll just put you _____ .

10 Is there anything else I can _____ this afternoon, Angela?

4 ◀) 7.03 Listen to the second phone call and answer the questions.

1 What information does the automated message ask for at first?

2 What problem does Angela have when responding to the automated system?

3 Why is Angela pleased to speak to Judith?

4 Why was Angela's phone bill higher than usual last month?

5 What does Angela want the phone company to do?

6 What does the agent advise her to do in future?

5 Look at the audioscripts for the two phone calls on page 150 and underline useful expressions for the customer side of the conversation.

6 Discuss these questions.

1 Why do you think customer service agents use a script to do their job? How does it make you feel as a customer?

2 How do you feel when a customer service agent uses your name frequently? Do you use their name?

3 How do you feel when a customer service agent uses the opportunity of your call to try to sell you something? Why do companies do this?

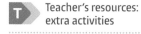

Teacher's resources: extra activities

Grammar Verb + *to*-infinitive or *-ing*

7A **Choose the correct options in italics. In one case both options are possible.**

Call 1

1 Do you have any mobile phone numbers you'd like *to add / adding* to your account?
2 Have you tried *to switch off / switching off* the wifi router and *to turn it on / turning it on* again?
3 Can you tell me if the lights start *to come on / coming on* on the router?
4 They've started *to come on / coming on*.
5 I'm just trying *to get / getting* into my email.

Call 2

6 I want *to query / querying* my mobile phone bill.
7 I don't remember *to use / using* the phone's data.
8 We always recommend *to contact / contacting* customer services to check roaming charges.
9 I'll certainly remember *to look for / looking for* a cheaper operator as soon as I can.

B **Look at the sentences above and complete the information with *to*-infinitive, *-ing* or *both forms*.**

1 After the verbs *would like* and *want* only use _____ .
2 After the verb *recommend* only use _____ .
3 After the verbs *remember, start* and *try* use _____ .

➡ **page 124** See Grammar reference: Verb + *to*-infinitive or *-ing*

8 **Write these sentences in a different way by using *to*-infinitive or *-ing*. Does the meaning of the sentence change or not?**

1 Did you remember sending the email?
2 They stopped to look at the new website design.
3 We continued to argue about the charges.
4 She went on to ask for a discount.
5 I forgot to pay the phone bill last month.
6 He began complaining about the poor service.
7 She tried not to get angry.
8 He prefers to sit at the front in the cinema.

9A **Complete this message that Angela Parsons wrote on her internet provider's forum page with the correct form of the verbs in brackets.**

My phone bill last month was three times more than usual. I couldn't afford [1]_____ (pay) this bill and I felt the company failed [2]_____ (inform) me clearly about the high roaming charges. The company risks [3]_____ (lose) lots of customers if it keeps [4]_____ (operate) like this.

The customer service agent I spoke to would not agree [5]_____ (reduce) the charge. So I am now seriously considering [6]_____ (go) to another provider because I want to avoid [7]_____ (get) a shock like this in future. Would you please agree [8]_____ (give) me a partial refund?

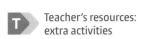

Teacher's resources: extra activities

B **If you were the company, how would you reply to Angela's request?**

➡ **page 117** See Pronunciation bank: Unstressed syllables at the end of a sentence

Writing **10A** **Why might a customer complain to one of these companies?**

| bank   internet service provider   insurance company   telephone company |

B **You want to write a message on a company's forum page to complain. Choose one of the companies in Exercise 10A or use your own ideas. Write about 100 words. Include the following details:**

• why you are writing to complain. • the action you want the company to take.
• how you feel and any relevant details about the service or product.

Self-assessment

• How successfully have you achieved the lesson outcome? Give yourself a score from 0 (I need more practice) to 5 (I know this well).
• Go to My Self-assessment in MyEnglishLab to reflect on what you have learnt.

Lesson outcome	Learners can use a range of expressions to manage customer relationships and support a colleague.

Lead-in 1A There is a saying in business: 'the customer is always right'. Work in pairs and discuss these situations. Is the customer right in each case?

1 A passenger boards an aeroplane wearing a hat with an offensive slogan on it. Other passengers complain, and the cabin crew ask the passenger to remove the hat. The passenger refuses.

2 A man orders a meal in a restaurant. The food takes a long time to come, and when it finally arrives it is cold. The man complains to the waiter.

3 A woman goes into a shop to buy a blouse. The shop assistant offers to help, but she says she is just looking. She tells him to leave her alone. Later she needs help from the assistant, but he is nowhere to be seen. The woman complains to the store manager.

B How would you react if you were the:

a pilot on the aeroplane?

b restaurant manager?

c store manager?

VIDEO 2A ▶ 7.3.1 Watch as Daniel talks to Beata and then calls Mateo.

1 What is the main issue they need to resolve?

2 What does Daniel think may be the reason for this?

3 What alternative reasons does Beata suggest?

4 Daniel says there are 'one or two small things' to discuss. How does Mateo respond?

B Do you think the phone call will go well? Why / Why not?

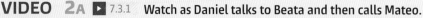

L Go to MyEnglishLab for extra video activities.

3A In small groups, discuss which is the best approach (Option A or B) for Daniel to take in the phone call with Mateo. As a class, decide which video to watch first.

Option A – Daniel should listen carefully to what Mateo has to say, but not make any comments about Beata's actions.

Option B – Daniel should listen carefully to what Mateo has to say, but make it clear that he fully supports Beata.

B Watch the two videos in the sequence the class has decided and answer the same questions about each video.

Option A ▶ 7.3.2 **1** What reasons does Mateo give to explain his position on the refrigeration issue?

Option B ▶ 7.3.3 **2** How does Daniel react to Mateo's arguments about the refrigeration issue?

3 How does Daniel respond to Mateo's criticisms of Beata?

4 What does Daniel promise to do after the telephone call?

5 How many times does Daniel refer to Beata?

4 How do you think Beata and Mateo felt at the end of each sequence? In pairs, discuss the advantages and disadvantages of Daniel's different approaches. Do you think he should have shown his support for Beata? Why / Why not?

5 ▶ 7.3.4 Watch the Conclusions section of the video and note down the points the speaker makes about the two approaches.

Reflection 6 Think about the following questions. Then work in pairs and discuss your answers.

1 Which approach would you prefer to use in such a situation? Why?

2 What is one advantage and one possible disadvantage of such an approach?

Functional language

Responding to customer concerns

7 Use the seven phrases from the video (a–g) to complete the gaps in the table (1–7).

a I am sure we'll [come up with a solution].

b [Beata] is correct about that.

c I just want to hear your side of things.

d [Beata] has filled me in on all of the details.

e Let me [do some calculations and speak to my people].

f [Beata] is absolutely right on this.

g [Please understand] I see your point.

A Explaining the reason for the conversation	1 _____ I just want to make sure everything is OK.
B Confirming you already have specific information	2 _____ Beata has told me about that.
C Supporting a colleague	3 _____ 4 _____ I have to say Beata [is right / has a point].
D Reassuring a customer	5 _____ 6 _____ I'm confident we'll come up with a solution.
E Outlining your next step	7 _____ I'll [go through all the details / double check all the data] with Beata.

A customer has asked to speak to a manager to discuss a bill, which he/she feels is too high. The manager's colleague has explained the situation: the customer has a card offering a 10 percent discount, but it does not apply to this product. The manager phones the customer.

8A Read the scenario on the left. What can the manager say to respond to the customer's concerns? Use phrases from Exercise 7.

Manager: Explain the reason for the conversation.

Customer: 'I think my bill is wrong. I told your colleague that he forgot to include the 10 percent discount.'

Manager: Confirm that you already have specific information.

Customer: 'Your colleague said the discount does not apply and that I should speak to you about this.'

Manager: Support the colleague.

Customer: 'I have to say I am not happy about this situation.'

Manager: Reassure the customer.

Customer: 'What are you going to do about it?'

Manager: Outline your next step.

T Teacher's resources: extra activities

B Work in pairs and roleplay the phone call.

>**TASK**

9A Work in groups of three. Turn to page 130 and choose one of the scenarios. Decide who will take the roles of the manager trying to control the situation, the unhappy customer and the observer.

B Read the complaint for the scenario you have chosen and the instructions for your role.

C Roleplay the telephone conversation between the manager and the customer. If you are the manager, try to uses phrases from Exercise 7.

D When you have finished, decide if the customer is now satisfied. Listen to the observer's feedback. Discuss what went well, what didn't go well and how you can improve next time.

Self-assessment

- How successfully have you achieved the lesson outcome? Give yourself a score from 0 (I need more practice) to 5 (I know this well).
- Go to My Self-assessment in MyEnglishLab to reflect on what you have learnt.

Lesson outcome Learners can use a range of expressions to generate and present ideas.

Lead-in **1** **Work in small groups and discuss the questions. Then share your ideas with the class.**

1 Why is it important for businesses to be good at generating ideas?

2 Whose responsibility is it to generate ideas: managers, staff or both?

Listening **2A** ◀) 7.04 **A group of employees are attending a staff training day on customer service. Listen to the manager introducing the session and answer the questions.**

1 According to the manager, when do we have ideas?

2 What happens to most ideas? Why?

3 What does the manager want to do in this meeting? Why?

4 What must the group come up with?

B **Complete the text using the words in the box. Then listen again to check.**

> enough   generate   lose   share   ways

So I want to hear your ideas about how we can ¹_____ more ideas, and how we can ²_____ them with each other. But it's not ³_____ just to have good ideas. What I want to do in this session is to brainstorm ⁴_____ we can capture those ideas to make sure we don't ⁵_____ them.

3 **Work in small groups. Discuss ways to generate ideas and how to capture them and not lose them. Then discuss your ideas as a class.**

4A ◀) 7.05 **Listen to six people presenting their team's ideas. Which techniques (if any) have you already discussed?**

B **Listen again. Tick the techniques which talk about ways to capture or record ideas.**

1 brainstorm   4 roleplay

2 use a notebook/smartphone   5 visualisation

3 mind mapping   6 play devil's advocate

C **Work in pairs. Use the words and phrases on the left to make short notes about each of the techniques in Exercise 4B.**

Functional language

Discussing and presenting ideas

5A Match the beginnings (1–10) with the endings (a–j) to make sentences from the audio.

1 We think **the first thing we need to do is** to
2 **So we should** brainstorm
3 **We suggest everyone needs to** get into
4 **Another way is to** use
5 The thing is, it's got to be easy,
6 Our team would like to push the idea of
7 **Basically,** starting with
8 **So it's a bit like**
9 **Our team came up with** the idea
10 What we want to do is make sure that

a a word or phrase, and then simply writing down all the ideas that come from that phrase.
b make lists.
c we really think through the issues.
d the habit of carrying a small notebook.
e the recorders on our smartphones.
f as many ideas as possible, and write them all down.
g mind mapping.
h otherwise we won't do it.
i brainstorming, which the first group mentioned.
j of visualisation.

B Look at the words in bold in the sentences in Exercise 5A. Which phrases introduce the idea, and which can be used to add a comment or explanation?

C Turn to the audioscript on page 150 and find more phrases to add to the categories in Exercise 5B.

6 Here are some opening statements about customer service. Use the phrases in Exercise 5 to add your own comments or explanations.

1 We think that it is important to have competent staff.
2 The first thing we need to do is to make sure that we offer a premium service.
3 We like the idea of giving the customer VIP treatment.
4 Our team would like to push the importance of good communication.

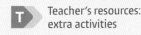
Teacher's resources: extra activities

→ **page 117** See Pronunciation bank: Introducing a topic

> **TASK**

7A You are going to discuss ideas to solve a problem or challenge which is common to everybody. Choose one of the topics in the box, or use your own ideas.

1 You have too much work.
2 You have no idea about future jobs.
3 You don't have enough money.
4 Your classes are too large.
5 You have a poor wifi connection.

B Work in small groups. Choose two techniques which you can use to generate ideas to deal with your problem or challenge. The techniques don't have to come from this unit, but it's important that everybody in the group understands how they work.

C Use the techniques to generate and discuss your ideas. Make sure you capture your ideas so that you can explain them later.

D Present your ideas to the class. Try to use phrases from Exercise 5.

E Reflect on the process you have just followed. Which technique did you prefer, and why? Discuss what went well, what didn't go well and how you can improve next time.

Self-assessment

- How successfully have you achieved the lesson outcome? Give yourself a score from 0 (I need more practice) to 5 (I know this well).
- Go to My Self-assessment in MyEnglishLab to reflect on what you have learnt.

WRITING
External 'thank you' email

Lesson outcome	Learners can write an email expressing thanks.

Lead-in 1A Read the 'thank you' email and choose the correct options in italics.

Dear Glen,

I am writing to thank you and your staff for the excellent service you ¹*provided / produced* organising our trade conference last week.

The ²*happening / event* ran very smoothly thanks to the hard work of **all** your staff. I would also like to ³*express / say* our appreciation for the prompt way in which your staff ⁴*dealt / handled* the problems there were with **some of** the catering facilities. Your customer service team ⁵*responded / replied* to the difficulties quickly and **none of** our guests realised that anything was wrong. In fact, they seemed to be able to ⁶*deal / handle* with **any** problems that came up.

We will certainly use your company again in the future and have already ⁷*proposed / recommended* you to other business contacts.

I would like to thank you and your staff once again and I look forward to working with you in the ⁸*close / near* future.

Kind regards,

Franz Benheim

B Work in pairs and check your answers.

Functional language

2 Complete the table with the words in the box.

> appreciated   definitely   helpful   much   once   recommended   replaced   smoothly
> sorted   take   wanted   writing

Beginning	Details	Closing
I am ¹_____ to thank you for your help …	The conference ran very ⁶_____ .	We will ¹⁰_____ use your company again in the future.
Thank you very ²_____ for your help …	Your staff ⁷_____ out the problems very quickly.	We have already ¹¹_____ you to other companies.
I would like to ³_____ this opportunity to thank you for …	Your customer service team were very ⁸_____ .	Thank you ¹²_____ again for all your hard work.
We really ⁴_____ all your hard work …	You ⁹_____ the damaged goods immediately.	
I ⁵_____ you to know how much we appreciate your work.		

 Teacher's resources: extra activities

L The email contains examples of *some (of), any, all (of), none (of)*. Go to MyEnglishLab for optional grammar work.

→ **page 124** See Grammar reference: *some (of), any, all (of), most (of), no, none (of)*

TASK

3A Turn to page 132 and read the short thank you email. In pairs, decide how you could improve it.

B Your company bought some new computers but some of them did not work properly. You were very happy with the way the company dealt with the problem. Write an email thanking the supplier. Use the notes on page 132. Write about 140 words.

C Exchange emails with your partner. In what ways is your partner's email different from yours? Having read your partner's email, how would you improve yours?

Self-assessment
- How successfully have you achieved the lesson outcome? Give yourself a score from 0 (I need more practice) to 5 (I know this well).
- Go to My Self-assessment in MyEnglishLab to reflect on what you have learnt.

Communication

> 'There is a world
> of communication
> which is not
> dependent on
> words.'
> Mary Martin,
> American actress

Unit overview

8.1 >	**Face to face?**	**Video:** Improving communication in the workplace
	Lesson outcome: Learners can use vocabulary related to office communication.	**Vocabulary:** Digital communication
		Project: Communication survey

8.2 >	**How to communicate**	**Reading:** Three tips for effective workplace communication
	Lesson outcome: Learners can use the first and second conditional to talk about likely and unlikely situations.	**Grammar:** First and second conditional
		Speaking: Solutions to communication problems

8.3 >	**Communication skills:** Closing a deal	**Video:** Closing a deal
	Lesson outcome: Learners are aware of ways to close a deal in a simple negotiation.	**Functional language:** Closing a deal
		Task: Trying to close a deal

8.4 >	**Business skills:** Talking about priorities	**Listening:** Setting priorities
	Lesson outcome: Learners can use a range of expressions to set and discuss priorities.	**Functional language:** Talking about priorities
		Task: Prioritising

8.5 >	**Writing:** Short report	**Model text:** A short report
	Lesson outcome: Learners can write a short business report.	**Functional language:** Introduction, findings and recommendations
		Grammar: Past Perfect Simple
		Task: Write a short report

8.1 ▶ Face to face?

Lesson outcome | Learners can use vocabulary related to office communication.

Lead-in **1A** **Choose the best ending for each sentence for you, or give your own answer.**

1 Text messaging is
  a convenient.   **b** a time-waster.   **c** an annoying interruption.   **d** something I never use.

2 I receive … emails.
  a way too many   **b** a manageable number of   **c** very few   **d** no

3 My phone is
  a one of my most important possessions.   **c** an annoying interruption.
  b useful, but I don't use it very often.   **d** something I almost never use.

B **Give your partner some extra information about each of your answers above.**
I use text messages with my friends, to make plans. We usually …
I use email a lot for work. Every day, I have to write …
I usually carry my phone with me, but I don't use it too much. I'd rather …

VIDEO **2A** **You are going to watch a programme about how a company improved communication in the office. Answer the questions.**

1 What types of communication do you think people in an office use frequently?

2 What kinds of problems with communication in an office do you think people might have?

B ▶ 8.1.1 **Watch the video and check your answers.**

3 **Watch the video again and complete the notes.**

1 the type of communication that is causing problems	
2 what employees were not allowed to do	
3 the type of communication employees must use in the office	
4 the employees' feelings about the changes	
5 the two things Cary Cooper wants employees to balance	
6 the atmosphere in the office after the experiment	

4 **Watch the video again and decide if these sentences are** *true* **(T) or** *false* **(F). Correct the incorrect sentences.**

1 Mike Brogan feels that it's important for his employees to work after hours.

2 One employee says he checks his email on holiday and at the weekends.

3 Cary Cooper doesn't want the employees to use email at all – even with customers or people outside of the office.

4 Cooper says there is no connection between what happens at work and what happens at home.

5 Most of the employees couldn't stop working after hours.

6 One result of the experiment was that the workers got to know their colleagues better.

7 The experiment was a success.

5 **Work in pairs or small groups. Discuss these questions.**

1 Would you be happy to stop using communication technology for a day? A week? A month? Why / Why not?

2 How would it change your life if you couldn't use communication technology? What would become more difficult? Would anything become easier?

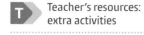
Teacher's resources: extra activities

Vocabulary Digital communication

6 Complete the text using the words in the box.

> catch   check   internal   master   overloaded   reply   servant   technology

I usually [1]_____ my email first thing in the morning, on my phone. But I don't
[2]_____ to any messages before I've had breakfast. I properly [3]_____ up on
my emails when I arrive at the office, first thing in the workday. I have customers all over
the world, so a lot email arrives overnight. Those are usually manageable. But emails
from my colleagues and from company management have often [4]_____ me.
These [5]_____ emails are a real problem. Sometimes, people write three different
emails, each with one question. Some people choose 'reply all' and I receive a copy of
a message that is of no interest to me. [6]_____ is great and makes a lot of useful
communication possible. But sometimes I worry that I am the [7]_____ of
technology rather than the [8]_____ . And that's a depressing thought.

7 Complete the questions with words from Exercise 6. Then work in pairs
and answer them.

1 Do you more often _____ to messages immediately, or take some time before
answering?

2 How often do you _____ your social media?

3 Do you consider yourself a _____ of technology, or its servant? Explain.

4 Do you have a special time when you _____ up on emails and other messages,
or do you look at them as they come in?

5 Are you _____ by communication?

Teacher's resources:
extra activities

Project: Communication survey

8A Make notes about the following.

1 List three methods of communication you use every day, or nearly every day.

2 For each method of communication, estimate how many minutes per day
you spend using it.

3 For each method, say 1–3 things you like (pros) about using it.

*It's convenient; I don't have to talk; It's cheap; It's a fast way to share
my thoughts ...*

4 For each method, say 1–3 things you don't like (cons) about using it.

*I communicate even when I don't have anything to say; I receive
messages all the time, so it's hard to concentrate; It is easy to make
mistakes in typing ...*

B Work in pairs or small groups. Write *Wh-* questions for a survey
to find out about how your class communicates. You have five
minutes to get your questions ready.

*What methods of communication do you use every day?
How many minutes per day do you ... ?
What are the pros ... ?*

C Ask some of your classmates the questions you prepared. Note down
their answers.

D Present the results of your survey to the class in pairs or small groups.

*The most common method of communication is speaking face to face. On average, people
spend three hours per day in face-to-face communication. People say that it's easy to
understand other people's feelings in face-to-face communication, but sometimes, people
chat too much, and it's a waste of time.*

Self-assessment

- How successfully have you achieved the lesson outcome? Give yourself a score from 0 (I need more
practice) to 5 (I know this well).
- Go to My Self-assessment in MyEnglishLab to reflect on what you have learnt.

8.2 ▶ How to communicate

| Lesson outcome | Learners can use the first and second conditional to talk about likely and unlikely situations. |

Lead-in 1 **Work in pairs. What are the advantages and disadvantages of working in a) a private office and b) an open-plan office?**

2 **Work in pairs or small groups. Do you agree with these statements?**

1 People shouldn't use social media in class or at the office.

2 Chatting with colleagues is a waste of time.

3 The most important communication in the workplace is formal communication.

Reading 3 **Read the article quickly. Match the headings (a–d) with the correct section (1–3). There is one extra heading you do not need to use.**

a Give workers some privacy   c Keep meetings short

b Encourage small talk   d Stay connected – but be careful!

Three tips for effective workplace communication

Good communication is very important for success and happiness in all areas of life – including the office. According to business expert Allan Webster, lack of communication and teamwork can make projects fail. Here are three tips from around the world for developing good communication at work.

1 _____

According to business blogger Tim Eisenhauer, if managers encourage more water-cooler chat (informal office conversation), their employees
5 will become happier, more productive and more interested in their work. Scott Bedbury, who worked as Nike's head of advertising, agrees. He said that the really useful conversations
10 between colleagues generally took place at the vending machine, in the cafeteria or in the gardens outside the office. Bedbury says that a company's internal communication needs to be
15 both formal and informal to help build the relationships necessary for success.

2 _____

Juriaan van Meel, author of _The European Office_, says that almost every office worker in both Sweden and Germany
20 has a private office. Though open-plan offices are intended to improve communication, research shows that the background noise often makes it difficult for workers to concentrate – and to
25 communicate. Sound expert Julian Treasure says that it's impossible to understand two people when both of them are speaking. Office design expert Alexi Marmot believes that if companies
30 provided a choice, productivity and happiness would increase. She says that people need both private space for concentrating and public space for open communication.

3 _____

35 According to the _South China Morning Post_, the WeChat social media app, with 889 million monthly active users in China, is quickly replacing phone calls, emails and even business cards for professional
40 communication in China. Though the app wasn't designed as a business communication tool, every day, 87.7 percent of its users use it for work communication, while phone, fax and text message are used by only 59.5
45 percent, and email by only 22.6 percent. Many Chinese businesspeople now connect on WeChat instead of giving each other business cards. However, the convenience of the app may have a downside. Some users
50 say that messages come in 24/7, and it's rude not to reply, so they feel they're always at work – a case of too much communication.

4 **Read the article again and answer the questions.**

1 According to Allan Webster, what happens without good communication?

2 What increases workers' productivity and happiness at work?

3 What effect does the combination of formal and informal communication have?

4 According to the text, what's the biggest problem with open-plan offices?

5 What does Alexi Marmot recommend?

6 What form of business communication is the least used, according to the _South China Morning Post_?

7 What's the biggest problem with using social media for business purposes?

5 **Work in pairs. Of the three tips in the article, which one do you think is the most useful for improving workplace communication?**

T Teacher's resources: extra activities

Grammar First and second conditional

6 Read sentences 1 and 2 from the article. Then answer questions a–c about each one.

1 *If managers encourage more water-cooler chat, their employees will become happier, more productive and more engaged with their work.*

  a What tense is used in the *if*-clause?

  b What time is the result clause referring to: future or present?

  c Is the situation described in the sentence likely or unlikely?

2 *If companies provided a choice, productivity and happiness would increase.*

  a What tense is used in the *if*-clause?

  b Is the sentence referring to the past?

  c Is the situation described in the sentence definitely going to happen, or is it less probable?

➜ page 125 See Grammar reference: First and second conditional

7 Complete the conditional sentences with the correct form of the verbs in brackets.

1 If you use social media for work, you _____ (be) connected 24/7.

2 We _____ (not have) space for private offices if we move to a smaller location.

3 If we give workers more breaks, they _____ (spend) more time chatting.

4 We _____ (have) better coffee breaks if we had a nice break room.

5 You would know your colleagues better if you _____ (talk) to them more.

6 If the management stopped workers using social media, people _____ (be) unhappy.

7 If we had our meetings in a café, they _____ (feel) less formal.

8 If you _____ (turn) off your phone at six o'clock every night, your kids would be happier!

T Teacher's resources: extra activities

➜ page 117 See Pronunciation bank: Conditional sentences

Speaking 8A Work in pairs. Match each communication problem (1–4) with two possible solutions (a–h).

Communication problems

1 Workers don't know each other very well. There isn't a strong sense of teamwork.

2 The open-plan office is too noisy to make phone calls easily.

3 We don't have a place where workers naturally meet for informal chats.

4 Employees complain that even when they're at home, they feel they're at work because of the constant texts and emails on their smartphones.

Possible solutions

a Take the entire team (75 people) on an adventure holiday.

b Move to a building that's three times bigger and give every employee a private office.

c Encourage more informal communication.

d Provide a few small, private rooms for employees to use when needed.

e Buy every employee a smartphone for work that they can turn off when they go home.

f Create a small break area near the water cooler with a couple of sofas and comfortable chairs.

g Encourage employees not to respond to work texts and emails outside of office hours.

h Buy the café next to the office building and turn it into a private break room.

B Discuss the problems and possible solutions. Use the first conditional for more likely solutions and the second conditional for less likely solutions.

If we wanted to develop a sense of teamwork, we could take the entire team on an adventure holiday.

If we encourage informal communication, workers will get to know each other better.

C For each problem, think of one additional solution. Explain it using the first or second conditional.

Self-assessment

- How successfully have you achieved the lesson outcome? Give yourself a score from 0 (I need more practice) to 5 (I know this well).
- Go to My Self-assessment in MyEnglishLab to reflect on what you have learnt.

Lesson outcome	Learners are aware of ways to close a deal in a simple negotiation.

Lead-in **1A** Discuss in pairs why the two points below are important in closing a deal.

'Closing a deal in a negotiation is all about making a sale. To close a deal successfully you need to 1) summarise what has been agreed and 2) work through any outstanding issues.'

B Experienced negotiators often talk about the importance of creating a 'win–win' situation in a business deal. This means that both sides end up with a good result. Work in pairs and discuss the questions.

1 Why is a 'win–win' situation a good thing for a long-term business relationship?

2 Why can a 'win–lose' situation be a bad thing?

VIDEO **2** ▶ 8.3.1 Watch the video. Work in pairs and discuss the questions.

1 Do Daniel and Beata feel they have a solution which Mateo will accept?

2 What does Daniel want Beata to focus on during the meeting?

3 What evidence is there that Mateo and Daniel have a good relationship? Do you think this relationship will help the discussion?

4 What is Daniel's plan for the meeting?

L Go to MyEnglishLab for extra video acitivites

3A In small groups, discuss which is the best approach (Option A or B) for Daniel and Beata to take in this important meeting. As a class, decide which video to watch first.

Option A – Explain the idea carefully, focusing on the technical detail, and make sure that everyone understands how it works.

Option B – Briefly explain the idea, and focus mostly on the benefits for Mateo.

B Watch the two videos in the sequence the class has decided and answer the questions for each video.

Option A ▶ 8.3.2 1 Work in pairs. Together redraw and label the sketch that Beata uses to explain the technical solution to the problem. Then explain the solution to each other. Use the following words to help you.

> container   five degrees   insulation   portable   power supply
> refrigerator   stable temperature   transport

2 Make a list of the benefits which Daniel and Beata mention.

Option B ▶ 8.3.3 1 Work in pairs. Together explain Beata's solution to each other. Use the following words to help you.

> container   insulated   power supply   refrigerator   stable temperature

2 Make a list of the benefits which Daniel and Beata mention.

4 In pairs, discuss what lessons you have learnt about closing a deal.

5 ▶ 8.3.4 Watch the Conclusions section of the video and make notes about the differences between the two approaches. How might you decide which approach to use?

Reflection **6** Think about the following questions. Then discuss your answers with a partner.

1 Which approach would you prefer to use in such a situation? Why?

2 What is one advantage and one possible disadvantage of such an approach?

Functional language

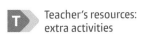

agreed	leaves	mean
return	sum	sums

Closing a deal

7A Complete these extracts from the video using the words in the box.

1 So that just about _____ it up.

2 We've _____ on the delivery dates.

3 That only _____ the same point as before.

4 Does that _____ up the situation as you see it?

5 So what you _____ is that I don't need to put the sensors into refrigerators?

6 In _____ we would need you to provide the power supply.

B Match the sentences in Exercise 7A with the categories (a–c) below.

a summarising   b clarifying   c referring to outstanding issues

C Match the sentences (1–6) with the categories in Exercise 7B.

1 To sum up, you provide the containers, and I provide the power supply.

2 If it is as you say it is, we will be able to go ahead.

3 But if we use these portable refrigerators, won't the cost go up?

4 We are prepared to cover the extra cost providing you buy enough sensors.

5 Do you have any information about how much power we would need?

6 As I understand it your local rules do not require the sensors to be refrigerated.

8 Complete the conversation using the phrases in the box.

as I understand it	to sum up
if you agree	that leaves
so what you mean is	

A: ¹_____ , I want to buy the computer and you want to sell it. And your price is $350?

B: Yes, that's correct.

A: ²_____ the problem of the mouse – it's broken.

B: I'm prepared to buy you a new mouse.

A: ³_____ , you will buy a new mouse, but the price stays the same?

B: Yes. ⁴_____ to pay cash now, the price will stay the same.

A: So, ⁵_____ , you get the cash now, and I get a computer with a new mouse. Yes, OK, that sounds fine.

B: Agreed. Thank you very much.

> **T** Teacher's resources: extra activities

> TASK

9A Work in pairs. Choose one of the items below. One of you is selling the item and the other is buying. Each item has a problem.

Item 1 – a kayak with a small crack in the side

Item 2 – a bicycle with worn tyres

Item 3 – a computer desk with a missing shelf

B Try to close a deal on the item you have chosen. Follow steps 1–7 below and use phrases from Exercises 7 and 8.

1 Summarise the situation.

2 Identify the outstanding issue.

3 Suggest a solution (e.g. repair the problem, replace the part, offer a discount).

4 Clarify/Discuss any outstanding issues (repeat 3 and 4 if necessary).

5 Agree on a solution.

6 Summarise the benefits for each side.

7 Close the deal.

C When you have finished, discuss what went well, what was difficult and how you could improve next time. Then share your ideas with the class.

Self-assessment

- How successfully have you achieved the lesson outcome? Give yourself a score from 0 (I need more practice) to 5 (I know this well).
- Go to My Self-assessment in MyEnglishLab to reflect on what you have learnt.

8.4 BUSINESS SKILLS
Talking about priorities

Lesson outcome Learners can use a range of expressions to set and discuss priorities.

Lead-in

1 Read this list and number the items in order of importance to you personally (1 is most important, 7 is least important). Are any of the items urgent?

Staying healthy
Spending time with family and friends
Doing well at your studies/job
Earning enough money to live
Earning enough money to live very comfortably
Having fun
Learning English

2 Work in pairs. Choose one item on the list and discuss what tasks you need to do in order to achieve it. Which tasks will you prioritise (do first)? Why?

Listening

3A 8.01 Look at the matrix and listen to a consultant talking about setting priorities.

1 What two things do you need to do to set priorities?
2 Why are *important* and *urgent* tasks not the same thing?
3 Label the four quadrants in the matrix as *important and urgent*, *important but not urgent*, *urgent but not important* and *not important or urgent*.

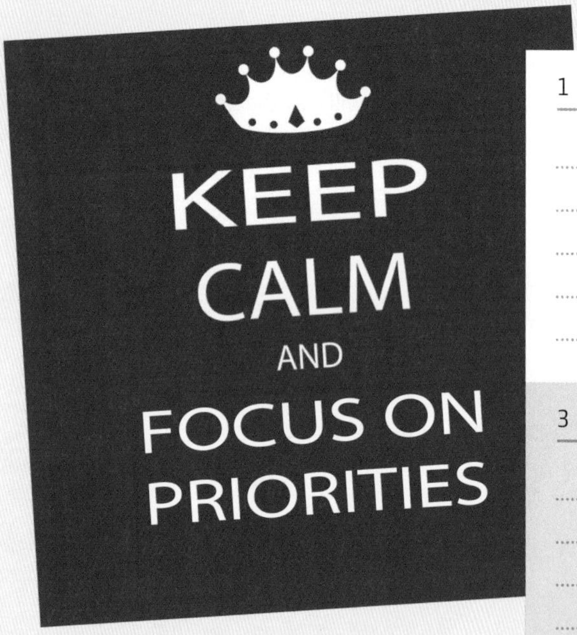

KEEP
CALM
AND
FOCUS ON
PRIORITIES

1 ______	2 ______
3 ______	4 ______

B 8.02 Listen to Part 2. The consultant goes through a list of tasks. Write the numbers of the tasks in the correct quadrant of the matrix.

C Work in pairs. Decide in what order you will do the tasks in the matrix. Compare your answers with other pairs in the class.

D 8.03 Listen to Part 3. The consultant ends with a useful tip. What is the 'real tip'?

Functional language

Talking about priorities

4A Choose the correct option in italics to complete the sentences for talking about priorities.

1 It's of the *utmost / entire* importance.
2 This is really *low / mini* priority.
3 You need to give this task a *great / high* priority.
4 This email is *really / well* urgent.
5 It's *largely / quite* important that we have this meeting.
6 The security check is *extremely / plenty* urgent.

B Match the beginnings (1–10) with the endings (a–j) to make sentences for setting priorities.

1 Don't
2 Put it in your
3 It is also of utmost
4 Make it your number one
5 Do it today if you have
6 It's a bit of a
7 Put it at the bottom of your list of things
8 Give it a
9 It's information
10 You can

a schedule.
b importance.
c put it off for a while.
d only.
e high priority, please.
f priority.
g waste time.
h distraction.
i to do.
j time.

5 Work in pairs. You are working on an assignment at your desk. Discuss how you would prioritise the following items.

1 Your manager/tutor sends you an email with high priority.
2 You get an unexpected message notification on your phone.
3 The fire alarm goes off – you suspect it may be a drill.
4 You receive a reminder about an interesting presentation later today.
5 A colleague asks you for some information you promised to send him/her last week.
6 You need to finish your English homework (due to be handed in next week).
7 You want to see the latest news online.
8 A colleague wants to see how fast you can solve the Rubik's cube.

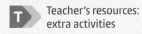

Teacher's resources: extra activities

> **TASK**

6A Think about all the tasks you have to do over the next few days. Make a list.

B Work in pairs. Share your lists with each other. Use the matrix in Exercise 3A to discuss and set priorities for your partner. Try to use phrases from Exercise 4.

C Find a new partner and repeat the process.

D Reflect on the process you have just followed. How useful do you find the matrix? Share your thoughts with the rest of the class.

Self-assessment

- How successfully have you achieved the lesson outcome? Give yourself a score from 0 (I need more practice) to 5 (I know this well).
- Go to My Self-assessment in MyEnglishLab to reflect on what you have learnt.

Lesson outcome	Learners can write a short business report.

Lead-in

1A **Read the brief report and complete it with the words in the box.**

> department   heads   issues   orders   policy
> reasons   stock   systems   technology   updates

> ### Introduction
>
> There have been some problems recently due to poor communication so we need to have a new communication ¹_____ for the company. This report looks at ²_____ for communication problems between departments and finally makes recommendations.
>
> ### Findings
>
> One of the key ³_____ is that warehouse staff are unhappy with sales staff who take ⁴_____ for goods which are out of stock. Last week we had a big order for fridge-freezers and there were none in the warehouse. It seems that the sales ⁵_____ **had not checked** ⁶_____ levels before accepting the order. The Sales Manager complained that no one **had updated** the stock records. Stock ⁷_____ ought to happen automatically but they do not. It seems that staff expect the ⁸_____ to do everything and will not talk to each other.
>
> ### Recommendations
>
> It is therefore recommended that department managers monitor ⁹_____ more closely and make sure that any problems are reported immediately so everyone is aware of them. There should also be morning meetings for all department ¹⁰_____ to exchange information.

B **Work in pairs and check your answers.**

Functional language

2 **Complete the table below with the words in the box.**

> aims   asked   found   key   looks   make   might
> purpose   recommendations   recommended
> seems   should   thing

Introduction
This report ¹_____ at reasons for the problems.
The ²_____ of this report is to …
The director has ³_____ me to write this report to …
This report ⁴_____ to analyse the reasons why …
Finally it will ⁵_____ recommendations …

Findings
One of the ⁶_____ problems is that staff do not …
The first ⁷_____ we noticed was that …
It was ⁸_____ that staff were unhappy because …
It ⁹_____ that staff do not speak to each other.

Recommendations
It is therefore ¹⁰_____ that …
The managers ¹¹_____ have morning meetings to …
Our ¹²_____ are to …
We ¹³_____ therefore need to change the system.

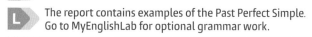

T   Teacher's resources: extra activities

L   The report contains examples of the Past Perfect Simple. Go to MyEnglishLab for optional grammar work.

→ page 125   See Grammar reference: Past Perfect Simple
→ page 117   See Pronunciation bank: Contractions in speech

> TASK

3A **Work in pairs. Read the short report on page 131. Think of ways to improve the phrases in italics. Then write the improved report.**

B **Look at the notes on page 132. Brainstorm some ideas for the report. Then, individually, write a short report of about 160 words.**

C **Exchange reports with your partner. In what ways is your partner's report different from yours? Having read your partner's report, is there anything you would change in yours?**

Self-assessment	• How successfully have you achieved the lesson outcome? Give yourself a score from 0 (I need more practice) to 5 (I know this well). • Go to My Self-assessment in MyEnglishLab to reflect on what you have learnt.

Business Workshops

1 **Global recruitment agency** p.88

Lesson outcome: Learners can discuss candidates for a job and choose the best person based on their online profile.

Reading: Job listing
Listening: Initial job interviews
Reading: Online candidate profiles
Task: Discuss job candidates

2 **Investing your money** p.90

Lesson outcome: Learners can ask and answer questions about companies and industries and present ideas and suggestions.

Listening: Investing
Speaking: Investor's checklist
Task: Choose a company to invest in

3 **The grand opening** p.92

Lesson outcome: Learners can participate in a project management meeting and make a decision on the main priorities for an event.

Listening: Understanding project priorities
Reading: Analysing follow-up emails
Task: Hold a project meeting

4 **Hand-made** p.94

Lesson outcome: Learners can consider market research and devise a marketing strategy.

Listening: Key factors for a global business
Speaking: Doing market research
Task: Choose market for a global strategy

5 **Smart fabric** p.96

Lesson outcome: Learners can understand the principles of the marketing mix and talk about products.

Reading and listening: Market research
Task: Choose a product to develop

6 **Visitor safety** p.98

Lesson outcome: Learners can assess safety and security procedures for visitors to office and factory buildings.

Reading: Safety and security
Listening: Risk assessment
Task: Prepare a visitor safety and security report

7 **Red Cushion Furniture** p.100

Lesson outcome: Learners can identify problems in customer service and find solutions.

Reading: Customer complaints
Listening: Dealing with unhappy customers
Task: Turn failure into success

8 **Global communication** p.102

Lesson outcome: Learners can identify and talk about communication problems.

Listening: Communication problems
Reading: Email exchanges about a problem
Task: Recommend ways to improve communication

Global recruitment agency

Lesson outcome	Learners can discuss candidates for a job and choose the best person based on their online profile.

Background

1 **Read the background and answer the questions with a partner.**

1 What service does JobNow provide?

2 Have you ever used this type of service?

3 If you could choose any field to work in, what field would you choose?

BACKGROUND

JobNow is a global recruitment agency – a company that matches jobs with job-seekers all over the world. Companies give details of vacancies to JobNow. The recruiter checks its database of job-seekers for someone with the right skills and experience, and also actively uses online professional networks to find suitable candidates. In addition, job-seekers can search the listings to find jobs to apply for. Companies pay JobNow a commission when they fill a position.

According to JobNow Director, Elena Paz, 'We look at thousands of online profiles, and it's amazing how many people leave out basic information – their university studies, the field they want to work in, some description of their skills.' She adds, 'We want to see specific information about actual experiences – tell us what you can do by showing us what you've done.'

A job vacancy

2A **Read the job listing that JobNow has received. In each category below, tick (✓) one item from each group that you think best matches this job. More than one answer may be possible, so prepare an argument to explain your choice.**

Medical Insurance Product Writer

London

We're looking for a graduate or experienced professional to write marketing and training materials for GIG – a growing medical insurance group. You will be responsible for working with several departments to develop documents for both internal company use and customer-facing product promotion, including website copy, social media updates and blogs. We will provide training as necessary.

Skills and experience:

- A degree in a related field • Good team player
- Confident, can-do attitude • Willingness to try new things
- Creative, with attention to detail

Degrees

- ☐ medicine
- ☐ engineering
- ☐ economics or finance
- ☐ English
- ☐ fine art (painting)

Professional experience

- ☐ retail sales – clothing
- ☐ nursing
- ☐ insurance sales
- ☐ accounting
- ☐ freelance writing

Other interests and activities

- ☐ playing team sports
- ☐ cooking
- ☐ volunteering in a local hospital
- ☐ travel
- ☐ reading and going to the movies

B **Work in pairs and compare your answers. Explain your choices.**

I think a finance degree would be the best match. Insurance is more about money than medicine.

I'm not sure. The job requires writing. Maybe a degree in English would be more useful.

3A ◀) BW 1.01 JobNow short-listed five job-seekers for the job with GIG. Listen to part of the initial interview with three of them. Match each name with two descriptions.

1 Maria
2 Agata
3 Taro

a has no professional experience.
b wants to try a different profession.
c is a little bit worried about the issue of age.
d enjoys sports.
e wants a steadier income.
f has travelled a lot.

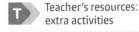
Teacher's resources: extra activities

B What skill or experience does each person have that could be useful for the job?

Online professional profiles

4 Read the three online profiles of applicants for the job of Medical Insurance Product Writer. Complete the table below.

JobNow

Agata

Three years ago, I moved from Reading to London to begin my studies in economics. I love my courses and I'm doing well in them so far. Outside of my studies, I love training for and playing football with a local club. I also work as a volunteer two evenings a week in a children's hospital near my university. When I graduate six months from now, I hope to find a position in the finance sector, ideally in an international environment.

Taro

When I graduated from Tokyo University with a degree in English, I wanted to see the world. After three or four months of travelling in Australia and New Zealand, I ran out of money and decided to try my hand at travel writing rather than return home. Since that time, my travel writing has been published in newspapers and magazines both in Japan and around the world. I'm currently looking for a permanent position as an in-company writer and would consider working in any sector.

Maria

When people are ill or in pain, you want to help them. Fifteen years ago, after completing my medical studies at Universidad Autónoma de Guadalajara, I opened a clinic in the town of Santa Clara. I hired two partners who helped the clinic grow and better serve the community. I usually work seven days a week, fifty weeks a year. I'm currently looking for an opportunity to change the focus of my work and use my skills in a different sector. I would be happy to move to a new area and to consider additional training.

	Activity or experience	Item mentioned in the vacancy listing
Agata	*studying economics, playing football*	*degree in a related field, good team player*
Taro		
Maria		

> **TASK**
> Discuss job candidates

5A Work in groups of three. You work for JobNow. Your client – GIG – wants to interview a total of three candidates for the position of Medical Insurance Product Writer. You've already sent two for an interview, so there's one place left. Discuss the pros and cons of Agata, Taro and Maria and choose which candidate to send.

- Talk about each candidate's skills, experience and interests and how they match the job. Use the table in Exercise 4.
- Think about the relationship between experience and salary. Which candidate will probably cost the employer the least?
- Decide on the best choice. Which candidate has the most to offer?

B Work in new groups of three with different people. Take turns explaining the decision your group made in Exercise 5A.

C As a class, vote on the best candidate for the job.

Sometimes, interviews are done as an online video chat.

Teacher's resources: extra activities

6 Write an online profile for yourself.

Self-assessment

- How successfully have you achieved the lesson outcome? Give yourself a score from 0 (I need more practice) to 5 (I know this well).
- Go to My Self-assessment in MyEnglishLab to reflect on what you have learnt.

> 89 <

BUSINESS WORKSHOP 2 » Investing your money

Lesson outcome	Learners can ask and answer questions about companies and industries and present ideas and suggestions.

Background

1 Read the background and answer the questions with a partner.

1 What do the three friends want to do?
2 Why do they join an investment club?
3 What are the key benefits of joining an investment club?
4 What are club members doing now?
5 What kind of business do you think you would invest in if you had the money?

BACKGROUND

Three friends, Melanie, Franco and Toni, want to invest their own money in the stock market but, individually, they did not have enough money so they decided to join an investment club. These clubs are set up to offer people with a limited amount of money the chance to invest in companies with other people. Everyone shares their ideas and knowledge about investing and makes joint decisions about which companies to invest in. As a result, they all share the risk as well as the benefits of investing. It is a great way for people who do not have a lot of experience to learn about investment. The club is now looking at the best industry to invest in. Each of the friends has decided to research different industries and select one they all agree on.

Investment possibilities

2A ◀)) BW 2.01 Listen to the conversation between Melanie, Franco and Toni and decide if these sentences are *true* (T) or *false* (F).

1 Melanie researched the graphite mining industry.
2 Graphite has been in pencils for a long time.
3 Graphene is both very strong and lightweight.
4 We already use it to upload data very quickly.
5 Nuclear waste includes some graphite.

B Listen again and complete the notes.

Graphene

- made from ¹_____ which is found all over world
- much stronger than ²_____ and extremely flexible
- good conductor of ³_____ and electricity
- used in phone and ⁴_____ touchscreens and sports equipment
- potential uses: could ⁵_____ phones in five minutes and clear up nuclear waste

3A ◀)) BW 2.02 Listen to Toni talking about her research. Put a tick (✔) by the things she mentions.

☐ hotels   ☐ camping   ☐ sports   ☐ package holidays
☐ train travel   ☐ cooking   ☐ spas   ☐ cruises

B Listen again and complete the notes.

¹_____ industry

- includes ²_____ travel providers, cruise companies, hotel ³_____ and mega-resorts
- mega-resorts provide everything a guest needs in one place
- companies are building huge new cruise ships

4 ◀)) BW 2.03 Listen to Franco talking about his research and answer the questions.

1 What industry does he want to invest in?
2 Which market is he interested in within the industry?
3 What kind of companies are making big profits?
4 Why does he think this is a good time to invest in this market?

T Teacher's resources: extra activities

5A Work in groups of three. Look at the charts on page 131. In your groups, compare the charts and discuss why you think each industry would be a good investment.

B Decide together which industry you think the club should invest in.

C Write a short summary for other investment club members, saying which industry you think seems to be the best one to invest in, and give your reasons.

Company investment checklist

6A Work in small groups. Discuss what you would like to know about a company before investing in it. Here are some factors to start with. See how many more you can add.

> profits   sales figures   size

B ◀)) BW 2.04 Listen to a podcast about investing in a company. Check to see how many of your ideas the speaker mentions, then add to the notes below.

Company ¹_____	Who ²_____ it _____ and _____ ?
Financial performance	look at financial ³_____ for last three years
	check what the company is ⁴_____
	identify trend in sales and revenues
	identify ⁵_____ _____ _____
⁶_____ **team**	assess ⁷_____ and skills
	How effectively do they use the skills of ⁸_____ ?
⁹_____ **plans**	How ¹⁰_____ are the plans?
Additional factors	environmental and ¹¹_____ responsibilities

C Work in pairs or small groups. Make a list of five questions you need to answer before you invest in a company. Use these ideas to help you.

> date founded   employee skills   management team

T Teacher's resources: extra activities

7A Work in three groups.
  Group A: Look at Company 1 on page 132.
  Group B: Look at Company 2 on page 134.
  Group C: Look at Company 3 on page 138.

- Study the company information.
- Think of ways to expand the information in the notes.
- Discuss the key factors which would interest potential investors.
- Decide how you will present the information to the class.

B In your groups, present your companies to the class. Follow these steps:
- Introduce each company and its history.
- Talk about current projects and future plans.
- Outline key factors which would interest investors.
- Ask the audience for any questions and answer them.

C As a class, discuss which of the three companies would be best to invest in and why.

> TASK
Choose a company to invest in

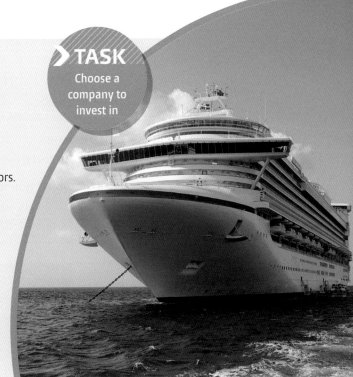

Self-assessment

- How successfully have you achieved the lesson outcome? Give yourself a score from 0 (I need more practice) to 5 (I know this well).
- Go to My Self-assessment in MyEnglishLab to reflect on what you have learnt.

Lesson outcome	Learners can participate in a project management meeting and make a decision on the main priorities for an event.

Background

1 Read the background and answer the questions with a partner.

1 What kind of business is Casa Paradiso?
2 Why is wind energy an important selling point for the hotel?
3 Would you choose to stay in this sort of hotel? Why / Why not?

BACKGROUND

Casa Paradiso, a new 20-room boutique hotel, is opening in the popular seaside resort of Miramar. The hotel will generate some of its electrical power using wind turbines on the roof – an important selling point. The owners have hired M&PR, a marketing and public relations firm, to create and manage the grand opening event to get media attention for the new business.

Decisions so far:
- The event will be held at the hotel.
- An A-list celebrity will attend and endorse the hotel.
- The guests – representatives of travel magazines and tour operators – will be treated as VIPs.
- A tour of the hotel will include a visit to the roof, to see the wind turbines and discuss the environmentally friendly nature of the resort.

With only two months to go, there is still a lot of work to do.

Understanding project priorities

2A ◆) BW 3.01 **Read the agenda for a meeting between Lily, M&PR's Account Manager and Carlos, the Project Manager for the grand opening. Then listen and match each item on the agenda with the time it should be completed (a–d).**

AGENDA

Project: Casa Paradiso grand opening

Meeting date: 1 August

Event date: 1 October

1) 'Save the date' invitations to guest list
2) Contract with actress Lana Gabler-Jones
3) Engineer to explain wind turbines
4) Food order for the event

a Can do tomorrow
b Don't need to do this
c Get Sarah to do this on 15 September
d Need to do today

B Read the project priority box. Match each item on the agenda with a number in the box.

	IMPORTANT	
	YES	NO
URGENT YES	**1** Do this now	**3** Delegate someone to do this
URGENT NO	**2** Decide when to do this before it becomes urgent	**4** Delete this – don't waste your time

T Teacher's resources: extra activities

Analysing meeting minutes

3A Read the document on page 134. Was it written before or after the meeting? How do you know?

B Answer the questions.

1 Did they discuss every item on the agenda?
2 What four tasks does Carlos now need to complete?

Analysing follow-up emails

4A Read the three emails. Match each one with a numbered item in the minutes in Exercise 3A.

Dear Constance,

I hope you're well. I'm writing regarding the grand opening of Casa Paradiso in Miramar. You may recall that I sent the contract six weeks ago for immediate signature, but I haven't received it back from you. We'd like to promote the event with Lana's photo, but we can't do that until we have a signed contract. I know you're busy, but would it be possible to get this sorted out today? Could we perhaps have a phone call?

Yours sincerely,

Carlos

Hi Sarah,

I'd like you to take care of the food order for the Casa Paradiso grand opening, please. The event is on 1 October, so we need to finalise the menu on 15 September. By that time, we should have an exact number of guests. We've already agreed the menu and paid a deposit. On 15 September, we need to give final numbers and pay 50 percent, minus the deposit. We'll pay the final 50 percent after the event.

Let me know if you have any questions.

Cheers,

Carlos

Dear Jim,

We spoke a few weeks ago about possibly getting one of your engineers to give a talk about the wind energy system at Casa Paradiso, for the grand opening. The owners have decided not to include that as part of the event. Thanks anyway for agreeing to help us.

All the best,

Carlos

B Decide if the sentences below are *true* (T) or *false* (F). Correct the incorrect sentences.

1 Carlos sent the contract to Constance about a month and a half ago.
2 Carlos wants to speak with Lana on the phone.
3 Carlos isn't sure how many people will attend the grand opening.
4 Carlos has already paid some money for the food.
5 The email to Jim is Carlos's first contact with him.
6 Carlos wants Jim to come to the grand opening.

 Teacher's resources: extra activities

❯ **TASK**

Hold a project meeting

5A Work in pairs. Student A is a representative of M&PR and Student B works for Casa Paradiso.

It's now 21 September, ten days before the grand opening. M&PR is meeting representatives from Casa Paradiso to finalise the plans for the grand opening. Here is the agenda for the meeting:

AGENDA

Project: Casa Paradiso grand opening
Meeting date: 21 September
Event date: 1 October

1) Progress of hotel construction   4) Music
2) Update on guest list   5) Food
3) Special celebrity guest   6) AOB

Student A: Go to page 135.
Student B: Go to page 137.
Work through the agenda for the meeting, sharing the information you have.

B As a group, decide what the current priorities are for the project and answer the following questions.

1 Will you try to continue the grand opening on the planned date? If so, where can you hold the event? If not, what date will be suitable?
2 If you decided to change the date, how does that affect other parts of the project? What additional changes do you need to make?

C Work individually. Write minutes for the meeting. Use the form on page 135.

Remember to:

• follow the structure of the agenda in Exercise 5A.
• include *Discussion*, *Decision* and *Action* for each numbered item, as in the minutes in Exercise 3A on page 134.
• decide who is responsible for each action.

D Work in groups. Compare your minutes. Are they similar?

Teacher's resources: extra activities

Self-assessment

• How successfully have you achieved the lesson outcome? Give yourself a score from 0 (I need more practice) to 5 (I know this well).
• Go to My Self-assessment in MyEnglishLab to reflect on what you have learnt.

| Lesson outcome | Learners can consider market research and devise a marketing strategy. |

Background

1 Read the background and answer the questions with a partner.

1 What does HappyPure make?
2 Who started the company and why?
3 Who are HappyPure's main customers at the moment?
4 What are HappyPure's future plans?
5 What kind of hand-made products have you used in the past?

BACKGROUND

HappyPure provides hand-made skincare creams for sensitive skin types. It was created by Isabella Barco from Venezuela when she could not find any suitable face creams on sale for her sensitive skin. Experimenting with different natural ingredients and essential oils, she found a formula which really worked. She gave it to her school friends who all wanted to try it and they became her first customers. They told their mothers who then told their friends until she had a solid customer base.

Isabella, who is now 18 years old and about to take her final school exams, works every weekend and every day after school to produce enough products to meet demand. Last month she opened an e-shop and was surprised by the demand for her products. Although she had planned to go to university, she realises that she has a really good business model and she wants to continue to expand the business full time. However, she does not have the business experience to do it herself. Last week she got requests from a chain of beauty salons in India who are interested in using her products and a request from a Russian supermarket to sell her products. She now has to decide how to take the business global.

Going global – what you need to know

2A 🔊 BW 4.01 **Listen to the first part of a radio interview with a Global Supply Chain Management Expert. Tick (✓) the things he mentions.**

- ☐ keeping costs low ☐ customer service ☐ cross-cultural problems
- ☐ delivering goods ☐ setting up a new business

B Listen again and complete these notes.

> **Key factors for going global**
> - having an efficient and ¹_____ supply chain
> - supply chain mustn't be ²_____ and difficult to control
> - supply chain needs to support both new and ³_____ customers

3A 🔊 BW 4.02 **Listen to the second part of the interview and answer these questions.**

1 Why does Greg mention horse meat?   2 What does he say about Google?

B Listen again and complete these notes.

> **Things to consider**
> - production increases, cost of ¹_____ , transport, payment terms, currency, amount of ²_____ needed
> - different ³_____ laws
> - product ⁴_____ must remain high
>
> **Global success depends on**
> - learning quickly and being ⁵_____

 Teacher's resources: extra activities

Supply chain 4A 🔊 BW 4.03 Listen to the expert talking about a simple supply chain model and complete the diagrams below.

1 Supply chain for organic apple juice start-up

1 _____ : local 2 _____	→	manufacturer and 3 _____ : Walter	→	4 _____ : friends and 5 _____

2 Supply chain for expanding apple juice company

new 6 _____	→	new manufacturer	→	warehouse and 7 _____	→	8 _____ → 9 _____
					↘	retailer → online 10 _____

B Work in pairs or small groups. Look at the problems below and indicate where they might occur in the supply chain.

1 stock running out
2 poor-quality product
3 production delays

4 increase in costs
5 customers can't find product in shops
6 online order deliveries delayed

Market research

5 Work in pairs. Discuss what kind of skincare products are popular in your country with both men and women. Consider why they are popular and who the target markets are. Do both men and women use skincare products?

6 Work in small groups. Discuss what research you think Isabella needs to do before selling into new markets. Consider these points and try to add at least four more of your own.

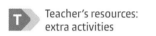

* rules and regulations / legal system
* potential customer base

* marketing
* shipping costs

 Teacher's resources: extra activities

7A Work in pairs or small groups.

Student/Group A: Look at the market research notes for India on page 135.
Student/Group B: Look at the market research notes for Russia on page 136.

* Exchange information about the two markets.
* Study the information together and discuss how HappyPure meets the market demands.
* Consider the potential difficulties of selling to those markets.
* Discuss what HappyPure must do now if it is serious about going global.

B Work in two groups with people from both A and B. Hold meetings to come up with a strategy for HappyPure to go global. Here is the agenda.

* Which market should HappyPure enter: India or Russia?
* What changes will the company have to make to go global?
* Manufacturing
* Pricing
* Branding and marketing
* Next steps / action points

C Share the results of your meeting with another group. Did you come to the same conclusions?

> TASK
> Choose a market for a global strategy

T Teacher's resources: extra activities

Self-assessment

* How successfully have you achieved the lesson outcome? Give yourself a score from 0 (I need more practice) to 5 (I know this well).
* Go to My Self-assessment in MyEnglishLab to reflect on what you have learnt.

Lesson outcome	Learners can understand the principles of the marketing mix and talk about products.

Background

1 Read the background and answer the questions with a partner.

1 What kind of company is eFAB?
2 What kind of company is TopCheng?
3 What would you make out of eFAB's new fabric?
4 Would you wear a T-shirt or jacket made from this material? Why / Why not?

BACKGROUND

eFAB, a British company that develops and manufactures cutting-edge, technically advanced textiles, was approached by TopCheng, a fashion design company in Taiwan, to develop a new type of cloth – a 'smart fabric'. TopCheng wanted the material to look and feel like normal cloth, but to include a very thin electronic element, allowing it to change colour, to display a variety of designs and even to light up. Initial market research shows that people love the idea, so eFAB's research and development team have created the new cloth and together with TopCheng's marketing department and product development team have produced several prototype T-shirts, dresses and jackets. Now the teams are working out how best to place the products in the market. The next step will be to carry out more detailed market research.

Market research

2A Read the extract from an email from the TopCheng Marketing Manager to the R&D Manager at eFAB. Answer the questions.

1 Who does TopCheng expect to sell the T-shirts to?
2 What do they say about the price?
3 What are they going to do next?

> After detailed consideration of the marketing mix of several possible products, we have decided to carry out further market research on a smart-fabric T-shirt. We have identified the target market as teens and early 20s who love technology. We can price the T-shirts at €35, so while that isn't cheap, they will be popular as a premium product. We plan to make them available online only at first, and to promote them on social media. The next step will be to test the product with focus groups.

B ◀) BW 5.01 **Listen to the focus group discussion about the smart-fabric T-shirt. Choose the correct words in italics.**

The focus group members …

1 *have already / haven't yet* worn the T-shirt.
2 *don't think / think* the shirt is fashionable.
3 *have a few / don't have any* ideas about other possible uses for the smart fabric.

C Listen again. Make notes about the feedback on the product.

Positive feedback	Negative feedback	Suggestions

The marketing mix

3A Match each of the five sections of the marketing mix diagram with the best explanation (1–5) below.

1 The location where a buyer can see and get the item or service _____
2 An item or service that is created to meet a need _____
3 The group of people who are expected to want the item or service _____
4 The way a manufacturer lets people know about the item or service _____
5 The amount of money a customer will pay for the item or service _____

B Answer the questions.

1 Which of the five circles represents eFAB's smart fabric, or things made from it?
2 Which of the five circles represents the advertisements eFAB might create to sell its smart fabric?
3 What does eFAB need to get high enough to make sure that the company earns enough money, and also low enough that customers will be interested?
4 Which circle represents the customers that eFAB will try to sell to?
5 If eFAB decides that their product will be available to order on the internet, which circle represents that?

Considering options

4A ◀) BW 5.02 Listen to a conversation between an eFAB Product Developer and a Marketing Manager. What product are they discussing?

B Listen again and make notes.

Product: _____
Target market: _____
Promotion: _____
Place: _____
Price: _____

T Teacher's resources: extra activities

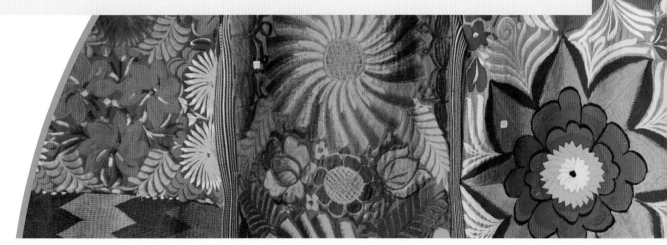

5A Work in pairs. Student A is a Product Developer at eFAB and Student B is a Marketing Manager. Take turns to ask and answer questions about possible products.
Student A: Go to page 133.   Student B: Go to page 129.

> TASK
Choose a product to develop

B Now decide which of the three products below eFAB should develop. Say why.

Think about which product might:

• have the biggest target market.
• earn the most money for the company.
• be the most popular.

☐ smart wallpaper
☐ road worker safety vest
☐ cycling safety vest

6 Work individually. Write an email explaining your decision about which product from Exercise 5 to develop. Use the email in Exercise 2A as a model.

Self-assessment

• How successfully have you achieved the lesson outcome? Give yourself a score from 0 (I need more practice) to 5 (I know this well).
• Go to My Self-assessment in MyEnglishLab to reflect on what you have learnt.

Lesson outcome	Learners can assess safety and security procedures for visitors to office and factory buildings.

Background

1 Read the background and answer the questions with a partner.

1 What kind of company is DIGAX?

2 What is happening in six months' time?

3 Why do you think their safety and security procedures haven't been updated?

4 What kind of new safety and security arrangements do you think the new manager might implement?

5 Have you had experience of your property being stolen at work or college? If you have, why do you think it happened?

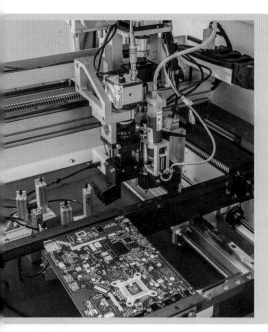

BACKGROUND

DIGAX Limited designs and produces innovative accessories for electronic devices. It is going to move its headquarters into a brand new office building and factory in six months. Security at the current premises has failed badly over the last year with staff property being stolen and competitors accessing confidential documents from company computers. The company has been in its current offices and factory for the past ten years. Unfortunately, the security is rather old-fashioned and consists mainly of CCTV cameras. There are several entry and exit points, which allow people to enter and exit the building without records being kept. Visitors have entered the offices and factory unnoticed without checking in at the reception desk first. There have also been several accidents in the factory because proper safety procedures have not been in place and one of these accidents involved a visitor. As a result of this, the company has now recruited a Safety and Security Manager who will be responsible for planning and organising the safety and security arrangements in the new offices and factory.

Safety and security

2A Work in small groups. Discuss potential hazards you might find in a factory. Use these signs to help you. Then share your ideas with the class.

B In your pairs, design another sign you might find in other business premises.

3A Scan the DIGAX report on page 137 about new approaches to safety and security and see if any of the potential hazards you came up with in Exercise 2A are mentioned.

B Read the report again and make a list of the following.

1 Problems that may occur in the factory now

2 Advantages of using robots

3 Potential problems using robots

4 Advantages of using biometrics

5 Potential problems of using biometrics

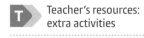 Teacher's resources: extra activities

Risk assessment

4A 🔊 BW 6.01 **Listen to part of an interview with an expert talking about risk assessment in offices. Complete the notes.**

Risk assessment notes

1 ¹_____ any hazards such as:
- trailing wires
- damaged ²_____
- machines without guards
- ³_____ and temperature of workspace
- ⁴_____ must be adequate
- office chairs – ⁵_____ results in sick leave

2 ⁶_____ risks

3 Create procedures to limit risk

B **Decide what risks you might find in a warehouse. Think about these things: heavy boxes, forklift trucks, ladders.**

C **Complete the risk assessment form below and then complete it for two other risks you talked about in Exercise 4B.**

RISK ASSESSMENT FORM   Please complete and hand in to your manager

1 Activity process   *Lifting heavy boxes*

2 Potential hazards

3 Who is at risk?   *Warehouse staff*

4 What have you already done to limit risk?

5 What risk is there of the action you've already taken failing?   *People might forget to lift properly*

6 What action must you take in an emergency?

Visitor information for factory visits

5A **Work in small groups. Discuss the following statement. Why do you think this might be true?**

'The person most likely to have an accident in a factory is a visitor.'

B **Discuss the questions.**

1 What things might visitors need to know about before visiting a factory? For example:
- equipment • clothes/shoes • vehicles • fumes from equipment • emergency procedures

2 What safety and security procedures should a company have for visitors to the factory? For example:
- ID • use of mobile phones • access to confidential areas

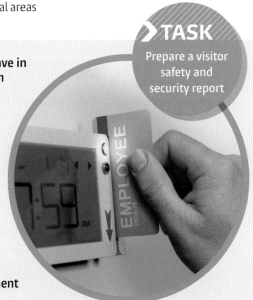

> **TASK**
> Prepare a visitor safety and security report

6A **Work in two groups, A and B. Discuss what procedures you will need to have in place at DIGAX for visitors. Use your ideas from Exercise 5B and make them specific to DIGAX.**

Group A: Discuss potential safety hazards in the factory and offices, e.g. equipment, electrical wires/cables, clothing, environment.

Group B: Discuss potential security problems, e.g. access to buildings (office and factory), ID systems, who should be allowed access.

Add any other information you think visitors need to know.

B **In your groups, prepare a presentation for the DIGAX management team giving details of the procedures which you think the company should put in place. Then discuss what signs you will need around the premises.**

C **Work in pairs, (one person from A and one from B). Present your ideas to each other and answer any questions your partner has. Then, using information from both presentations, write a full report for the management team. Use the report in Exercise 3 as a model.**

Self-assessment
- How successfully have you achieved the lesson outcome? Give yourself a score from 0 (I need more practice) to 5 (I know this well).
- Go to My Self-assessment in MyEnglishLab to reflect on what you have learnt.

Red Cushion Furniture

| Lesson outcome | Learners can identify problems in customer service and find solutions. |

Background

1 Read the background and answer the questions with a partner.

1 How did Red Cushion start?
2 What does the company do?
3 When did their problems start?
4 What problems is the company facing now?
5 Why do you think they have been unable to deal with the problems?

BACKGROUND

Red Cushion, a furniture manufacturer based in Mexico, was founded by Alejandro Roja, who started designing and making furniture in his workshop at home. Today, Red Cushion has grown into a multi-million-dollar business producing modern, stylish domestic and commercial furniture made from sustainable natural woods. It has a large domestic market and exports to North and South America and, more recently, some European countries. Over the years it has built up a reputation for providing excellent quality and style within a moderate price range.

Unfortunately, since expanding their export market, there have been a few problems and complaints from both new and old customers. Firstly, their raw material suppliers have been unable to supply the increased amounts of wood required and the production line has stopped several times due to equipment breakdowns. As a result, orders have not been getting out on time. Furthermore, several key design staff and craftsmen have left the company. In addition, the customer service department is unable to deal with the increased number of complaints.

Did customer services get it right?

2A Work in two groups.

Group A: Read the two case histories below.

Group B: Read the two case histories on page 137.

How well do you think each company dealt with the problem? Why do you think the company behaved in this way?

Case history A

A business executive arrived at his hotel late in the evening after a very long flight. He had an important meeting the following day in the afternoon, so he put the 'Do not disturb' sign outside his room so that he could sleep late to recover from the flight. The next morning, at seven o'clock, he was woken up from a deep sleep by a cleaner in his room. He was furious and asked the cleaner to stop but she did not, probably because she did not understand him. He called the Front Desk Manager who said there was nothing he could do. The guest then demanded to speak to the General Manager but was told that he was on holiday and that there was no one who could help him. Angrily, the executive got ready for his meeting, which did not go well.

Case history B

One day, a man was flying to visit his ninety-year-old father, who was dying. He needed two flights to get there, but the first one was delayed, so he would miss his connecting flight. He told the airline crew about his situation. The captain radioed head office and asked if they could do anything to make sure that the man caught his onward flight. When the plane arrived forty-five minutes late, he had missed the connecting flight by ten minutes. However, when he landed, an airline staff member took him straight over the runway to another plane. It was his connecting flight, which the airline had held for him. He got to see his father just before he died.

B Work in pairs, one person from Group A and one from Group B. Present your case histories to each other.

 Teacher's resources: extra activities

C Work in small groups. Discuss what you would do differently in each situation.

Dealing with angry customers

3A Read the customer emails on page 135 complaining about a Red Cushion product or service. Note down the answers to these questions for each one.

1 What is the problem?

2 What upset the customer about the customer service?

3 What does the customer want the company to do?

B Work in small groups. Share your answers to the questions, then together, decide what the best course of action would be for each one.

4A 🔊 BW 7.01 Listen to a customer services expert explaining how to deal with angry customers and customer complaints. As you listen, complete the key notes with one word in each gap.

Dealing with unhappy customers

1 _____ as fast as you can to sort out problem

2 Check _____ first before making any offers

3 For written communication: reply immediately: apologise and promise to look into it and _____ them asap

4 Consider each problem as a _____

5 Find _____ as fast as possible

6 Create _____ customers by offering more than they expect

Company policy

7 Ensure that _____ staff have authority to make decisions

8 Provide good _____

9 Create culture of _____ for the customer

10 Keep good _____ of all communication with the customer

B Work in pairs. Choose one of the complaints from Exercise 3A and roleplay the conversation between the Customer Service Manager and the customer. Take turns to be the customer and the manager.

> **TASK**
> Turn failure into success

5A Work in small groups. You work for Red Cushion and need to decide how to deal with the customer service problems that the company is currently experiencing. Look at the problems and complaints on page 136.

- Prioritise the complaints and decide what you should do first.
- Decide how to deal with each complaint (phone, email, letter to customer).
- Decide how to avoid these problems in the future.

B In your groups, present your analysis and solutions to the class. Include the following in your presentation:

- an explanation of how you prioritised tasks.
- how you decided which was the best method of communication to use.
- why you chose the ways to avoid the problems and complaints in the future.

C In the same or different groups, use notes from the presentations to prepare an information sheet that customer service staff can use in future.

Self-assessment

- How successfully have you achieved the lesson outcome? Give yourself a score from 0 (I need more practice) to 5 (I know this well).
- Go to My Self-assessment in MyEnglishLab to reflect on what you have learnt.

| Lesson outcome | Learners can identify and talk about communication problems. |

Background

1 Read the background and answer the questions with a partner.

1 What sort of company is DaneAv?

2 What is the main language of communication within the company?

3 What problem is DaneAv currently experiencing?

4 Have you ever experienced a communication problem because of language or culture? What happened?

5 When people are communicating in a second language, what can they do to try to make sure they have communicated clearly?

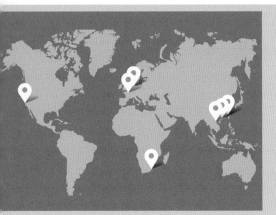

BACKGROUND

DaneAv is a Danish manufacturer of aviation navigation equipment. They have subsidiaries in Vietnam and China, where they make their products, and sales and support offices in Hong Kong, Durban, Dubai, Paris and San Francisco. Employees in all of the offices communicate with each other on a regular basis using email, text messaging, video conferencing, telephone calls and face-to-face meetings – always conducted in English. While the business is generally very successful, employees at all levels in the company often complain that they feel that clear communication can be a real problem, and that misunderstandings are common. Some employees have even said that simple communication problems with days, dates and numbers have led to lost business. Top management is aware of the problem and would like to solve it, but they aren't sure what to do.

Identifying communication problems

2A ◀)) BW 8.01 Listen to two DaneAv employees talking about communication problems. From the list below, choose the type of communication problem (a–d) each speaker is having.

Speaker 1 _____   Speaker 2 _____

a an accent that is very difficult to understand

b different cultural approaches to communication

c important information not shared

d paperwork overload

B Listen again and answer the questions.

1 a Which two nationalities were involved in the situation?

   b What did the speaker expect of the dinner meeting?

   c What did the speaker learn?

2 a How often is the speaker supposed to provide a sales activity report?

   b How often would she like to write the report?

   c How does she describe the performance of the sales team?

C Answer the questions.

1 How would a Vietnamese businessperson travelling to South Africa probably expect to do business? And what would he/she probably experience doing business in South Africa? How do you think he/she would feel about it?

2 Which culture is more like your home culture – Vietnam or South Africa?

 Teacher's resources: extra activities

3A Read the email exchange on page 138 between the Denmark-based Product Manager, Frederik Jensen, and Research and Development Manager, Mr Lau. Are the plans for Frederik's trip going well so far? Why? / Why not?

B Read the next email exchange on page 136. Answer the questions.

1 What does Mr Lau report?

2 Will Frederik need to change his presentation plans? Why / Why not?

4A 🔊 BW 8.02 **Listen. Decide if these sentences are *true* (T) or *false* (F).**

1 Frederik feels that the situation is more stressful than it should be.

2 He blames Mr Lau for the incorrect placement of the power switch.

3 He doesn't understand why Mr Lau needed to ask him what to do.

B 🔊 BW 8.03 **Listen. Choose the correct option in italics.**

1 Mr Lau *knew / didn't realise* the placement of the power switch was important.

2 Mr Lau asked for Frederik's advice *because he didn't know what to do / to show respect*.

3 Mr Lau's actions were based on *his own cultural understanding of / company rules about* how people should work together.

C **At this point, how does Frederik feel about the situation? How does Mr Lau feel?**

Think about who:

• thinks the other person should have behaved differently.

• has worked hard to make sure the model is correct and the presentation will go well.

• wants the company to succeed.

• is aware of how the other person thinks and feels.

Solving problems

5 **Read the email. What problem does it discuss? What solution does it offer?**

Thursday, 4 May | 15:07 Guangzhou (09:07 Copenhagen)

To all employees,

We are aware that recently, many of you have felt that communication among the offices globally has at times been difficult. We would like to address the issue by hiring a specialist consulting firm to deliver some training in cross-cultural communication. We feel that as a global company, this will help all of us to improve our communication skills, and increase the chances that we're all playing by the same rules.

We will be in touch again soon with more information about the times and locations of the training.

We will review the situation again after six months.

If you have any questions, please don't hesitate to get in touch.

Igmar

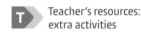 **T** ▶ Teacher's resources: extra activities

6A **Work in small groups. Igmar has suggested cross-cultural communication training for employees. Decide which of these other ideas might be effective.**

• Gather key employees from all offices for a formal meeting to discuss ways to improve communication

• Arrange an informal weekend away for all employees at a beach resort, so people can get to know one another

• Offer employees more opportunities to work in offices outside their own country for two or three months at a time

B **Using the email in Exercise 5 as a model, write an email explaining your solution.**

> **Remember to:**
> • explain the problem that you are addressing.
> • explain the solution you have chosen.
> • give reasons why you think the solution will work.
> • invite employees to ask questions or give feedback.

C **Work in pairs with someone from another group. Present your ideas. Did you reach the same conclusions?**

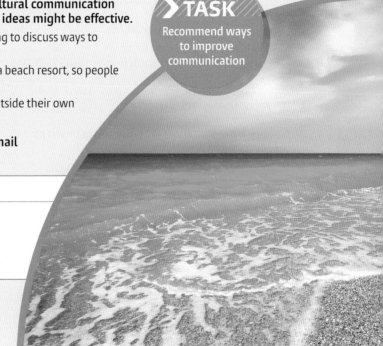

> TASK
Recommend ways to improve communication

Self-assessment

• How successfully have you achieved the lesson outcome? Give yourself a score from 0 (I need more practice) to 5 (I know this well).

• Go to My Self-assessment in MyEnglishLab to reflect on what you have learnt.

1.1 Transferable skills

1 Complete the text using the words in the box.

> attitude communication determination
> goals integrity player outside thinking

Geoff works hard and has a can-do [1]_____ ,
which makes him a very good team [2]_____ .
He has a lot of [3]_____ and never gives up when
things are difficult. He also uses critical [4]_____ to
solve problems and is able to think [5]_____ the
box. He sets realistic [6]_____ for himself and his
team. Geoff shows he has great [7]_____ – he
never blames other people for his mistakes. All this,
together with his excellent [8]_____ skills, makes
him a valuable employee.

2 Complete the sentences with the correct form of the words in capitals.

1 Ewa is very _____ and can work in
many different job areas. ADAPT

2 We need _____ people to do
this kind of work. RESOURCE

3 _____ is an important quality for this job.
We can't have someone who is often late
or off sick. DEPEND

4 He doesn't have as much _____
as we would like. CONFIDENT

5 I would like to see more _____
in the way he works. FLEXIBLE

6 We want someone who is _____
to reach the top level. AMBITION

7 I am _____ about the work I do. PASSION

8 I'd like a job which gives me a lot of
_____ to make my own decisions. INDEPENDENT

1.2 Advice and suggestions

3 Complete the sentences with the correct form of the verbs in brackets.

1 You should _____ (write) a blog about your
work placement.

2 Why don't you _____ (go) to a networking
meeting?

3 How about _____ (give) me an example of your
creative skills?

4 He could _____ (send) his details to the company.

5 Why not try _____ (use) social media to find
a job?

6 You shouldn't _____ (list) all your hobbies, just
a few.

7 You ought _____ (find) out about the company
before the interview.

Functional language

1.3 Asking questions to build rapport

4 Complete the conversation with one word in
each gap.

A: So, you worked in Brazil. How [1]_____ did you
work there?

B: A couple of years.

A: [2]_____ exactly did you work?

B: Recife. Do you [3]_____ it?

A: No, I don't. [4]_____ did you like best about it?

B: It was a great place to live and work.

A: [5]_____ did you come back to live in the UK?

B: Last month.

1.4 Networking at a careers event

5 Put the words in the correct order.

1 me / experience / about / tell / more / could / your / you?

2 you / put / in / with / me / charge / the / touch / person /
in / can?

3 questions / like / ask / a / the / few / about / to / you / I'd
/ company.

4 your / for / you / time / thank.

5 your / are / job / enjoying / how / you / new?

6 week / you / a / give / could / call / next / I?

1.5 Introducing yourself

6 Complete the email using the phrases in the box.

> any questions appointed as by email feel free
> hope to meet similar position to meeting you
> would like to

Dear colleagues,

I [1]_____ introduce myself. I have just
been [2]_____ the new Sales Manager
for KINDLO plc. Before I joined KINDLO, I was
working in a [3]_____ in a much smaller
company.

I [4]_____ you all on Friday, but please
[5]_____ to contact me [6]_____ or
phone if you have [7]_____ before then.

I very much look forward [8]_____ all in
person.

Kind regards,

2 REVIEW

2.1 Sectors and industries

1 Complete the sentences using the words in the box.

> automotive agriculture card drilling
> extraction financial manufacturing primary
> retail secondary tertiary

1 Alia works in _____ services and has a job in a credit _____ company. This kind of business is in the _____ sector.

2 Most economic activity is in the _____ sector with most of the population working in _____ (animal farming, crop growing, etc.).

3 We make furniture in our factory, which means that we're in the _____ industry. Therefore our business is part of the _____ sector.

4 The Japanese _____ industry is strong, with their vehicles sold worldwide.

5 That supermarket chain is one of the most successful companies in the _____ industry.

6 The _____ of raw materials is part of the primary sector and includes things such as coal mining, and gas and oil _____ .

2.2 Past Simple and Past Continuous

2 Complete the text with the Past Simple or Past Continuous form of the verbs in brackets.

A few years ago, while I [1]_____ (study) engineering at university, I [2]_____ (have) to spend three months as an intern in a large engineering company. One day, I [3]_____ (work) in the office when I [4]_____ (meet) someone who changed my life. While I [5]_____ (explain) one of the projects I [6]_____ (be) responsible for to a visitor who [7]_____ (own) a company, he suddenly [8]_____ (offer) me a job with his company. At first I [9]_____ (not hear) what he said, so he [10]_____ (repeat) the offer. He [11]_____ (wait) for me to reply when my manager [12]_____ (interrupt) us and asked the visitor, 'What are you doing?' 'I've just offered your intern a job!' he replied. I'm now Senior Engineer in a very successful company.

Functional language

2.3 Interrupting and dealing with interruptions

3 Complete the conversation using the phrases in the box.

> before we speak can I for interrupting
> going back to I was making just say something
> sorry to interrupt

Anna: Let's look at the new project in Paraguay first.

Benito: I'm [1]_____ , but I think we should discuss the construction project in Rio first.

Anna: Well, [2]_____ about that, let me just say that Paraguay is the most urgent item on the agenda.

Carlos: Can I [3]_____ here? Benito's right. Rio's more urgent at the moment.

Anna: [4]_____ what I was saying, I know Rio's important, but if we don't finalise Paraguay first …

Dina: Excuse me [5]_____ but …

Anna: [6]_____ just finish my point? The point [7]_____ was that Paraguay is really urgent at the moment.

2.4 Leaving a voicemail message

4 Choose the correct option in italics to complete the text.

Hello, [1]*this / here* is Johannes Marks from JOHAMA Supplies. This is a [2]*phone / message* for David Kiteman. I'm [3]*returning / getting back* your call. Please [4]*call back to me / call me back* so we can discuss the contract in more detail. And, er, can you call me on my mobile please as I'm away from the office all day? Could you [5]*get / call* back to me by the end of the day? I look forward to [6]*hearing / returning* from you.

2.5 Emails – Action points

5 Complete the email using the words in the box. There are three extra words you do not need to use.

> aware by decision decide involve know
> organise meeting with

As you [1]_____ , we're going to build a new factory. The project will [2]_____ a lot of planning, so we had a [3]_____ to discuss the next stages. Here are the key action points:

• [4]_____ on location for factory
• choose construction company
• [5]_____ permissions (Barbara)
• plan schedule (Juan [6]_____ end of month)

3 ◀ REVIEW

3.1 Managing projects

1 Choose the correct option in italics to complete the sentences.

1 We have reached an important *milestone / setback* in the project, so we're celebrating.
2 There has been another *risk / setback* with the project and it's now behind schedule.
3 We don't *anticipate / manage* any further problems or delays with the project.
4 It's impossible to accurately *anticipate / predict* the future.
5 A Project Manager is responsible for *milestone / risk* management – planning for possible problems.

Word building – verbs and nouns

2 Complete the email using the correct form of the words in the box.

> add   attach   decide   construct   identify
> investigate   solve   suspend

Dear all,

I've made a ¹_____ to change the project schedule after several ²_____ problems delayed the building project. We failed to ³_____ problems with the quality of some materials and were unable to find a ⁴_____ to the problem quickly. In ⁵_____ to this, poor weather conditions are also causing delays. Therefore we decided to ⁶_____ all work for a week while we ⁷_____ why we had quality issues.

Please see ⁸_____ for further details.

3.2 Comparatives and superlatives

3 Complete the text with the correct comparative or superlative form of the words in brackets.

This is our ¹_____ (big) project at the moment but it is progressing ²_____ (quickly) than we would like. One problem is that not all employees are ³_____ (experienced) as we would like and we are currently looking for people who are ⁴_____ (experienced). Everyone is working ⁵_____ (hard) as they can to try to finish the project on time. Secondly, although the budget is ⁶_____ (large) than any of our other budgets, there are problems with a new material. We used it because it was the ⁷_____ (expensive) – everything else cost much more – but the quality is not ⁸_____ (good) as we expected. As a result, the job is taking us much ⁹_____ (long) to complete. Next time we must use ¹⁰_____ (good) quality materials.

Functional language

3.3 Giving and responding to instructions, standing your ground

4 Complete the dialogue using the phrases in the box.

> can do it   compromise on   leave it
> like you to think about   need you to meet
> no problem   there's no flexibility   up to speed

Piotr: Can you bring James ¹_____ on the project so far?
Alicia: Of course. It's going well but we really ²_____ the new deadline.
James: Sure, ³_____ .
Alicia: We'd also ⁴_____ shift work, too, so you can complete the work on time.
James: The staff refuse to work shifts. They won't ⁵_____ this. We can't afford to lose them.
Piotr: I'm sorry, ⁶_____ on this. We've decided this is the best way forward.
James: I think we ⁷_____ without the need for shift work. ⁸_____ with me. I'll sort it out.

3.4 Asking for and giving updates

5 Choose the correct option in italics to complete the sentences.

1 The new design is *in progress / up to date* and I expect to complete it today.
2 *Where / What* are we with the new design?
3 What's the *last / latest* on the Indian contract?
4 Can you please give me *a schedule / an update* on the construction?
5 How are we *happening / doing* with the project scheduling?
6 I don't see any *impediments / deadlines* at the moment.
7 We hope to *finish / follow up* drawing up the plans today.

3.5 Email requesting an update

6 Match the sentence halves.

1 I'd like to know
2 Would you mind
3 I'd like to
4 Could you let
5 Would it be
6 I'd appreciate
7 Could you
8 I'd be very

a me know what supplies you need?
b possible to visit the site tomorrow?
c grateful if you could do this for me.
d if the project is on schedule.
e request a meeting with the project manager.
f it if you could give me some more information.
g sending me the staff files?
h possibly send me photos of the site?

4.1 Global markets: adjective and noun collocations

1 Complete the sentences using collocations made from the words in the box. Use the clues in brackets to help you.

> brand consumer goods local luxury marketing preferences strategy target territories

1 What are your _____ ?
(*the countries you want to sell to*)

2 What's your _____ ?
(*plan for selling the product*)

3 We sell _____ to wealthy people. (*high-end products*)

4 You have to know what the _____ are. (*what different markets want*)

5 We are a major _____ .
(*a well-known product bought by individuals*)

Word building

2 Complete the sentences with the correct form of the words in capitals.

1 The _____ of luxury goods has decreased in the past year.   CONSUME

2 We _____ in making leather goods.   SPECIAL

3 It is _____ to involve local people in the marketing.   PREFER

4 We need to _____ the system so everyone has the same information.   STANDARD

5 We have seen a considerable _____ in sales in the last two months.   GROW

4.2 Present Simple and Past Simple passive

3 Complete the text with the passive form of the verbs in brackets.

We produce healthy food products, which ¹_____ (sell) around the world. The business ²_____ (found) in 2004 when only three people ³_____ (employ). After six months my kitchen, which was our production facility, ⁴_____ (expand) and in two years a new factory ⁵_____ (build). Healthy food products ⁶_____ first _____ (export) in the second year, when they ⁷_____ (ship) to the USA for the first time. This expansion meant that six offices ⁸_____ (opened) in different U.S. cities. Currently 3,000 staff ⁹_____ (employ) worldwide and food ¹⁰_____ (produce) in ten countries.

Functional language

4.3 Changing the subject and staying on track

4 Complete the conversation using the phrases in the box. There are two extra phrases you do not need to use.

> a good moment   come to that   get back   I forget
> plenty of time   reminds me   wonder if we could

A: Excuse me, I ¹_____ talk about the new office?

B: Yes, of course. The building's nearly complete. We'll open on schedule, next month.

A: Is this ²_____ to start talking about the opening party?

B: We'll ³_____ later. We need to have a video walkthrough of the furniture layout first.

A: That ⁴_____ , my new sofa's coming today. I've got to go home to wait for it.

B: OK, but before you go, can we get back to the furniture?

A: Of course. But before ⁵_____ , we need to order more desks. Is that OK?

4.4 Reaching agreement

5 Complete the conversation with one word in each gap.

A: I think we ¹_____ change the design of our logo.

B: I'm sorry but I don't agree ²_____ you. Why ³_____ we just change the colour?

A: Actually, that's not a ⁴_____ idea. It'd look better in red and green.

C: Sorry, I'm not ⁵_____ I agree. We need to do something, but changing the colour isn't enough. How ⁶_____ if we ask the staff what they think?

4.5 Letter confirming an order

6 Choose the correct option it italics to complete the text.

¹*This / That* is to confirm your order no. 4536 for 100 BK workstations. I also confirm that we will ²*distribute / deliver* the workstations to your head office on Friday.

The ³*unit / item* price of the workstations is £200 and, in addition, we are offering you a ⁴*refund / discount* of 10 percent providing you pay for the goods on time. Our ⁵*payment / account* terms are 30 days after invoice date and I ⁶*enclose / involve* full terms and conditions for your records.

We ⁷*appreciate / thank* you for your business and look forward to ⁸*supplying / receiving* you again in the future. If you have any ⁹*orders / queries*, please do not ¹⁰*hesitate / stop* to contact us.

5.1 Technological innovation

1 Choose the correct option in italics to complete the text.

Today, customers are always looking for something different. This is probably because in today's [1]*disrupted / automated* world full of [2]*innovation / interaction*, everyone seems to follow the same trends and ends up with the same products despite the fact that there is far more [3]*choice / custom* than ever before. Furthermore, many people spend their days [4]*swiping / interacting* with machines rather than other people, so they may feel a little disconnected. Consequently, by offering [5]*customised / disrupted* products, companies offer something a bit different and perhaps make customers feel more human and individual again.

Describing innovative products

2 Complete the sentences with the adjective form of the words in brackets.

1 I think the new car design is very _____ (style).
2 This phone uses the most _____ (advance) technology available.
3 It's important to offer user-_____ (friend) products.
4 The company has a reputation for making very _____ (good, design) products.
5 People want to buy a brand whose quality is _____ (depend).

5.2 Present Perfect Simple with *just*, *already* and *yet*

3 Write sentences or questions in the Present Perfect Simple using the words in brackets.

1 (already) we / build / three factories this year.
2 (yet) they / not export / to USA.
3 (just) Mr Kite / become/ Sales Manager of the Year.
4 (yet) you / finish the designs for the new product line?
5 (just) Liam / get / a new job?
6 (just) the boss / send me an email.
7 (yet) I / not / start my new job.
8 (already) she / finish the report.

Functional language

5.3 Asking open and closed questions

4 Decide if these questions are *open* (O) or *closed* (C).

1 Tell us about the new product line.
2 Have you worked in packaging design before?
3 How long will it take to finish the product?
4 Can we change the meeting from today to tomorrow?
5 What do you mean exactly?
6 Has the machine stopped working?
7 Where did the delivery go?
8 Why did the customer make a complaint?

5.4 Describing features and benefits

5 Match the sentence halves.

1 The new dishwasher comes with
2 The new machine comes in
3 It is designed
4 The use of special crystals
5 There are no handles,
6 This makes it easier
7 There are two widths: one

a allows it to heat up without using electricity.
b to fit the machine neatly into a kitchen.
c measures 60 cm and the other 50 cm.
d lots of new features.
e silver, white and black.
f which means that there are no bits sticking out.
g for daily family washes.

5.5 Product review

6 Complete the review with one word in each gap. The first letter is given to help you.

HLX Multi-cooker
Rating: ★★★★☆

We [1]c_____ this cooker because the adverts said it [2]p_____ more economically than most competitors, which is true. It also has a long-lasting battery in case there is a power cut. I was [3]i_____ by this innovation, which means that you can cook for six hours even if there is no electricity. [4]A_____ good thing is that it has a built-in microwave so everything is in one unit. However, [5]w_____ I liked most how was how quickly everything cooks in the main oven.

[6]O_____ thing I didn't like was the colour – there is no choice, only black – but the main [7]d_____ is the price, which is about 10 percent higher than other similar cookers. Nevertheless, if you want an efficient cooker, we [8]r_____ the HLX Multi-cooker.

6.1 Health and safety

1 Complete the paragraph using the words in the box.

> defenders drops fit handle hold injures
> issue masks pose record resistant visibility

Companies must evaluate anything which could
[1]_____ a risk of injury to their employees.
Therefore they must [2]_____ staff with protective
clothing such as high-[3]_____ jackets and
personal safety equipment such as face [4]_____ ,
cut-[5]_____ gloves and ear [6]_____ if
necessary. When working with machinery, the company
must make sure they [7]_____ side guards to all
dangerous equipment. If the job involves waste material,
staff need to know how to [8]_____ it correctly
and the company must [9]_____ regular training
programmes. Companies must [10]_____ all
accidents that happen on their premises. So, if someone
[11]_____ a box on their foot and [12]_____
themselves, it must be written down.

6.2 Modal verbs of prohibition, obligation and no obligation

2 Choose the correct option in italics to complete the sentences.

1 Everyone *must / needs* sign in at reception.

2 You *don't have / mustn't* to leave your phone at reception.

3 However, you *must / have* to turn it off while you are on the premises.

4 When I visited the factory last week, I *didn't have / don't need* to wear goggles like last time.

5 We *need / must* always accompany visitors when they are in the building.

6 You *didn't need to / didn't have* check the stock yesterday. I did it two days ago.

7 Do we *need / have to* work late tonight?

8 *Do we have / Must we* wear our visitor badges while we are in the building?

Functional language

6.3 Explaining rules and requirements

3 Complete the table with one word in each gap.

Explaining rules	The machine [1]_____ be switched off at the end of each day.
	You [2]_____ to deliver the items by Friday latest.
Stating your [3]_____	[4]_____ you deliver the goods today or we will find another supplier.
	We can't finish [5]_____ you increase the budget. We need more money.
Maintaining a positive [6]_____	I'm sure we want the same [7]_____ .
	I can [8]_____ you've already done a lot of work on this.

6.4 Resolving a conflict

4 Complete the conversation using the phrases in the box.

> come to a compromise   from both sides
> how you feel   not happy with   really appreciate
> suggestion is   to an agreement   we proceed
> why don't we

A: We need to find a solution to this supply problem as fast as possible.

B: I totally agree. However, I can see it [1]_____ .
We can't produce the stock quickly enough and you have customers waiting. So how do [2]_____ ?

A: I [3]_____ it's difficult for you, Jack, but I've got an idea.

B: Go ahead.

A: My [4]_____ that we get another factory to produce the extra stock for now while we expand our own capacity as soon as possible.

B: I'm sorry, but I'm [5]_____ that. I think we need to find a new permanent supplier immediately.

A: I know [6]_____ but we've had a long business relationship. I think we need to [7]_____ on this.

B: OK. [8]_____ discuss the details with the supplier you were thinking of? Maybe we can come [9]_____ on this that's good for all of us.

6.5 Instructions and warnings

5 Choose the correct option in italics to complete the sentences.

1 *Don't / Mustn't* enter the factory without the correct footwear.

2 *Careful / Beware* of all moving machinery.

3 *Make / You must* sure you are wearing your ID badge at all times.

4 You are *forget / not allowed* to take anything out of the factory.

5 You *don't / mustn't* take any photographs.

6 Don't *beware / forget* to put any valuables in a locker.

7 *Watch / Make* out for overhead cables!

8 Be *careful / sure* of slippery floors.

7.1 Customer service

1 Choose the correct option in italics to complete the sentences.

1 Our *premium / 'no-frills'* service offers customers extra quality and features.

2 We also offer *class / priority* boarding so you can board the plane before other passengers.

3 His *body / business* language showed he felt uncomfortable – he kept moving around.

4 We like the *personal / priority* attention we get from the staff.

5 We finally reached a very *satisfactory / satisfied* conclusion.

6 The job is very *undemanding / demanding* and stressful, so I get very tired.

7 They were *apologetic / apologise* about the mistake and gave us a free flight.

8 John's *handling / handle* of the problem was really good.

2 Complete the paragraph with the correct preposition.

Sophie was always anxious ¹_____ travelling. She usually travelled by train, but was never satisfied ²_____ the service on them. Nearly every time she travelled, she complained ³_____ the train company ⁴_____ something or other.

7.2 Verb + *to*-infinitive or *-ing*

3 Complete the sentences with the correct form of the verb in brackets.

1 I don't like _____ (wait) a long time for someone to answer the phone.

2 We can't afford _____ (waste) time.

3 We can't avoid _____ (make) changes to the company structure.

4 They forgot _____ (pay) their energy bill last week.

5 Do you remember _____ (sign) the contract with the supplier last year?

6 The company agreed _____ (refund) customers' money.

7 He failed _____ (tell) his boss what he was doing.

8 Joanna didn't want _____ (find) a new job.

9 The phone kept _____ (ring) all day.

10 He promised _____ (help) me finish the report.

Functional language

7.3 Responding to customer concerns

4 Complete the conversation using the phrases in the box. There are two phrases you do not need to use.

> absolutely right   confident we'll   correct about   filled me   have to say   let me speak to   told me   wanted to make sure that

Pablo: Hello, Pablo here from PabKitchdesign. I just ¹_____ everything is OK. Jorge has ²_____ in on the problem with finishing your kitchen.

Customer: He said that it's going to take another week to finish the job. That's not acceptable.

Pablo: He's ³_____ that. It's going to take longer than planned, but your kitchen will look fantastic.

Customer: I ⁴_____ that I'm really not happy about this. We've got a party this weekend and we need the kitchen working. You promised it would be finished this week.

Pablo: ⁵_____ Jorge again and see if we can speed things up. I'm ⁶_____ come up with a solution.

7.4 Discussing and presenting ideas

5 Choose the correct option in italics to complete the text.

We think that it's important to have competent staff so I think the first thing we ¹*need / should* do is brainstorm as many ideas as possible and we ²*want / suggest* everyone writes them down. ³*Otherwise / Basically*, it's about getting as many ideas as possible. Then we can see what we all ⁴*come / get* up with. ⁵*What / That* we want to do is make sure that we really think through all the ideas before we choose the best ones.

7.5 External 'thank you' email

6 There are seven incorrect words in the email. Write the correct words below.

We are ¹**sending** to thank you and your staff ²**with** your help with organising our conference. I would also like to ³**make** this opportunity to thank Ms Anita Freund who was especially ⁴**unhelpful**.

The conference went very smoothly despite a few initial problems, which your staff ⁵**handled** out very quickly.

Thank you ⁶**over** again for all your excellent work and we look forward to working with you again ⁷**at** the future.

1 _____   5 _____

2 _____   6 _____

3 _____   7 _____

4 _____

8.1 Digital communication

1 Choose the correct option in italics to complete the text.

It seems that people are ¹*overloaded / caught* by emails these days. People are always ²*replying / checking* their emails and social media sites on their phones. Are you a ³*master / servant* or a slave to technology? How quickly do you ⁴*reply / check* to emails and messages? Some people have a special time when they ⁵*catch / write* up on these instead of interrupting what they are doing and responding immediately the messages come in.

2 Complete the sentences using the correct form of the words in the box.

benefit   organise   perform   produce   transform

1 The company is hoping to increase _____ in the factory next month.

2 We plan to _____ a large staff party to celebrate the company anniversary next year.

3 The staff have just had their _____ review and I think we need to discuss some changes.

4 The company offers great _____ to its staff such as health insurance.

5 We have seen a huge _____ in the way people work in the last few years.

8.2 First and second conditional

3 Complete the paragraph with the correct conditional form of the verbs in brackets.

If we move to bigger premises it ¹_____ (be) very disruptive for staff and customers during the relocation. If I ²_____ (be) the boss, I ³_____ (think) very carefully about making this decision. I ⁴_____ (not spend) all my profit on a relocation at this stage. Staff ⁵_____ (have) to travel much further to get to work if this move goes ahead. And it won't affect just staff, but customers as well. Feedback from customers suggests that they will look for other suppliers if the company ⁶_____ (do) this. If we communicated better with the staff, we ⁷_____ (see) that this is not the solution. If I ⁸_____ (have) my own company, I ⁹_____ (not do) anything without talking to staff and customers first. If the move goes ahead, there ¹⁰_____ (be) many problems.

Functional language

8.3 Closing a deal

4 Complete the dialogue using the words or phrases in the box.

leaves   sums   sum up   return   understand

A: So that just about ¹_____ it up. We've agreed on the delivery dates.

B: But that still ²_____ the question of a discount. We really need 10 percent.

A: So what you mean is, you won't give us this order if we can't offer 10 percent?

B: That's right.

A: As I ³_____ it, we're still much cheaper than our main competitors. Our last offer is 8 percent. But if you increase your orders to £10,000 per month, then in ⁴_____ we would be prepared to give you 10 percent.

B: So, to ⁵_____ , you'll give us a bigger discount.

8.4 Talking about priorities

5 There are five incorrect words in the dialogue. Write the correct words below.

A: We must complete this report on time. It's of the ¹**entire** importance. Please ²**do** it your number one ³**importance**. You can't put it ⁴**on** any longer.

B: Not possible, I'm afraid. I'm meeting clients today but I'll put it in my ⁵**security** right now for first thing tomorrow.

A: Thanks. I appreciate it.

1 _____   3 _____   5 _____
2 _____   4 _____

8.5 Short report

6 Complete the short report using the phrases in the box.

it is recommended   it looks at why   it also seems that
it was found   it will make recommendations
one of the key problems   this report aims to

¹_____ outline the causes of customer complaints, which have risen dramatically in the last two months. ²_____ customers are unhappy and analyses why the complaints occurred. Finally, ³_____ about action to take now and the changes required to avoid a repeat of these problems .

⁴_____ is that customer orders are late or incorrect. ⁵_____ that staff in packing and distribution were unhappy because of shift changes. ⁶_____ some of them are not checking the orders properly. ⁷_____ that we discuss the shift changes with staff and try to come to an agreement which is good for both sides.

Introduction

Pronunciation is important because even if you use the right words and the right grammar, you won't be able to communicate effectively if listeners can't understand your pronunciation easily. Awareness of the key elements of pronunciation will also help you to understand spoken English better.

Syllables, stress and intonation

Different words have different numbers of syllables:

1 syllable	*grow, growth*	4 syllables	*in·ter·view·er, co·or·di·nate*
2 syllables	*prod·uct, re·port*	5 syllables	*char·ac·ter·is·tic*
3 syllables	*in·ter·view, pro·duc·tion*	6 syllables	*re·spon·si·bil·i·ty*

In words with more than one syllable, one of the syllables is stressed, i.e. clearer, louder and longer than the other syllables, and it carries the main intonation, i.e. the movement of the voice up or down:

PRODuct INterview INterviewer
rePORT proDUCtion coORdinate

In longer words and compound nouns there is often a secondary stress, i.e. a less strong stress earlier in the word:

characteRIStic responsiBILity mobile PHONE

Stress is important in making words recognisable, and stress and intonation are used to highlight important information:

A: Are you still using that same old comPUter? **B:** No, I've got a NEW one.
A: Did you get it as a PREsent? **B:** No, I BOUGHT it.

The sounds of English

These are the sounds of standard British English and American English pronunciation. See also the section 'Varieties of English' on the following page.

Consonants	
Symbol	Keyword
p	**p**en
b	**b**ack
t	**t**ea
t̬ (*AmE*)	ci**t**y
d	**d**ay
k	**k**ey
g	**g**et
tʃ	**ch**ur**ch**
dʒ	**j**u**dg**e
f	**f**act
v	**v**iew
θ	**th**ing
ð	**th**is
s	**s**oon
z	**z**ero
ʃ	**sh**ip
ʒ	plea**s**ure
h	**h**ot
m	**m**ore
n	**n**ice
ŋ	ri**ng**
l	**l**ight
r	**r**ight
j	**y**et
w	**w**et

Vowels		
Symbol	Symbol	Keyword
BrE	AmE	
ɪ	ɪ	k**i**t
e	e	dr**e**ss
æ	æ	b**a**d
ʌ	ʌ	b**u**t
ʊ	ʊ	f**oo**t
ɒ		**o**dd
ə	ə	**a**bout
i	i	happ**y**
u	u	sit**u**ation
iː	i	f**ee**l
ɑː	ɑ	f**a**ther
ɔː	ɔ	n**or**th
uː	u	g**oo**se
ɜː	ɚ	st**ir**
eɪ	eɪ	f**a**ce
aɪ	aɪ	pr**i**ce
ɔɪ	ɔɪ	b**oy**
əʊ	oʊ	n**o**
aʊ	aʊ	m**ou**th
ɪə	ɪr	n**ear**
eə	er	f**air**
ʊə	ʊr	j**ur**y

/t̬/ means that many American speakers use a voiced sound like a quick /d/ for the /t/ in words like *city, party, little*.
ː shows a long vowel

Sounds and spelling

In English, the relationship between spoken and written language is particularly complicated.

The same sound can be spelt in different ways, e.g.

- /əʊ/   sl**ow** g**o** l**oa**n t**oe** alth**ough** kn**ow**
- /s/   **s**ell **sc**ien**ce** **c**ent

The same letter can be pronounced in different ways, e.g.

- the letter *u* can be pronounced /ʌ/ as in **c**ut, /ʊ/ as in f**u**ll, /ɔ:/ as in s**u**re in British English or /ɪ/ as in b**u**sy;
- the letter *s* can be pronounced /s/ as in **s**ell, /z/ as in ea**s**y, /ʃ/ as in ten**s**ion or /ʒ/ as in deci**s**ion.

Using a dictionary

Once you are familiar with the phonetic symbols in the table in The sounds of English section, you will be able to use a dictionary to find the pronunciation of any word you are unsure about. As well as the sounds in a word, dictionaries also show word stress. Look at this dictionary entry for *controversial*:

> **con·tro·ver·sial** /ˌkɒntrəˈvɜːʃəl/ *adj* causing a lot of disagreement, because many people have strong opinions about the subject being discussed

- The ' sign shows you that the syllable immediately after it is stressed.
- The ˌ sign shows you that the syllable immediately after it has secondary stress.
- The ː sign shows you that the vowel is long.

Simplifications

In normal everyday speech, however, words often do not have the same pronunciation as shown in dictionaries. This is important for listening. Vowels in stressed syllables are usually pronounced clearly, but otherwise speakers make various simplifications:

- Some sounds are missed out, e.g. *facts* can sound like 'facs', *compete* can sound like 'cmpete', *characteristic* can sound like 'charrtristic'.
- Some sounds are merged together, e.g. *on Monday* can sound like 'om Monday', *ten groups* can sound like 'teng groups', *this show* can sound like 'thishow'.

Varieties of English

English is of course spoken by some people as a first language, but it is spoken by much larger numbers of people who learn it as an additional language and use it as a lingua franca for international communication.

There is a large amount of variation in how English is pronounced:

- Variation among traditional 'native' accents such as British, American and Australian. There are even considerable differences between the accents of different regions of the United Kingdom.
- Variation among accents of English as a lingua franca, with many of the differences caused by the influence of speakers' first languages, e.g. Japanese speakers often do not distinguish between /l/ and /r/, and Spanish speakers often add an /e/ at the front of words beginning with /sp/, /sk/ and /st/.

Consonant sounds are generally similar in different varieties, but there is much more variation in vowel sounds – both the number of vowel sounds used and the exact quality of the sounds.

In the audio and video recordings which accompany this course – and in your everyday life and work – you will hear speakers from various English-speaking and non-English-speaking backgrounds communicating successfully with each other despite such differences in pronunciation. For example, many speakers do not use the /θ/ sound of '**th**ink' and the /ð/ sound of '**th**en', but this does not generally affect their ability to make themselves understood. Particularly important things to concentrate on include:

- word stress,
- stress and intonation in phrases and sentences, for highlighting important information,
- consonant sounds,
- groups of consonants at the beginning of words – e.g. **str**ong,
- the difference between long and short vowels.

Good pronunciation does not necessarily mean speaking like a 'native' speaker; it means being understood by others when communicating in English. Awareness of pronunciation principles and regular pronunciation practice will help you improve your speaking, but also your listening comprehension.

Lesson 1.1 >
Word stress

We can record the stress pattern of a word by using a large circle for the stressed syllable and small circles for the unstressed syllables. For example: *performance oOo* This word has three syllables, per·form·ance, and the second syllable is stressed.

1 Work in pairs. Write the words in the correct place in the table according to their stress pattern.

adaptable   adaptability   computer   confident
dependability   flexible   independent   motivation
passion   people   reliable   resourceful

1 Oo	
2 Ooo	
3 oOo	
4 oOoo	
5 ooOo	
6 oooOoo	

2 ◀)) P1.01   Listen and check. Then listen again and repeat.

3 Work in pairs. Clap one of the stress patterns in Exercise 1. Your partner says one of the words that has this stress pattern, and uses it in a phrase or sentence.

Lesson 1.2 >
Voice range

Using a wide voice range will help you to sound interested and enthusiastic.

1 ◀)) P1.02   Listen to two versions of these questions. Which version sounds more interested and enthusiastic, the first or the second? Tick (✓) a or b.

1 Why don't you send an email to some companies?   **a** ☐   **b** ☐

2 How about setting up your own website?   **a** ☐   **b** ☐

3 Why not try making a video for YouTube?   **a** ☐   **b** ☐

2 ◀)) P1.03   Listen and repeat the more interested versions.

3 Work in pairs. Take turns to ask one of the questions, sounding either interested and enthusiastic or not, and to give one of these answers in the same style.

1 That's a good idea.

2 Yes, I think I'll do that.

3 Thanks for the suggestion.

Lesson 2.2 >
Stress in compound nouns and noun phrases

In compound nouns and noun phrases the main stress may fall on either word:
climate change, fossil fuel
Stress on the first word is more common.

1 Work in pairs. Underline the word with the main stress in these compound nouns and noun phrases.

backup power   electricity bill   energy supply
global warming   greenhouse gases   power cut
solar panel   wind energy

2 ◀)) P2.01   Listen and check. Then listen again and repeat.

3 Work in pairs, A and B. Takes turns to be A and B. Student A says *one* word from the box in Exercise 1. Student B, without looking at Exercise 1, says the compound noun or noun phrase in a sentence.

Lesson 2.3 >
Stress in phrases for turn taking

Some turn-taking phrases have characteristic stress patterns. For example:
Sorry to interrupt

1 Work in pairs. Mark where you think the two main stresses will be in the phrases.

1 Please continue.

2 As I was saying, …

3 The point I was making …

4 Excuse me for interrupting.

5 Please go ahead.

2 ◀)) P2.02   Listen to the sentences and repeat.

Lesson 3.1 ❯❯
Stress in derived words

When we add endings to words, the stress sometimes stays on the same syllable. For example:
manage → *management*
Sometimes it moves to a different syllable.
For example:
finance → *financial*

1 Work in pairs. Look at the words. In which pairs does the stress stay on the same syllable? In which pairs does it move?

> add → addition
> construct → construction
> investigate → investigation
> suspend → suspension

2 🔊 P3.01 **Listen and check. Then listen again and repeat.**

3 Work in pairs. Take turns to say one of the words, and the other says a word derived from it.

> attach   communicate   describe   detail   happy
> identify   interest   move   perform   person
> present   reason

Lesson 3.2 ❯❯
Weak forms in comparisons

In comparatives, the words *as* and *than*, and the ending *-er*, are pronounced as weak forms, with the /ə/ **vowel.**

1 Work in pairs. Take turns to say the sentences and tell each other if you used the weak forms or not.
1 The Panama Canal was cheaper than expected.
2 The Panama Canal wasn't as easy to build as the Suez Canal.
3 What's more amazing than the length of the Grand Canal is its age.
4 Work on the Grand Canal began more than 2,500 years ago.
5 The Suez and Panama Canals aren't as wide as the Grand Canal.
6 The Suez Canal route isn't as difficult or time-consuming as the journey round Africa.

2 🔊 P3.02 **Listen to the sentence and repeat.**

Lesson 4.3 ❯❯
Pronunciation of -(e)s endings

When we add *-s* or *-es* to a verb or noun, we sometimes add an extra syllable. For example:
go (1 syllable) → *goes* (1 syllable)
age (1 syllable) → *ages* (2 syllables)

1 Work in pairs. Write the words in the correct place in the table.

> agenda → agendas   decide → decides
> bus → buses   manage → manages
> choice → choices   office → offices
> client → clients   talk → talks

extra syllable	
no extra syllable	

2 🔊 P4.01 **Listen and check. Then listen again and repeat.**

3 Work in pairs. Make sentences using the words in Exercise 1.

Lesson 4.4 ❯❯
Consonant–vowel linking between words

In spoken English, a consonant sound at the end of a word is often linked to a vowel at the beginning of the next word.

1 🔊 P4.02 **Listen and repeat these phrases. Notice the consonant-vowel links.**
1 everybody's‿opinion
2 a moment‿of silence
3 break‿into smaller groups

2 Work in pairs. Mark where there will be consonant-vowel links in these phrases.
1 meet again next week
2 just an example
3 not a bad idea
4 I'm afraid I disagree
5 I want to remind everybody
6 decide as a group
7 listed on the board
8 narrow it down if possible

3 🔊 P4.03 **Listen and check. Then listen again and repeat.**

4 Take turns to say the phrases in Exercises 1 and 2.

Lesson 5.1 ❯
Numbers of syllables in words

> The number of syllables in a word is not always obvious from the number of vowels. For example: *meal* (one syllable), *create* (two syllables). **Sometimes the number of syllables is reduced in fast speech. For example:** *ordering* → *ord'ring* (two syllables).

1 Work in pairs. How many syllables are there in these words?

1	friends	**4**	automated	**7**	business
2	able	**5**	different	**8**	designed
3	unique	**6**	financial		

2 🔊 P5.01 Listen and check. Then listen again and repeat.

3 Work in pairs. Which syllables in these words may disappear in fast speech?

1	restaurant	**3**	similar
2	delivering	**4**	necessary

4 🔊 P5.02 Listen and check.

Lesson 5.2 ❯
Contrastive stress

> We can use stress to contrast two different or opposite ideas. For example:
> *I wouldn't enjoy <u>testing</u> musical instruments because I can't <u>play</u> one.*

1 🔊 P5.03 Listen and underline the two words with contrastive stress in each sentence.

1 People think I spend all my time playing the games, but I'm actually working all the time.

2 I've never really played the games – I try to find problems with them.

3 It's fun, but it's also hard work.

4 I've always enjoyed gaming, but I never expected to get a job in the industry.

2 Work in pairs. Student A says the first part of a sentence from Exercise 1, and Student B says the whole sentence.

3 Work in pairs. Underline the other word in each sentence that you think will have contrastive stress.

1 What do you think is the <u>worst</u> and the best part of being a product tester?

2 I was surprised to hear he's <u>left</u> his new job. He only started it last week!

3 I haven't become <u>bored</u> with it yet – in fact I still love it.

4 🔊 P5.04 Listen and check. Then listen again and repeat.

Lesson 6.2 ❯
Phrasing and pausing

> When giving a presentation, it is important not to speak too fast, and to pause in appropriate places.

1 🔊 P6.01 Listen to two versions of the beginning of this presentation. Which version is more effective, a or b?

Retail theft, also known as shoplifting, is a major problem for shops. In the past, prevention measures were more personal and low-tech. Shopkeepers and employees had to watch customers closely and the security system didn't need to be any more sophisticated than that.

2 🔊 P6.02 Work in pairs. Listen to the more effective version and mark where the speaker pauses on the text above.

3 Practise saying the beginning of the presentation with pauses in the same places as the speaker on the recording.

Lesson 6.4 ❯
Stress in phrases

> A lot of phrases typically have a two-stress pattern. For example:
> *to <u>meet</u> our <u>deadline</u>   I <u>totally</u> a<u>gree</u>*

1 Work in pairs. Mark the two stressed syllables in each phrase in italics.

1 It's important to *avoid conflict*.

2 Now it's *over to you*.

3 Believe me, I *know how you feel*.

4 OK, then, *what's the solution*?

5 Let's do the job as *quickly as possible*.

6 I think we can *come to a compromise*.

7 So, *what do you suggest*?

8 So, *how do we proceed*?

2 🔊 P6.03 Listen and check.

3 Work in pairs. Student A says one of the sentences in Exercise 1 and Student B claps on the two stressed syllables.

Lesson 7.2 »
Unstressed syllables at the end of a sentence

> The main stress is often near the end of the sentence. **For example:**
> *Let's go for a <u>walk</u>.*
> **Sometimes, however, after the main stress, there is a sequence of unstressed syllables which add no new information. For example:**
> *Yes, I'd <u>like</u> to go for a walk.*

1 ◀) P7.01 **Listen and repeat.**

Let's go for a <u>walk</u>.   Yes, I'd <u>like</u> to go for a walk.

2 **Work in pairs. Take turns to suggest and answer, as in Exercise 1. Complete each response.**

1 **A:** Why don't you take a few days off work?
B: I can't a<u>fford</u> to …

2 **A:** Why don't you phone customer services?
B: I <u>hate</u> …

3 **A:** Maybe it's better not to join the project?
B: I've already a<u>greed</u> to …

3 ◀) P7.02 **Listen and check. Then listen again and repeat.**

Lesson 7.4 »
Introducing a topic

> We often use a phrase with its own stress pattern to introduce a topic, and we often pause before we go on to say something about the topic.

1 ◀) P7.03 **Listen to these examples and repeat.**

1 In today's meeting, I want us to brainstorm ways of capturing ideas.

2 Mind-mapping is a kind of brainstorming.

2 **Work in pairs. Student A asks one of the questions (1–4), and Student B answers (a–d), putting the heaviest stress on the underlined words.**

1 What's the most important thing?

2 Whose responsibility is it to generate ideas?

3 What do your team think?

4 What happens to all our good ideas?

a <u>We</u> think the important thing is to have competent <u>staff</u>.

b <u>Generating</u> <u>ideas</u> is <u>everybody's</u> responsibility.

c <u>Our</u> team would like to push the importance of good <u>communication</u>.

d <u>Most</u> of the time, the good ideas we have simply <u>disappear</u>.

3 ◀) P7.04 **Listen and practise again.**

Lesson 8.2 »
Conditional sentences

> The two parts of a conditional sentence often have their own stress and intonation patterns.
> **For example:**
> *If you're <u>ready</u>, / we can <u>go</u>.*
> *We can <u>go</u> / if you're <u>ready</u>.*

1 ◀) P8.01 **Work in pairs. Listen and mark the main stress in each part of each sentence.**

1 If we give workers private offices, they'll be less distracted.

2 I'd stop to chat more often if I wasn't so busy.

3 If we encourage our employees to chat with each other, they'll get to know each other better.

4 I'd stop using social media at work if I were you.

2 **Practise saying the sentences.**

Lesson 8.5 »
Contractions in speech

> Contractions of auxiliary verbs (e.g. *be*, *do*, *have*) are widely used in speech and informal writing.

1 **Work in pairs. Which contractions will probably be used when these sentences are spoken?**

1 The sales department had not checked stocks before accepting the order.

2 Staff will not talk to each other.

3 Stock updates ought to happen automatically, but they do not.

4 The economic situation has not helped.

5 When I contacted the warehouse, they had ordered more stock.

6 It has been decided that we should make our brand more attractive to younger customers.

7 There have been a few problems.

8 Problems should be reported immediately, so that everyone is aware of them.

2 ◀) P8.02 **Listen and check. Then listen again and repeat.**

1.2 ❯ Advice and suggestions

We use **should**, **shouldn't**, **ought to** and **could + infinitive** to give advice:

*You **should** give detailed information about your experience.*

*You **shouldn't** use words like 'passionate' on your profile.*

*You **could** include information about your interest in hiking.*

*You **ought to** think outside the box.*

We use **Why not** and **Why don't you + infinitive** to make suggestions:

***Why not** try connecting with people in other industries?*

***Why don't you** give more information about your latest project?*

We use **What about** and **How about** + **-ing form** to make suggestions:

***What about** changing your profile picture?*

***How about** giving more details about the website you designed?*

1.5 ❯ Adverbs of degree

We can make adjectives weaker or stronger by using adverbs of degree.

- **Making adjectives stronger**

  very, really

  *I was working in a similar position in a **very** small company.*

  *I am **really** excited to be working for this company.*

- **Making adjectives weaker**

  quite, a bit

  A bit is used with negative words.

  *The meeting was **a bit** boring.*

  Quite is used with positive words.

  *This company is **quite** large compared to my last company.*

- **Making comparative adjectives stronger**

  much, a lot

  *The company is **much** bigger than I expected.*

  *The job is **a lot** more interesting than my last one.*

- **Making comparative adjectives weaker**

  a bit, a little

  *The company is **a bit** bigger than my old one.*

- **Making verbs stronger**

  very much, really, a lot

  Very much can go before or after the verb (and object).

  *I **very much** look forward to meeting you all in person.*

  *I look forward to meeting you all in person **very much**.*

  Really goes before the verb.

  *I **really** like this job.*

  A lot goes after the verb and object.

  *I like this job **a lot**.*

2.2❯ Past Simple and Past Continuous

- **Past Simple**

*Suddenly all the electricity **went out**.*

*I **thought** we really must do something about this.*

*She **walked** into the room, **made** herself a cup of coffee and **turned on** her computer.*

Form:

regular verbs: infinitive + -*ed*

Many of the most frequently used verbs have an irregular form, e.g. *think – thought, go – went*.

Use:

We use the Past Simple to talk about completed actions and events in the past. We also use the Past Simple to describe a sequence of completed events and actions.

- **Past Continuous**

*It **was snowing** all last night.*

*About 9 o'clock we **were** just **watching** TV.*

Form:

was/were + verb + -*ing*

Use:

1 We use the Past Continuous to talk about actions and situations happening at a specific moment in the past.

*A: What **were** you **doing** at 10 o'clock this morning?*

*B: I **was waiting** at the airport for the visitors to arrive.*

2 We use the Past Continuous in a story to give 'background' details, e.g. the weather, the location, the season, or extra details about someone's life at the time.

*She **was spending** the summer studying English in London when she met him.*

3 We use the Past Continuous to talk about a situation or action in progress which is interrupted by another event or action (expressed in the Past Simple).

1 *About 9 o'clock last night we were just watching TV.*

2 *Suddenly all the electricity went out.*

8.50 p.m.	②	9.15 p.m.

*I **was talking** on the mobile when the battery ran out.*

4 We use the Past Continuous with *while* to talk about two events or actions happening at the same time.

*She **was preparing** the presentation **while** he **was organising** the chairs in the meeting room.*

5 We generally use *when* before the Past Simple for actions and events of a shorter duration.

*I was talking on the mobile **when** the battery ran out.*

6 We generally use *while* with the Past Continuous for actions and situations of a longer duration.

__While__ I was reading the report, I made notes about the main points.

We often use the Past Simple and the Past Continuous tenses together.

Notice the important difference between these two sentences:

When we arrived, Janet was giving her presentation.

(Janet started her presentation **before** they arrived.)

When we arrived, Janet gave her presentation.

(Janet started her presentation **after** they arrived.)

Note: stative verbs

Verbs which describe states or feelings do not take the continuous form:

I ~~was liking~~ the book. ✗ I liked the book. ✔

He ~~wasn't agreeing~~ with my opinion. ✗

He didn't agree with my opinion. ✔

Some verbs can be both a state or action verb, depending on meaning:

I thought the book was interesting. ✔ (think = be of the opinion that)

I was thinking about writing a book. ✔ (think = consider)

2.5❯ *will, going to*

Going to is used for

- **a plan:**

*We **are going to** build a factory in Indonesia next year.*

- **an expected event:**

*The boss has arrived. He**'s going to** inspect the factory.*

Time expressions used with *going to*

- *soon, this evening, tonight, tomorrow, next week, next month*

Will is used for

- **opinions about the future:**

*The project **will involve** a lot of organisation and planning.*

- **decisions made at the moment of speaking about the future:**

*I**'ll do** it straight after the meeting.*

- **offers:**

*I**'ll help** you if you like.*

3.2 > Comparatives and superlatives

We can use adjectives in their base form with *as … as* to say two things are more or less equal or *not as … as* to say that one thing does not match another.

*The new computers are **as good as** the old ones.*

*The new computers are **not as good as** the old ones.*

*Doing calculations on paper **isn't as easy as** using a calculator.*

Comparatives

We use comparatives to say how two or more people or things are different.

To form comparative adjectives, we use *-er* or *more/less*:

*Having a meeting on Skype will be **easier than** talking face to face.*

*Finishing the project in six weeks will be **more difficult than** finishing it in eight or ten weeks.*

*For this project, the schedule is **less important than** the budget.*

With one-syllable and some two-syllable adjectives, we form comparatives using *-er*.

new → newer, short → shorter, narrow → narrower

With adjectives that have two or more syllables, we form comparatives using *more* or *less*:

expensive → more expensive, less expensive, modern → more modern, less modern

Some adjectives are irregular:

good → better, bad → worse, far → further

Sometimes we change the spelling when we add *-er*.

* Change *-y* (after a consonant) to *-i*:

  happy → happier

* Double the final consonant on adjectives ending with consonant + vowel + consonant in one-syllable adjectives:

  big → bigger

We form comparative adverbs in the same way as comparative adjectives, using *-er* or *more/less*:

*You work **harder** than I do.*

*They finished **less quickly** than we did.*

Some adverbs are irregular:

well → better, badly → worse

Superlatives

We use superlatives to say that one thing has more or less of a quality than any other thing in the same group.

To form superlative adjectives, we use *-est* or *most/least*:

*The Amazon is **the longest** river in the world.*

*This is **the most expensive** hotel in Lisbon.*

*Driving my car is **the least convenient** way to get to work because there's no parking.*

Note: we use *the* with superlatives.

With one-syllable adjectives, we form superlatives using *-est*:

new → newest, short → shortest

With adjectives that have two or more syllables, we form superlatives using *the most* or *the least*:

expensive → the most expensive, the least expensive

Some adjectives are irregular:

good → best, bad → worst

Sometimes we change the spelling when we add *-est*.

* Change *-y* (after a consonant) to *-i*:

  happy → happiest

* Double the final consonant on adjectives ending with consonant + vowel + consonant in one-syllable adjectives:

  big → biggest

We form superlative adverbs in the same way as superlative adjectives, using *-est* or *most/least*:

*He ran **the fastest**.*

*She worked **the most efficiently** of anyone in the office.*

*They responded **the least quickly** to my emails.*

Some adverbs are irregular:

well → best, badly → worst

3.5 > (not) enough

We can use **enough** with adjectives, adverbs and nouns. *Enough* means 'as much as you need'. *Not enough* means 'less than is needed or necessary'.

adjective + *enough*

*The manager is **experienced enough** for the job.*

*We can't work today. The weather isn't **good enough**.*

adverb + *enough*

*I'd like to know if the first stage of the building project is moving **fast enough**.*

*The project isn't moving **fast enough**.*

***enough* + noun**

*The CFO is now worried that there aren't **enough funds**.*

adjective/adverb + *enough* + *to* and *enough* + noun + *to*

*I understand that weather conditions were not **good enough to** start the second stage.*

*We haven't got **enough funds to** finish the project.*

4.2 ❯ Present Simple and Past Simple passive

We make Present Simple and Past Simple **passive forms** using the appropriate form of the auxiliary verb *be* + **past participle** of the main verb.

We use the passive form when we don't know who or what is responsible for an action (the agent), or the agent isn't important, or when we simply want to emphasise the importance of an action rather than the person or thing responsible for doing it.

We often use the passive instead of the active form to describe systems and processes and in formal writing (reports, manuals, etc.). When we include the agent we use the preposition *by*. For example:

Agent not known or not important

Present Simple

*These ceramic bowls **are made** by hand.*

*The ring **isn't made** of silver.*

***Are** the goods **shipped** worldwide?*

Past Simple

*Alibaba **was launched** in China in 1999.*

*Most of the concert tickets **weren't sold** directly to fans.*

*When **was** the website **started**?*

Agent known

*Several companies **are owned by** the Alibaba group.*

*All the jewellery in the store **was designed by** him.*

4.5 ❯ Verbs + prepositions

Some verbs are followed by a dependent preposition.

verb + *to*

- *belong, complain, listen, talk, write* and *speak*
  *We **are writing to** you to confirm the order.*
  *I need to **speak to** the boss.*

BE CAREFUL!

verbs that <u>don't</u> use *to*

- *ask, answer, phone, thank*
  Thank you for your business.

verb + *about*

- *complain, read, talk, think*
  *When we **talked about** your order, ...*

BE CAREFUL!

verbs that <u>don't</u> use *about*

- *discuss*
  We discussed the payment terms last week.

verb + *for*

- *apply, look, pay, wait, work*
  *I **work for** a bank but I'**m looking for** a different job now.*
  *He **applied for** the marketing job.*

verb + *at*

- *arrive, look, laugh, point*
  *I **looked at** the contract carefully after he signed it.*

verb + *with* + person

- *agree, disagree, do business*
  *I **agree with** the manager.*

verb forms after prepositions

If a verb comes after a preposition then you need the *-ing* form:

*They talked **about changing** the order.*

5.2 Present Perfect Simple with *just*, *already* and *yet*

We use the Present Perfect Simple to talk about actions that are very recently completed or not yet complete, within an unfinished period of time (*today*, *this week*, *this year*, *never*, *ever*).

- We use *just* directly before the verb to say that an action has been very recently completed:

  *A: You look tired! Have you **just** woken up?*
  (Did you wake up a few minutes ago?)

  *B: No! I've **just** come back from the gym.*
  (I returned a few minutes ago.)

  It is unusual to use *just* in a negative sentence.

- We use *already* in affirmative sentences, either directly before or directly after the verb to say that an action is completed at some time before the present, without saying exactly when:

  A: Have you finished your homework?

  *B: Yes, I've **already** finished. OR I've finished **already**.*

  We use *already* in questions, usually to express surprise that something has already been done:

  *A: It's only eight o'clock. Has everyone gone home **already**?*

  B: Yes, everyone was really tired.

- We use *yet* in questions to ask about actions that we think have happened or will happen soon. In questions, *yet* always comes at the end of the sentence:

  *Have you finished **yet**?*

- We use *yet* in negative sentences to say what hasn't happened:

  A: Have you finished yet?

  *B: No, I haven't finished **yet**.*

Yet most often comes at the end of the sentence, but it's also possible to put it directly in front of the verb. This usage sounds somewhat formal and old fashioned:

*We're hungry. We haven't **yet** eaten.*

We don't use *yet* in affirmative sentences.

5.5 Order of adjectives before nouns

When you have more than one adjective before a noun, they need to go in the following order.

- **Order of adjectives**

Opinion	lovely	interesting	
Size	big		small
Age		young	
Colour	black		blue
Origin		Japanese	
Material			wooden
+ noun	desk	manager	box

*The **practical strong** packaging the phone came in ...*

*The **stylish silver** phone has a **lovely large** screen.*

- We do not usually put more than three adjectives together. If you need more, then you should either change the sentence structure or start a new sentence:

*The **excellent**, **small**, **long-lasting** lithium battery works very well.*

*The **small long-lasting** lithium battery is **excellent** and works very well.*

or

*The **small long-lasting** lithium battery works very well. It is an **excellent** battery.*

- **Making adjectives stronger**

  We can make adjectives stronger by using *extremely*, *really*, *very*:

  *The **extremely stylish** silver phone.*

- **Making adjectives less strong**

  We can make adjectives less strong by using *pretty* (informal), *rather*, *fairly*, *slightly*:

  *It is **pretty good** value for money.*

  *The phone offers a **fairly good** performance.*

  *The battery life was **rather good**. (usually indicates that it is surprising)*

  *The phone is **slightly more expensive** than its main competitors.*

- **Using *quite* and *rather* + adjective before a noun**

  We need to add the indefinite article *a/an* after *quite* or *rather* and before the adjective.

  *It's **quite a good** phone.*

  *It was **rather a long** meeting.*

6.2❯ Modal verbs of prohibition, obligation and no obligation

1 We can use *have to*, *need to* or *must* to talk about obligations and actions that are necessary.

- *have to* + infinitive

  Staff **have to wear** ID badges at all times.

  Visitors **have to report** to reception.

  We **had to change** the security system after the theft.

  These obligations can include laws, rules and regulations.

  In British English it's also common to use *have got to* when speaking:

  I**'ve got to change** my password again.

- *need to* + infinitive

  Staff **need to wear** ID badges at all times.

  Visitors **need to report** to reception.

- *must* + infinitive

  Staff **must wear** ID badges at all times.

  Visitors **must report** to reception.

  We can generally use either *have to*, *need to* or *must* in most cases. However, we use *have to* and *need to* more frequently for external rules or regulations and *must* more frequently for obligations we make for ourselves:

  I **have to get** to work early tomorrow. There's a meeting at 9 o'clock.

  My boss says I **need to finish** this report before I go home.

  I **must get** to work early every day. It's when I get my best work done.

  We use *have to* and *need to* in both the past and present form:

  We **have / need to start** work at 9 o'clock every day.

  All visitors **have / need to sign in** at reception.

  I **had / needed to leave** work early yesterday.

  Did you **have / need to use** a password for the photocopier?

2 We use *mustn't* + infinitive to say that something is not allowed or permitted or that something is prohibited by law:

  You **mustn't use** your personal email account for work.

  Staff **mustn't talk** about company security in public places.

3 We use *don't have to* + infinitive or *don't need to* + infinitive to say that it is not necessary or compulsory to do something, but that you can do it if you want:

  You **don't have to / don't need to use** the lift but it's quicker than the stairs.

  I **don't have to / don't need to work** tomorrow. It's a public holiday.

  We also use *needn't* + infinitive:

  I **don't have to work** tomorrow. It's a public holiday.
  = I **needn't work** tomorrow.

BE CAREFUL!

Mustn't has a very different meaning from *don't have to / don't need to / needn't*:

You **mustn't** do that. = This is not permitted.

You **don't have to** do that. = This is not necessary.

You **needn't / don't need to** do that. = This is not necessary.

6.5❯ Linking words for time

before, after, when

These words are often used when we give instructions and warnings. We often use the *-ing* form of the verb after these words in written English:

Put on protective clothing supplied **before entering** the room.   written

Put on protective clothing supplied **before you enter** the room.   spoken

Make sure you put everything away in its correct place **after using** it.   written

Make sure you put everything away in its correct place **after you use** it.   spoken

Be careful **when standing** next to moving machinery.   written

Be careful **when you stand** next to moving machinery.   spoken

while

This is similar to *when* but it is used for continuous actions:

Be careful not to distract people **while they are working** on the equipment.

until

This word tell us when a situation finishes:

Stay there **until** the fire brigade rescues you.

as soon as

This means 'immediately when':

Report any problems with equipment **as soon as** you notice them.

BE CAREFUL!

When we are referring to the future we use the present tenses after *before*, *after*, *when*, *while*, *until* and *as soon as*.

while vs. during

We use *while* with a verb and *during* with a noun:

Do not use your phone **while you are operating** the equipment.

Switch your phone off **during meetings**.

7.2 **>** Verb + *to*-infinitive or *-ing*

When a verb is followed by another verb, the first verb dictates the form the second verb takes. There are various possibilities:

- **verbs which take *to*-infinitive**

  afford, agree, arrange, attempt, claim, decide, demand, deserve, expect, fail, guarantee, hesitate, hope, learn, manage, offer, plan, prepare, promise, refuse, seem, tend, would like

  She **decided to change** her mobile phone company.

  I**'d like to talk** to someone about my slow internet connection.

- **verbs which take *-ing***

  avoid, consider, delay, deny, dislike, enjoy, finish, involve, justify, miss, postpone, practise, risk, suggest

  He **avoided offering** the client a reduction in her phone bill.

  They **postponed launching** the new service for six months.

- **verbs which take *to*-infinitive or *-ing* with little or no change in meaning**

  begin, continue, hate, intend, like, love, prefer, start

  The agent **began talking / to talk** about a special offer.

- **verbs which take *to*-infinitive or *-ing* with a change in meaning**

  forget, go on, remember, stop, try

  I **forgot seeing** this film when I was a child.
  (here *forget* means not remembering something you have done)

  I **forgot to pay** my phone bill and they cut me off.
  (here *forget* means you didn't do something that was necessary to do)

  He **went on talking** for hours. (here *go on* means to continue an action)

  He **went on to show** some slides with the financial results.
  (here *go on* means to change action and do something else, often the next stage in a process)

  I **remember phoning** my husband a couple of times.
  (here *remember* refers to a past action, something the person knows happened)

  I'll **remember to look for** another mobile provider when I have time. (here *remember* refers to a future action, something the person needs to do)

  We **stopped to have** lunch. (here *stop* means to end one activity in order to start another)

  We **stopped talking**. (here *stop* means that an activity or event does not continue)

  I**'ve tried to get into** my email, but the connection is slow.
  (here *tried* refers to something the person wants to do, but is having difficulties doing it)

  Have you **tried switching** the router **off** and **on**?
  (here *tried* refers to an experiment that might help to do something or not)

7.5 **>** *some (of), any, all (of), most (of), no, none (of)*

Some, any

These are used when we do not want to say the exact number or amount of something.

- **affirmative sentences = *some***

  Some companies have really good customer service departments.

- **negative sentences = *any***

  You didn't have **any** problems dealing with the situation.

- **questions without a noun**

  Use *some* if you want a positive answer:

  A: Would you like **some** more time to think about it?

  B: Yes, please.

  Use *any* if you are not expecting a positive answer:

  A: Do you need **any** more time to finish the report?

  B: No, thanks.

- **without a noun**

  Did you find any problems? No, we didn't find **any**.

  Unfortunately, we found **some**.

- ***any* – with a different meaning**

  They seemed to be able to deal with **any** problems that arose.

  Here *any* means it doesn't matter which or what kind of problems.

Some of, most of, all of, none of, no

- We use *of* when *some/most/all/none* come before words like *this, it, the, them*:

  There were problems with **some of the** catering facilities.

  None of our guests realised that anything was wrong.

  Most of the problems were resolved quickly.

- *all* – we can leave out *of* after the word *all*:

  ... thanks to the hard work of **all of your** staff

  OR ... thanks to the hard work of **all your** staff

- Talking about things in general – we do not use *of*:

  All companies must look after the welfare of their staff.

  Most computer problems are caused by people.

  Having **no** holidays from work is bad for you.
  (notice the affirmative verb)

8.2❯ First and second conditional

- **First conditional**

  We form the first conditional with *if* + Present Simple, *will* + infinitive. We use it to talk about things that might happen in the future.

  *If we **give** workers private offices, they**'ll be** less distracted.*

  We can use *if* in two possible places in the sentence:

  ***If** we encourage our employees to chat, they'll get to know each other better.*

  *They'll get to know each other better **if** we encourage our employees to chat.*

- **Second conditional**

  We form the second conditional with *if* + Past Simple, *would/could/might* + infinitive. We use it to talk about situations that are:

- possible, but not probable.

  *If we **gave** everyone a private office, we**'d need** a much bigger office building!*

- impossible.

  *If I **were** you, I**'d stop** using social media at work.*

- imaginary.

  *If I **were** CEO, I**'d give** everyone a private office.*

  In the second conditional we usually use the verb *were* with *I*, *he*, *she*, *it*. However, in informal speech, people often use *was* with *I*, *he*, *she* and *it*:

  *If I **wasn't** so busy, I**'d stop** to chat more often.*

- **Remember**

  If I were you is a fixed phrased and we always use *were* with *I*.

8.5❯ Past Perfect Simple

The Past Perfect Simple shows that something happened before something else in the past.

Form: *had* + past participle

- **Past Perfect Simple**

  *It seems that the sales department **had not checked** stocks before accepting the order.*

  We understand: *before the order was accepted*

- **Past Perfect Simple vs. Past Simple**

  *When I contacted the warehouse, they **ordered** more stock.*

  = They only ordered more stock **after** I contacted them.

  *When I contacted the warehouse, they **had ordered** more stock.*

  = They ordered more stock **before** I contacted them.

- **already**

  We often use the Past Perfect with the word *already*:

  *The warehouse manager **had already ordered** more stock.*

- **with reporting verbs**

  We often use the Past Perfect with reporting verbs like *said*, *complained*, *told*, *thought* if the original sentence was in the Past Simple or Present Perfect:

  'No one has updated / updated the stock records,' complained the Sales Manager.

  *The sales manager **complained** that no one **had updated** the stock records.*

- **Remember**

  When we talk about the past we usually use the Past Simple. We only use the Past Perfect when we need to stress that something happened before an action in the Past Simple.

Lesson 1.2 ▶ 12

> I'm a recent graduate. I'm hard-working, creative and good with numbers. I'm looking for any job that uses my skills.

The person who wrote the above profile:

- has a degree in mathematics.
- graduated with honours.
- had a part-time job during their university studies, working as a cleaner.
- wrote stories that were published in a university magazine.
- played for a city league football team in secondary school.
- hopes to find a job in the financial services industry.
- would consider working in other industries if a job looks interesting.

Lesson 1.2 ▶ 13A

Student A

1 Give your partner advice about how to improve an online profile. Give advice about how to *show* skills online. Use the language from the Grammar section where possible.

Begin: *How would you describe yourself? What qualities do you want your profile to include?*

Other useful expressions:

You should consider putting that in your online profile.

You also said you're good with numbers. Could you give me an example of that?

You say you're a good leader. How about telling me something that shows it?

2 Make up at least one specific example from your life for each of the skills below. Then answer Student B's questions.

You are:

- hard-working.
- a good communicator.
- creative.

Lesson 1.3 ▶ 8A

Student A

	Student A
Location	Barcelona – stayed in cheap hostel, Las Ramblas
Purpose	Weekend with some friends
Timing	3 years ago, at university
Duration	Long weekend
Likes	The food, especially tapas

Lesson 1.4 ▶ 5A

Student A (recruiter)

Your World

Sector:	Web design
Established:	2010
CEO:	Kofi Smith
Capacity:	8 designers
Location:	West London
Target markets:	fashion, creative industries and start-ups
Turnover:	£1.6m in 2017

Lesson 1.5 ▶ 3A

> To all staff
>
> I'm Gabriela your new HR Manager. I started work today. Come and meet me, but book an appointment first. I'm sure we'll get on really well.
>
> See you soon.
>
> Gabriela de Souza

Lesson 2.1 ▶ 10A

The agricultural industry in Spain

One of the most important activities in the primary sector in Spain is agriculture, particularly olive, cereal and grape crops in central and southern Spain. In addition, citrus fruits (oranges and lemons) and vegetables are grown on the Mediterranean coast and in Andalusia.

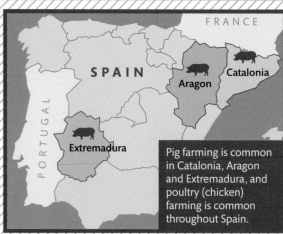

Pig farming is common in Catalonia, Aragon and Extremadura, and poultry (chicken) farming is common throughout Spain.

Spain is the world's largest producer and exporter of olive oil, the European Union's second-largest producer of fruit and the world's third-largest wine producer.

According to the Spanish government, today agriculture accounts for about 3 percent of the country's annual economic output (GDP) and 7 percent of all jobs in Spain.

Lesson 2.2 ▶ 9A

Student B

Complete the article using the Past Simple or Past Continuous form of the verbs in brackets.

How it started

Jan Koum and Brian Acton are the founders of WhatsApp. Koum, born in Ukraine, first ¹_____ (meet) Acton in 1997 while he ²_____ (study) in a state university in Silicon Valley and working for a computer security firm, inspecting Yahoo!'s advertising system. Acton was an engineer at Yahoo!

Within a year, Koum ³_____ (also / work) as an engineer at Yahoo! During their time at the company their friendship ⁴_____ (grow). They both left their jobs on the same day in 2007 and spent a year travelling around South America together.

In early 2009, Koum ⁵_____ (watch) movies at a friend's place when he had the idea for WhatsApp. It started as an idea to send notifications to friends, but soon ⁶_____ (become) an instant-messaging app that allowed any smartphone user to text without paying SMS fees.

But by June 2009, nobody, not even Jan's friends, ⁷_____ (use) the app. Both men ⁸_____ (live) off their savings and still unemployed. Koum told Acton that he ⁹_____ (think) about looking for a job. Acton encouraged him to give it a few more months.

When Koum released the second version of the app, he asked Acton to become a co-founder and Acton got his friends from Yahoo! to invest $250,000 in the business. In February 2014 Facebook ¹⁰_____ (buy) WhatsApp for $19 billion.

Lesson 2.3 ▶ 9B

Your company or place of study wants to:

1 introduce a compulsory system of car sharing for anyone using the car park.

For	Against
It's economical/cheaper.	It's not practical.
It's better for the environment.	Some people will have a longer journey.
Staff can make new friends.	It is less flexible because people will have to wait for each other.
It can improve team-building.	
It will save space in the car park.	

2 close the onsite company restaurant.

For	Against
It will create additional space in the building.	It may be difficult to find restaurants/cafes nearby.
It will reduce company recruitment costs.	Staff will need a longer lunch break to reach suitable places to eat.
Employees will be able to choose what they want to eat.	There will be less opportunity for team-building.

3 relocate to cheaper premises several kilometres away.

For	Against
It will reduce the running costs of the building.	The cost of moving.
It will reduce energy costs.	The disruption to work/studies and related costs during the move.
Some employees will have a shorter journey to work.	Some employees will have a longer journey to work.
	The company may need to provide company transport to the new site.

Lesson 2.2 ▶ 10A

This happened one day in March a few years ago. I was working late at the office so there weren't many people in the building.

Suddenly I looked out of the window and saw it was snowing. I was amazed because it never snows here at that time of year. I decided to get in my car and go home immediately. But when I got outside I saw it was impossible to drive. So I went to the train station but the service was cancelled because of the weather. Then a woman in the street told me that the metro station three kilometres away was open. I had to walk all the way there. It was very difficult and I felt very cold, especially my toes.

Fortunately, the metro was operating when I got there. Eventually, I got home that evening. I was very lucky; some of my colleagues spent the night in their cars because roads and motorways were blocked.

1 Background
Give some background details to introduce the story, such as the weather, location and date.

2 Details
Explain the main sequence of events. Use linkers to help you, e.g. *then, after that, at the same time, eventually.*

3 Conclusion
Say what finally happened. Was there a funny, sad, surprising, memorable ending to the story? How do you feel about it now?

Lesson 1.2 ❯ 13A

Student B

1 Make up at least one specific example from your life for each of the skills below. Then answer Student A's questions.

You are:
- good at problem solving.
- good with numbers.
- a good leader.

2 Give your partner advice about how to improve an online profile. Give advice about how to show skills online. Use the language from the Grammar section where possible.

Begin: *How would you describe yourself? What qualities do you want your profile to include?*

Other useful expressions:

You say you're hard-working. How about telling me something that shows that you're hard-working?

You should consider putting that in your online profile.

You also said you're creative. Could you give me an example of that?

Lesson 1.3 ❯ 8A

Student B

	Student B
Location	Barcelona – stayed in cheap hostel, Las Ramblas
Purpose	Summer holiday with a group of friends
Timing	3 years ago, at university
Duration	2 weeks
Likes	The people

Lesson 2.4 ❯ 3C

Daniella Rossi called re terms of new contract. Please call back on 07654 322 187 before 2 p.m. today or leave message with Elliot Barber, Ext 5238. Also please resend copy of contract.

Lesson 2.5 ❯ 3A

Points
- letter to employees explaining situation
- get customer feedback
- meeting with all staff
- ask staff for their opinions
- contact with individual customers
- email inviting staff to meeting
- press release

Lesson 1.4 ❯ 5A

Student B (candidate)

Profile 1:

A recent graduate of Nottingham Trent University, I'm a web designer specialising in the creative industries.

I design professional-looking, user-friendly websites using the latest software. My favourite programmes are Wordpress, Photoshop and Flash for animation.

When not in front of my computer, I'm behind a camera lens, photographing local bands.

Profile 2:

I'm a passionate graphic designer for web or print projects, specialising in the creative field. Tech-savvy, as well as proactive, reliable and enthusiastic. I love what I do and each project receives my full attention.

I graduated in 2017 from the Glasgow School of Design where I completed internships with local fashion houses, such as Lucie Lou's and Vintage Look.

Profile 3:

I was an IT consultant with a passion for fashion before I retrained to become a graphic designer. I have just completed an internship with Louis Vuitton in Paris and am now ready for a new and exciting challenge. Available immediately and looking forward to helping you make a successful contribution to the fashion world!

Lesson 2.4 ❯ 5A

Student A

Leave a message for Thomas Feldmann (Student B), Sales Representative of a family-owned bookseller. Include the following information in your message.

Caller:	Alysha/Ali Khan
Number:	0033 6 45 77 92 10
Reason for call:	You are calling about the order for 150 copies of *Communicate Better!* (you've lost the details of the order).
Action required:	You want the other person to check it has been dispatched, re-confirm the expected delivery date and time, and send you a copy of the order number (you want to be able to track it online).

Lesson 4.3 ❯ 10A

Supplier

Your ultimate aim is to sell your company's app. Start by getting your partner to start talking about how he/she manages business contacts. If this is too difficult, try and find out as much as you can about your client and his/her workplace context. Take a few moments to think about the language you need to use.

Lesson 3.3 ▶ 9B

Scenario 1

One of you does not want to leave the room. You think you should shelter under a table. The other believes that you should leave the building as fast as possible and get into the open air.

Scenario 2

One of you thinks it is important that the sightseeing should include a trip to a restaurant to try some local food. The other believes that the visitors would like to see some entertainment, not just the sights.

Scenario 3

One of you has a bad back and does not want to carry anything heavy. The other has a brother who owns a truck.

Lesson 3.5 ▶ 3A

Your head office is being refurbished and you want to find out from the project leader how the refurbishment is going. Write the exact questions you could ask.

- deadline
- new finish date
- work completed
- work not completed
- reasons
- furniture/equipment
- problems

Lesson 4.2 ▶ 7B

1 T
2 F – If your item sells, eBay charges 9 percent of the selling price to a maximum of $50.00. Alibaba charges a commission of 2 percent to 5 percent for each transaction.
3 T
4 F – Hotels are allowed to list on Airbnb as long as they don't hide the fact.
5 T
6 T
7 F – eBay does not belong to Google.
8 T (It currently costs $0.20 to publish a listing on the marketplace. A listing lasts for four months or until the item is sold.)

Lesson 5.5 ▶ 3A

⟨ ⟩

XB Watch – the new activity watch

Tracks all exercise activity, monitors sleep and syncs with phone app

Good points: long battery life, waterproof, app easy to use

Bad points: rather big and ugly

Does what is says. OK, if you don't mind how it looks.

Lesson 4.5 ▶ 3A

Dear Mr Jack Meadows,

I'm writing to you to say thanks for the order, which is great.
We think we can deliver on time but we have got some problems.
You must pay when you get the invoice or we will take the goods back.

Yours,

Dietger

BUSINESS WORKSHOP 5 ▶ 5A

Student B

1 **Ask Student A questions to complete the table.**

Product:	
Price:	
Promotion:	
Place:	
Target market:	

B: What's your product idea?
A: It's a safety jacket for road workers.
B: OK, can you tell me more about it?
A: Sure. It displays lights …

2 **Use the information below to answer Student A's questions.**

Product:	smart wallpaper – allows people to change the colour or pattern of their wall; allows people to write messages for special occasions (requires connection to a computer)
Price:	a premium product – the cheapest wallpaper is about €6 for a 10-metre roll; other premium wallpapers cost €50 to €100 per roll; it costs €48 to produce one roll of smart wallpaper
Promotion:	home design and decoration magazines
Place:	high-end department stores; online design shops
Target market:	people with plenty of money who are decorating their home; designers and decorators who help people with home decoration and design

A: What's your product idea?
B: Smart wallpaper.
A: OK, can you tell me more about it?
B: Sure. It allows people to change the colour …

Lesson 1.4 ▶ 5A

Student C (observer)

Listen to the conversation and make notes on the language Students A and B use to start and end the conversation, and show interest. Give feedback on what went well, what didn't go well and how they can improve next time. Use the tables below to help you give feedback. You may need to correct the expressions Students A and B use.

Student A

Rating: 1= effective, 2 = needs some improvement, 3 = poor

	1	2	3	Expression(s)
Started the conversation:				
Showed interest in the other person:				
Closed the conversation:				

Student B

Rating: 1= effective, 2 = needs some improvement, 3 = poor

	1	2	3	Expression(s)
Started the conversation:				
Showed interest in the other person:				
Closed the conversation:				

Lesson 2.4 ▶ 5A

Student B

Leave a message for Su Chen (Student A), Ticket Officer for UK Travel. Include the following information in your message.

Name: Josie/Joseph Makonga

Number: 0049 8529 990312

Reason for call: You are calling about fifteen first-class tickets from London to Glasgow for your colleagues to go on a team-building course. You ordered the tickets three weeks ago and you are still waiting to receive them by post. The team leaves tomorrow evening.

Action required: You want the supervisor to call back by 10 a.m. tomorrow with an explanation and/or to provide a suitable solution.

Lesson 4.5 ▶ 3B

Item:	printers catalogue ref: PR765 *OK*
Quantity:	100
Unit price:	€230
Discount:	8 percent on orders over 80 units *agreed last week*
Terms:	30 days *after invoice*
Delivery to:	Unit 14 Felton Business Park, Cross Street, Edinburgh
Delivery date:	5th May *send business terms and conditions*

Lesson 7.3 ▶ 9A

Scenario 1

'Your technician came to our house yesterday to fix our satellite dish which was broken in a storm last week. He arrived late, but that was OK. He spent two hours on my roof, but he did not fix the problem. My TV still doesn't work. I tried calling your office to complain, but all I got was a busy tone. Nobody answered the phone. What are you going to do about my satellite TV?'

Student A (manager): Think about whether or not you want to try to support your technician.

Student B (unhappy customer): Be prepared to challenge the manager if you are not satisfied with what he/she says.

Student C (observer): Listen to the conversation and note down the language the manager uses to respond to the customer.

Scenario 2

'Your cleaner came to our office yesterday to clear up after an office party. Unfortunately, the job was not well done, and the office is still dirty. Specifically, the kitchen is still full of dirty dishes, bins have not been emptied and the windows have not been cleaned. Please tell me what you are going to do about it.'

Student A (manager): Think about whether or not you want to try to support your cleaner.

Student B (unhappy customer): Be prepared to challenge the manager if you are not satisfied with what he/she says.

Student C (observer): Listen to the conversation and note down the language the manager uses to respond to the customer.

Scenario 3

'Your restaurant supplied food for our office party yesterday. Unfortunately, the food arrived late and was less than what we had ordered. Although the food was delicious, many of our staff expressed disappointment at the limited amount. I would like to talk to you about a reduction in the bill.'

Student A (manager): Think about whether or not you want to try to support your staff.

Student B (unhappy customer): Be prepared to challenge the manager if you are not satisfied with what he/she says.

Student C (observer): Listen to the conversation and note down the language the manager uses to respond to the customer.

Lesson 5.4 ❯ 6A

SPECIFICATIONS	Officejet Pro 2 Printer
Weight:	12 kg
Dimensions:	40.48 x 49.95 x 33.91 cm
Print resolution:	576,000 pixels
Print speed B&W:	35 pages per minute
Printer technology:	inkjet
Screen:	6.75 cm/touch-sensitive
Inks:	order to your door / monthly price plan
Other:	print from mobile device
Price:	£99.99

SPECIFICATIONS	Instata Print
Weight:	11.5 kg
Dimensions:	42.31 x 50 x 35.28 cm
Print resolution:	576,000 pixels
Print speed B&W:	40 pages per minute
Print speed colour:	29 pages per minute
Printer technology:	inkjet
Inks:	annual price plan
Other:	wireless printing
Price:	£98.45

Lesson 6.3 ❯ 9B

Student C (observer)

Listen to the conversation and make notes on the language Students A and B use to explain rules and requirements, state their position and maintain a good relationship. Give feedback on what went well, what didn't go well and how they can improve next time. Use this checklist to help you give feedback. You may need to correct the expressions they use.

Student A

Rating: 1= effective, 2 = needs some improvement, 3 = poor

	1	2	3	Expression(s)
Explaining the rules:				
Stating your position:				
Maintaining a positive relationship:				

Student B

Rating: 1= effective, 2 = needs some improvement, 3 = poor

	1	2	3	Expression(s) used
Explaining the rules:				
Stating your position:				
Maintaining a positive relationship:				

BUSINESS WORKSHOP 2 ❯ 5A

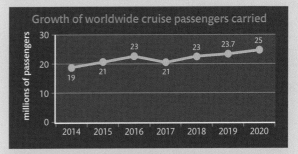

Growth of worldwide cruise passengers carried

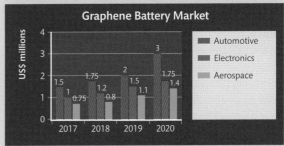

Graphene Battery Market

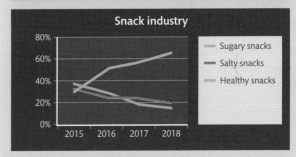

Snack industry

Lesson 4.3 ❯ 10A

Client

You are interested in learning about the app, but that will come later. For now, talk about everything except the app. Your aim is to learn as much personal information as you can about your supplier, and find out if he/she can be trusted as a business partner. Try not to talk about yourself too much. Take a few moments to think about the language you need to use.

Lesson 8.5 ❯ 3A

[1]*I'm writing this report because* my boss wants to know how the staff feel about the changes that are going to take place next month. [2]*I'm going to talk about* what those changes are, how the staff will be affected, and how they feel.

[3]*A very big problem is* the staff have not been told exactly what the changes are. As a result, they are very worried and unhappy. [4]*I also discovered* that some staff are applying for other jobs. This means we would lose some very experienced staff. [5]*I think* that this has caused a really bad feeling in the company.

[6]*I think it's important to tell* staff exactly what is happening and ask them for any ideas they might have to help with the changes. [7]*Let's do this* very quickly to solve the problems.

Lesson 6.4 ▶ 4B

Student A (Supervisor)

You are supervising a new intern who arrived a week ago. You are very pleased with his/her work so far. However, some of the staff have complained he/she often uses his/her mobile phone in the office and it is disturbing them.

Company rules on mobile use:

Keep your phone on silent or vibrate mode.

Don't take personal calls in your own time – use your lunch break or coffee break.

In an emergency, you must take your call in the corridor or outside the building.

Arguments:

Company rules are very clear.

It creates noise in the office and disturbs your colleagues.

You are using company time for personal matters.

You can ask people to contact you by text message.

Lesson 6.5 ▶ 3A

Student A

How to handle heavy loads

Before you lift any heavy loads it's important to follow certain procedures and gather information. For example, you need to know how big and heavy the load or package is and how far you have to take it. When you've worked out the destination, check it for any potential obstacles such as tight corners, narrow aisles and things you could possibly trip over. After that you should see if there is any equipment you could use to help you carry the load. Then clear the route of any obstacles which you could trip over.

When you are happy that the route is clear, you need to prepare for lifting. In order to do that, you need to make sure that you know how to lift correctly so you don't do any damage to your back. So, first of all you must get your body in the correct position by standing with your feet apart and your knees and hips relaxed. If your body is not in a good position to start with, you are more likely to hurt yourself. Then bend your knees, while keeping your back straight. You must have a firm hold on the load, so you need to get hold of the bottom of it firmly. Moving steadily and smoothly, lift the load, keeping your back straight and the load close to your body. When you put the load back down, you must follow these instructions in reverse.

There are two main things to beware of. For example, you must never twist your body while you are carrying a heavy load and you should definitely not try to lift anything which is obviously too heavy for one person.

Lesson 8.5 ▶ 3B

> *Requested by: HR Manager*
>
> *Why: too many staff leaving after one year*
>
> *Findings: salary not competitive, communication bad, too much work (add your own details)*
>
> *Recommendations: use your own ideas*

BUSINESS WORKSHOP 2 ▶ 7A

Group A

Company name	Best
Location	based in Germany
Company vision	to provide healthy free-from snacks using organic produce
Company history	founded in 2007 by Gabriela Santos, who realised that more and more people were snacking, but that the snack market only offered very unhealthy snacks
Current product range	gluten-free fruit bars low in sugar and salt; snacks containing whole nuts and super grains
Markets	Europe, USA and Australia
Financial performance	previous three years' sales revenue: $59m, $67m, $89m; projected sales for next two years: $100m, $130m
Management team	young team all passionate about healthy eating and keeping fit
Future plans	bringing out new range of healthy organic fruit and vegetable juices aimed at the teenage market; expand into the Asian market
Additional factors	providing food and shelter for homeless people

Lesson 7.5 ▶ 3A

Subject: Order XT/3401

Hi!

Well done getting the extra supplies to us earlier than promised.

You can still be our supplier.

Thanks.

Bye

Lesson 7.5 ▶ 3B

Notes for email

Problem with new computers

Call with supplier

- help desk staff – friendly, knowledgeable
- apologised
- offered new items or engineer to repair computers
- chose new computers
- one week later, customer services called to check all OK

Lesson 5.3 ➤ 9A

Student B

Read the feedback for Student A's presentation and prepare for his/her questions. You can also invent other details if you wish.

	Strength	Specific detail
Slides	very good	easy to read, good use of images
Body language	positive in general	at beginning of presentation – communicated well with audience, smiled, used good eye contact

	Weakness	Specific detail
Time management	poor	introduction too detailed, 10 minutes too long
Content	too basic	didn't know subject well, sometimes read information from slides, didn't use enough examples to demonstrate points
Delivery	average	monotonous tone of voice, too quiet

Ask Student A for feedback on your presentation by asking mainly open questions. Begin with:

What did you think of my presentation?

Lesson 6.3 ➤ 9B

Scenario 1: Working from home one day a week

Pros:

Employee can spend more time with family/children.

Employee's desk space can be used by other employees.

Employee will have a more flexible working day.

Working at home, employee will be able to focus better on important tasks.

Cons:

Employee may miss important meetings.

There's a minimum number of hours the employee must spend in the office per week.

Scenario 2: Requesting time off to take an advanced course in computer skills

Pros:

This will give the employee valuable computer skills.

This will add valuable computer skills for the company.

The company needs advanced skills for a particular project.

Without these skills it will be very difficult to complete the project on time.

The company needs to employ a new staff member with these skills.

Cons:

The cost of the course.

It's not clear who is going to pay for the course.

Who completes the work usually carried out by the employee while he/she is away?

BUSINESS WORKSHOP 5 ➤ 5A

Student A

1 Use the information below to answer Student B's questions.

Product:	safety jacket for road workers – displays lights that are visible at night; can produce patterns and messages
Price:	€35 to €40 to produce a jacket; standard safety jackets cost €20 to €30, so the retail price of this product will be a lot higher
Promotion:	construction trade magazines; special displays in building supply stores
Place:	in building trade shops; online
Target market:	companies that carry out road works and supply work uniforms; local governments that carry out road works and supply work uniforms

B: *What's your product idea?*

A: *It's a safety jacket for road workers.*

B: *OK, can you tell me more about it?*

A: *Sure. It displays lights ...*

2 Ask Student B questions to complete the table.

Product:	
Price:	
Promotion:	
Place:	
Target market:	

A: *What's your product idea?*

B: *Smart wallpaper.*

A: *OK, can you tell me more about it?*

B: *Sure. It allows people to change the colour ...*

Lesson 6.4 > 4B

Student B (Intern)

You started your internship a week ago and you are enjoying it, although you have a lot of responsibility. You are staying with a friend in his/her one-room flat, which is not very practical. You are having difficulty finding somewhere to live.

Possible arguments:

Other employees use their mobile phones in the office.
You try to take the calls outside when possible.
There's nowhere private to speak.
You are waiting for important calls about your new accommodation.

Lesson 6.5 > 3A

Student B

What to do in a fire

It's very important for everyone in a building to know what to do if there is a fire. Therefore, companies should prepare easy-to-follow guidelines for staff.

Firstly, everyone needs to know where the fire exits are and where they must meet outside – these are called assembly points. If someone finds a fire, they must keep calm and leave the office as quickly as possible with all their colleagues and sound the fire alarm. However, they must not use a fire extinguisher unless they have had the correct training.

There are certain procedures people should follow as they escape from the building. Firstly, they must shut the door once everyone is out of a room. Secondly, they need to check that doors aren't too hot before trying to open them as they escape. If there is a lot of smoke, they should cover their mouths and noses and get as close to the floor as possible whilst they are moving towards the nearest exit point. When they get outside, they should go to their assembly point. Unfortunately, it may not be possible to leave the office. In this case people should try to block gaps around the doors to stop the fire and smoke entering the room. Then they should open a window and shout loudly for help.

There are a couple of things which people should never do in the event of a fire. Firstly, they may want to take personal items and can waste precious time gathering them together. Secondly, they might try to use the lifts, which is extremely dangerous. Finally, once they are safely outside, they should never go back into the building until they are told it is safe.

Lesson 6.3 > 8

Colleague A

- Maintain a positive relationship (you know the colleague has already done a lot).
- Explain the situation (the end of the week is the deadline).
- State your position: the most important thing in this project is keeping to the schedule.

BUSINESS WORKSHOP 2 > 7A

Group B

Company name	Graf Industries
Location	based in USA
Company vision	to continue to create innovative products using graphene
Company history	founded in 2011 by a group of scientists who came up with ways of using graphene; 2015 opened factory to produce graphene-based batteries for electric vehicles
Current product range	batteries for cars, bicycles and motorbikes
Markets	USA, Canada and Europe
Financial performance	previous three years' sales revenue: $201m, $225m, $275m; projected sales for next two years: $325m, $340m; large R&D investment
Management team	dynamic, forward-thinking experts with good leadership skills
Future plans	new joint venture planned with South American graphene producer
Additional factors	supplying batteries to local communities

BUSINESS WORKSHOP 3 > 3A

MINUTES

Project: Casa Paradiso grand opening
Meeting date: 1 August
Attendees: LJ, CE

1) 'Save the date' invitations to guest list
   Discussion: Email approved
   Decision: Send email 2 August
   Action: CE to send email to guest list
2) Contract with actress Lana Gabler-Jones
   Discussion: Lana Gabler-Jones's contract not signed
   Decision: Need contract today
   Action: CE to email LG-J's agent today to get contract signed
3) Engineer to explain wind turbines
   Discussion: Decided a few weeks ago to hire an engineer to explain wind turbines – not necessary
   Decision: We don't need an engineer
   Action: CE to cancel engineer
4) Food order for the event
   Discussion: Catering company chosen
   Decision: Order food two weeks before event
   Action: CE to ask Sarah to place order

BUSINESS WORKSHOP 3 ❯ 5A

Student A: M&PR representative

As you work through the agenda, explain the following to the representatives from Casa Paradiso and listen to any information they have for you:

- Update on guest list: Good news: 125 people have said they would like to attend the party, and more than half of them will fly in from other countries to attend the opening. Should we try to get 25 more guests to attend, or stop at 125? We haven't confirmed with any guests yet.
- Special celebrity guest: More good news – Lana Gabler-Jones signed the contract and agreed to come to the party. The next day, she will fly to China to begin work on a new film, so we were lucky to get her. She will be in China for three months.
- We noticed that the invitation email mentions live music. Did the Casa Paradiso team hire a music group? M&PR didn't hire one – this may be a big problem.
- Sarah, who was supposed to order the food, went off work sick ten days ago and didn't make the order. Also, the caterers had the 1 October date as TBC, and are now no longer available on that date.

BUSINESS WORKSHOP 3 ❯ 5C

Project: Casa Paradiso grand opening
Meeting date: 21 September
Event date: 1 October

1) Progress of hotel construction
   Discussion: *125 guests will attend*
   Decision:
   Action:
2) Update on guest list
   Discussion:
   Decision:
   Action:
3) Special celebrity guest
   Discussion:
   Decision:
   Action:
4) Music
   Discussion:
   Decision:
   Action:
5) Food
   Discussion:
   Decision:
   Action:
6) AOB
   Information discussed:
   Decision:
   Action:

BUSINESS WORKSHOP 4 ❯ 7A

RESEARCH NOTES A

Indian skincare market

- rapidly growing market – huge potential
- customers want natural, organic ingredients which include things like vitamins, aloe and herbs
- demand for products with organic ingredients predicted to grow by 20 percent in next three years
- damage from environmental pollution growing, causing skin problems
- more awareness of need for sunscreen in products
- heat could be a problem for safety of products
- low import tax beneficial for foreign businesses
- pricing key to success – highly competitive and customers look for discounts
- markets different in each region – so need to adapt to local demands

BUSINESS WORKSHOP 7 ❯ 3A

1

From:	NoahDubango@OragaPty.com
To:	Customer Service Manager, Red Cushion
Subject:	Unwanted delivery

Your Customer Service Manager was extremely rude to me this morning when I rang to ask if you could come to collect the chairs, which you sent to us in error last week. We notified you immediately they arrived and you promised to collect them the following day. I have called every day since then and each time one of your agents has apologised and promised to collect them the following day. Instead I received an invoice by email this morning for the goods, which I hadn't even ordered. What sort of company are you running?

Noah Dubango

Purchasing Manager

2

From:	GeoffMeyers@MballHoldings.com
To:	Customer Service Manager, Red Cushion
Subject:	Order #23401 20 dining sets ref RC/D6

Dear Sir/Madam,

You invoiced us for twenty of the above dining sets but we only received ten. We emailed you last week about the problem but have still not received a reply. We will not pay for any of the sets until we receive the full order.

BUSINESS WORKSHOP 8 ❯ 3B

Thursday, 4 May | 15:07 Guangzhou (21:07 Copenhagen)

Frederik,

I received the design model for the HM-02 today. However, there is a problem. The main power switch has been placed in the wrong location. It works, but it doesn't look right. What should we do?

Mr Lau

Friday, 5 May | 8:03 Copenhagen (14:03 Guangzhou)

Mr Lau,

I was out with my family last night, so I didn't see your email until this morning. The power switch absolutely needs to be in the right place. Please have a new design model made. How quickly can this be done and sent out to Paris?

Frederik

Friday, 5 May | 8:05 Copenhagen (14:05 Guangzhou)

Dear Frederik

If I send it back this afternoon, we can have the new one in Paris on Monday morning.

Mr Lau

Lesson 5.3 ❯ 9A

Student A

Read the feedback for Student B's presentation and prepare for his/her questions. You can also invent other details if you wish.

	Strength	Specific detail
Content	interesting	knows his/her subject well, good use of examples to demonstrate points
Time management	excellent	demonstrated good time-management skills

	Weakness	Specific detail
Slides	difficult to read	font too small, too much information on the slides
Delivery	sometimes difficult to hear	pronunciation unclear, sometimes spoke too quickly
Body language	negative	looked bored, didn't communicate with audience, arms folded

Ask Student B for feedback on your presentation by asking mainly closed questions. Begin with:

Did you like my presentation?

BUSINESS WORKSHOP 4 ❯ 7A

RESEARCH NOTES B

Russian skincare market
- skincare market is one of the largest in the world
- women regularly buy more beauty products than in Europe and USA
- women aged 45–54 are largest consumers of products
- desire to look good and keep young is driving industry – anti-aging market very strong
- younger market mainly want facial products to keep skin clear from spots, etc.
- customers prepared to pay more for products which treat their specific needs
- supermarkets and hypermarkets are main distribution channel for skincare products, but internet sales are beginning to have an impact on these sales
- products which contain minerals, herbs and traditional Russian medicine are popular

BUSINESS WORKSHOP 7 ❯ 5A

1 – email

Order #23399 25 Office desks and matching filing cabinets ref RC/ODFC

We received the order from you ten days late and when we unpacked the desks, four of them were damaged. We are very unhappy with the quality of your goods and wish to cancel our order.

J. Long, Boston, USA

2 – social media

Don't buy any furniture from Red Cushion. It falls apart and is very ugly and looks nothing like the adverts.
Sonja #uglychairs   9/3/18 / 6:32pm

Rubbish – it's cheap furniture. Legs fell of my table and chairs were broken when they arrived. Customer service never replies to messages. Beware of this company!
#BewareRedCushion   9/3/18 / 7:11pm

3 – phone message

I've called you all day and all I get is 'Sorry, all our agents are busy at the moment. We care about your call. Please hold and a customer service agent will be with you soon.' But you wait and nobody comes on. You play awful music and it's costing me a fortune in phone calls. I want to speak to a person who can solve my problem. This is the worst company I've ever had to deal with.

BUSINESS WORKSHOP 6 ❯ 3A

Report on new approaches to safety and security

Introduction

Due to problems regarding safety and security on company premises, management asked me to investigate new approaches to safety and security.

1 Risk assessment review

It is clear that the company needs to review risk assessments for the factory and other premises. The following new approaches could be considered for the new safety and security policy.

2 Robots and factory safety

2.1 It has been proved that robots can greatly improve safety in hazardous environments. For example, we have to train human staff about potential hazards, such as equipment, chemicals, poor ventilation, heat, etc. They must also wear protective clothing to reduce the risk of harm. Nevertheless, instructions not to remove safety guards from equipment are still sometimes ignored to save time and some employees leave tools on the floor, creating trip hazards.

2.2 Robots, however, are never forgetful and always do as programmed. They do not daydream or distract co-workers and they follow procedures, unlike human employees who can get distracted, become tired, angry or bored. They are never late or off sick. Furthermore, the lack of emotion makes robots productive and reliable and, therefore, profitable. Problems only occur due to human error: for example, programming faults, incorrect installation or failure to follow maintenance procedures.

3 Security – Biometric ID

3.1 Biometrics means methods of recognising people using physical characteristics such as face, fingerprints, iris or retinal (eye) or behaviour patterns such as handwriting, or voice. Banks, online shopping companies and other businesses use biometrics to improve security. Facial or fingerprint recognition is already used in various companies and is familiar to many mobile phone users. Some airports and airlines use facial recognition to move passengers through the airport more quickly.

3.2 However, there are issues of privacy with biometrics and criminals can easily hack into these systems by photographing people's fingers from photos posted on social media, and recreating a fingerprint so that a scanner believes it is dealing with the person.

Conclusion

Firstly, the risk assessments need to be reviewed. Secondly, we should consider using robots in the factory to improve safety and, ultimately, save money. Regarding secure identification and entry to premises, biometrics potentially offers a secure system, but further investigation into this area is needed.

BUSINESS WORKSHOP 7 ❯ 2A

Case history C

A family were travelling to Bali with their young son who had some serious food allergies and therefore needed to have special milk and eggs. As a result, the family had packed these in their suitcase. Unfortunately, during the flight the eggs had broken and the milk had leaked so they had no food for their young son. They told the hotel what had happened and the hotel promised to try and find replacement food in town. However, they looked everywhere in Bali and couldn't find the right products. Then the Executive Chef remembered that you can buy them in Singapore, where his wife was from. He called his mother-in-law and asked her to buy them and then fly to Bali with them, which she did.

Case history D

A company was celebrating its 50th anniversary and the managers decided to have a party at their favourite restaurant where they usually took their guests and visitors for business lunches or dinners. Everyone enjoyed the party and had a good time although there were some issues with some of the food; it was not as good as it usually was so the Office Manager, who had organised the party, mentioned this to the Restaurant Manager. When she checked her phone after she got home, she discovered that the restaurant had posted some very negative comments about her company on social media, saying that they were the rudest customers ever. The next morning she contacted the manager and asked him about it. He said he didn't know anything about it and it was someone having a laugh.

BUSINESS WORKSHOP 3 ❯ 5A

Student B: Casa Paradiso representative

As you work through the agenda, explain the following to M&PR and listen to any information they have for you:

- Progress of hotel construction: The construction of the swimming pool is behind schedule, and so the area will not be ready for the party. There is no other suitable location at the hotel. It should be ready by 15 October. We need to change the party date to 16 October. Need to inform guests.

- Update on guest list: We've budgeted for food for 100 guests, and we think that is a comfortable number of people to enjoy the evening without it feeling too crowded.

- We have spoken with a DJ who could do a disco and also a local band who have appeared on TV and are becoming very popular. The band is a lot more expensive, but may be worth it. Both are available for 1 October, but we aren't sure about 16 October.

- The wind-power electrical system is complete and working very well. Should we email some pictures of it to our guest list?

BUSINESS WORKSHOP 2 › 7A

Group C

Company name	Palace Sea Magic
Location	based in Ecuador
Company vision	to provide upmarket cruises on small boutique-style ships, offering higher-quality service than found on bigger cruise liners
Company history	founded in 2003 by two businessmen who worked for the larger cruise companies for 20 years; they bought one small ship, refurbished it and started their business which now has three ships
Current product range	cruises around Central and South America and the Galapagos Islands
Markets	South America, USA, China and Australia
Financial performance	previous three years' sales revenue: $150m, $100m, $265m; projected sales for next two years: $375m, $450m; poor figures two years ago due to bad weather conditions (hurricanes/storms which damaged one of the ships)
Management team	experienced cruise industry experts with efficient team of employees
Future plans	new cruise ship in two years
Additional factors	supporting environmental projects in the places the cruises visit

BUSINESS WORKSHOP 8 › 3A

Monday, 1 May | 16:23 Copenhagen (21:23 Guangzhou)

Mr Lau,

As you know, I'm going to Paris next Sunday, 9 May to present the HM-02 on Monday to some key clients. I will need the new design model on that day, in the afternoon. Can you please confirm it will be ready in Paris on Monday?

Thanks.

Frederik

Tuesday, 2 May | 9:07 Guangzhou (3:07 Copenhagen)

Frederik,

I am expecting the design model on Thursday this week and will send it out overnight immediately. It will be in Paris on Saturday at the latest.

Mr Lau

Lesson 6.3 › 8

Colleague B

- Maintain a positive relationship (you know the colleague hasn't taken a holiday this year).
- Explain that the HR Director, who is away til Monday, must approve.
- State your position : you must find someone to cover the work.

1.1.1 P = Presenter YB = Yvonne Buysman
AH = Ashley Hayward RB = Ruth Badger
LS = Lord Sugar RF = Richard Farleigh

P: The twenty-first century workplace is constantly changing. In many countries, the idea of a career for life is long gone. What employers want are skills that can be applied to a range of tasks and roles. As a result, they look for flexible people who can demonstrate transferable professional skills as well as personal qualities that will benefit the company. Here's an insider's guide to the skills and qualities that will get you hired and also help you survive in today's job market.

A large part of the academic experience is based around individual performance.

In business, however, things are quite different. You need to develop a range of transferable skills. And one thing that many recruiters put at the top of their list is the ability to work in teams.

YB: I would look at ... can this candidate fit into the team well, do they work well with people, are they passionate about the topic, do they think outside of the box?

AH: Employers value teamworking skills very highly indeed, so if you're studying, it's really important you try and get some experience. Now, obviously, an internship's an ideal way to do this but you can also do it through part-time jobs, through vacation work, through voluntary work, or helping with societies and clubs while you're at university.

RB: Your experience at school is really, really important. So, if you played in a team – guess what? You're a team player – you set goals, you can achieve.

P: Twenty-first century careers involve a lot of movement, not just between jobs, but also between industries and countries. It's no good if your skillset locks you into one industry or even into one company, and this is where flexibility is important.

AH: Be prepared to develop attributes that are transferable across sectors so you can make the best moves for your career. I'm talking about things like critical thinking, which means analysing information very carefully, communication skills, problem solving, being able to influence people. Make sure you work on your communication skills – in person, on paper, face to face, in small groups, in large groups – you'll need to do this wherever you work, whatever job it is, across all sectors – communication skills are absolutely key. Employers are not just hiring a package of skills, they're hiring a person, and it's personal qualities that are of key importance: honesty, flexibility, enthusiasm – these things matter a lot.

YB: Be passionate – if you're really going to apply to a company that you're interested in, make sure your passion comes through and be genuine and authentic about that passion. You're going to work hard, you're going to play hard but you have to be passionate to be successful.

LS: It's their own determination that's gonna get them a job, right? Employers, you know, are gonna look at them not necessarily for the skills that they may have, but for the passion that they may, you know, express.

RF: Convince them that you have integrity. You know, integrity is very important, obviously. And convince them that you have ability, that you'll do everything you can to make that job work.

RB: If you are motivated and have a can-do attitude, you will get wherever you want.

P: So to sum up our insider's guide ... You need professional skills that can transfer from one job to another, especially the ability to be a good team player. And don't forget that employers look at the person behind the CV or résumé to identify the personal qualities they value in the workplace.

1.3.1 D = Daniel A = Alex J = Jessica
B = Beata

D: Hi, I'm Daniel Smith. I'm heading up the Diabsenor project here at Evromed. It's a new treatment for type 1 diabetes.
There's a lot of excitement about it, which I love. There's also a lot of work to do, which means a lot of stress. So I'm putting together a small team of our trainee graduates. Hopefully, none of them will be as nervous on their first day as Alex was

A: I heard that!
Is that Beeta? Batta? Barta?

D: Beata. She's Polish. I spoke to her on the phone. Great CV. Very promising. Business school in Krakow, five years' experience in Japan. Confident ... but not *too* confident.

A: Ah. Good. Hopefully she'll get on with Jessica then.

J: I'm Jessica Scott. Evromed is a small family-owned business dealing in the pharmaceutical sector. As CEO, I'm looking for the right attitude in an employee. Confident, but not arrogant. And sometimes I feel that overconfidence can come across as arrogance.

B: Hello. Daniel, isn't it?

D: That's me. And this is Alex. He's been here just over a year.

A: A year already? That's hard to believe. Twelve months in this crazy place!

B: Sorry?

D: Don't worry, Beata. Alex is just a bit of a joker, that's all.

1.3.2 B = Beata A = Alex D = Daniel
J = Jessica

B: That's OK. I was just confused for a moment. Nice to meet you.

A: You, too. I hear you lived in Tokyo. Where exactly did you live?

B: Suidobashi. Do you know it?

A: Ah, yes, near the baseball park. I lived there myself for a while. Loved it. How long were you in Japan for?

B: Five years. When were you in Tokyo?

A: 2013 to 2015. About eighteen months.

B: What did you do there?

A: Teaching English, mainly.

B: Teaching. Interesting. What did you like best about it?

A: Mainly the food!

D: This is Jessica Scott. She's our CEO.

B: Hello, Ms Scott. Beata Kowalska. Nice to meet you.

J: Please, call me Jessica. I hear you worked with one of our main competitors in Tokyo?

B: You mean MEDilink?

J: You must have learnt a lot while you were there.

B: Absolutely. But I'm very keen to learn even more here.

J: Well, you're going to be working with a great team. Daniel and Alex really know their stuff. How about we chat in a couple of weeks' time?

B: Sounds great. Thank you, Jessica.

J: Nice to have you on board.
I was very impressed with Beata. Confident but not arrogant. Just the right balance.

D: Beata made a great first impression. I'm sure she and Alex will have lots of Tokyo stories to share. And even Jessica liked her!

1.3.3 B = Beata J = Jessica D = Daniel

B: Oh. Right. So I'm working on the Diabsensor project, yes? What will I be doing exactly?
Hello, Ms Scott. Beata Kowalska. Very nice to meet you. Let me tell you about myself. I have lots of experience working in project management and have recently completed an internship in another medical supplies company in Japan. MEDilink. I'm sure you know it?

J: I'm aware of our biggest competitor, yes.

B: How is the Diabsensor project coming along? I'd like to discuss my ideas, if possible.

J: Well ... it's probably best if you get to know the product and the company first. Daniel and Alex will look after you for the next few days.

B: Yes. Of course.

J: Welcome to Evromed.
Beata? Hmm. Honestly, I'm not sure. I love her enthusiasm, but ... she seemed a little arrogant with it.

D: Beata meant well, I'm sure. But Jessica didn't respond well to her, which is a shame. Perhaps she needs to work on her communication skills a little more.

1.3.4

Basically building rapport is about getting on well with people, individually or in a group. Once you build rapport, you generally find communication flows more easily and it's usually more effective too. Sometimes rapport just happens naturally, but other times you need to use simple techniques to develop a link with the other person.

If we observe Beata in Option A, she doesn't have any problems building rapport with Alex. They both have an interest in Japan and rapport seems to come naturally. It's not the same with Jessica. In Option A Beata comes across as confident, which Jessica seems to appreciate, and this way the two create a bond. It's quite different in Option B, where Beata tries too hard to show how much she knows.

There are different ways of building rapport. One way is to find out what you have in common with the other person. It's not difficult – start by asking simple questions; business travel is often a good place to start. There are also simple non-verbal techniques you can use. Try to keep an open posture when you're speaking and smile. And eye contact will help you develop rapport in most cultural contexts, but make sure it's not too intense.

2.1.1 P = Presenter CG = Carlos Ghosn

P: Different countries often dominate in different industries. When we think of luxury goods, we think of France and Italy, and we associate internet technology with the USA. Japan is well known for its strong consumer electronics and car-making industries. Let's take a closer look at the country's economic development over the past decades.
Japan's industrialised, free-market economy is the third largest in the world. In the past, the country's been seen as a mystical land of cherry blossoms and samurai. Nowadays, it's better known as one of the world's leading high-tech economies.
Japan enjoyed rapid expansion after World War Two. It recovered from devastation to become the world's second-largest economy by the 1960s. Japan's service sector, which includes finance, trade, entertainment, tourism, retail and transportation, accounts for a massive three-quarters of Japan's total economic output. It isn't surprising therefore that within the financial world, the Nikkei is one of the most important markets, and that many Japanese banks are global players. But it has been Japan's manufacturing industries that have made the most global impact.
The automotive industry has been particularly successful. Japanese car manufacturers enjoy a reputation for producing reliable, high-quality and innovative vehicles. They pioneered technological advancements in the use of robots, which enabled the Japanese auto industry to produce cars to a high standard and very efficiently.
In the 1970s Japanese car makers became aggressive and successful exporters. The cars were cheap, reliable and popular with consumers. This meant domestic car makers in the USA and Europe lost market share.

Japanese vehicles' continuing popularity enabled Japan to become the largest car-producing nation in the world in 2000.

Despite increasing competition, Japanese automakers continue to innovate – the Toyota Prius was the first, and is still one of the best-selling, mass-produced hybrid cars. In 2010, Nissan released the world's first all-electric car: the Leaf.

CG: This car represents a real breakthrough. For the first time in our industry history a car manufacturer will mass-market a zero-emission car, the ultimate solution for sustainable mobility.

P: It isn't only the automotive industry, however, that provides world-beating products.

Japanese electronics companies are known for producing small, well-designed and often innovative products. Some of these have been so original that they have changed the way we live, work and play.

In 1979, Sony released the Walkman, a small and portable cassette player allowing consumers to listen to music while on the go – a concept that was revolutionary back then.

In the realm of video game technology, Japanese company Nintendo is credited with producing the best-selling handheld console in history – the DS, while electronics giant Sony claims the highest selling console of all time in the Playstation 2.

As we've seen, in the twentieth century Japan was very successful in using technology to innovate in areas like the automotive and electronics industries. Will it be able to use twenty-first century technologies as effectively? That is the challenge.

2.3.1 B = Beata   J = Jessica

B: The CEO is holding an induction meeting today so I thought I'd prepare a little over my morning coffee. Evromed … family-owned business … 145 employees … main market share in Europe … And suppliers based in China … in Shenzhen … newer projects in South America … New contract in Rio to supply hospital with device for diabetes patients. A trip to Rio would be very nice at this time of year … or any time of year …

J: Please feel free to ask questions as we go along.

2.3.2 J = Jessica   B = Beata   G1 = Graduate 1

J: Please feel free to ask questions as we go along.

B: How does the new product work, Jessica?

J: Good question. Who hates the sight of blood? Wow. It's not often meetings come to a consensus so quickly. Now, imagine you have to prick your finger several times a day just to check your blood sugar levels. With the Diabsensor, you don't have to. It's a real breakthrough –

B: Sorry, Jessica, when you say 'blood sugar', do you mean 'glucose'?

J: Yes, that's right.

B: And how does it work?

J: It analyses the patient's glucose level. A sensor collects the data through a patch on the skin and then sends it to a remote monitor. Basically it's a reliable and pain-free way to manage diabetes. Does anyone have any other questions …

B: How big is it?

J: Small. It fits in the palm of your hand, weighs about 35 grams. I actually have a prototype handy. Would anyone like to see it?

B: And the assembly process? I understand it's made in China?

J: The components come from China, yes. But we assemble the product at our plant here in Manchester. Just across there, in fact.

G1: Sorry, Jessica, if I could just …

B: Why don't you assemble the product in China? Isn't it cheaper?

J: Beata, I like your enthusiasm. But maybe someone else has a question? Please, yes, go ahead.

G1: What was the reaction to the product?

J: Very good initially …

B: I probably asked too many questions, I think. But to be honest no one else seemed very interested, which is a shame because it's a really innovative product. My mum has type 1 diabetes and this device would make her life so much easier. It's also one of the reasons I wanted to do this graduate programme. But yes … Jessica was getting a little irritated by my interruptions. I should be more careful about that next time.

2.3.3 G1 = Graduate 1   J = Jessica   B = Beata   G2 = Graduate 2   G3 = Graduate 3

J: Please feel free to ask questions as we go along.

G1: What can you tell us about the product? It sounds very innovative.

J: Good question. And it is very innovative. But here's a quick question for you first. Who hates the sight of blood? I bet we're all scared of spiders, too. Anyway. Imagine you hate the sight of blood, but you have to prick your finger several times a day just to check your blood sugar levels. Yes?

B: Sorry to interrupt, Jessica.

J: That's OK. Please go ahead.

B: When you say 'blood sugar', do you mean 'glucose'?

J: Glucose. Exactly. Yes.

G2: Ah, good, thanks. I was wondering about that, too.

J: So, as I was saying … no more pricking of fingers. The Diabsensor uses a sensor to read the patient's glucose level. It collects the data through a patch on the skin and then sends it to a remote monitor. Basically it's a reliable and pain-free way to manage diabetes.

G2: How big is it?

J: Small. Handheld. It weighs about 35 grams. How about I pass round a prototype for you to have a look?

B: Excuse me, Jessica, can I just ask … ? I understand the components are made in China. Is that right?

J: Yes, they *are* made in China … but we assemble the product here in our Manchester plant. Just across there, in fact. Any more questions?

B: I'd like …

G3: Yes, please can …

J: Yes, please, go ahead.

G3: Thanks. What was the reaction to the product?

J: Very positive, actually. There are several articles in medical journals. I can send you some links.

G3: That would be great. Thanks.

J: So … no more questions? Alright, then. My assistant Carol will be here soon and she'll take you to meet the production team.

B: That went really well. I had so many things I wanted to ask – but it was important to let others speak, too. Such a relaxed, friendly atmosphere. I think I'm really going to enjoy working with these guys.

2.3.4

It's clear Beata is highly motivated, not only by the programme, but also by the product.

In Option A, we see how she dominates the meeting; she interrupts continuously and even criticises the production process. She's clearly focused on getting answers to her questions. As a result, she gets information on the product but she makes a bad impression.

In Option B we see her using a more balanced approach. She's much more respectful, not just to the speaker but to the other participants as well. This time, she makes a better impression.

So here's my advice. We all have our own agenda when we attend a meeting. The important point is to respect the other participants, and that includes the presenter. Two things: first, this means knowing when to listen. And second, we should remember to watch the other participants so we know when to interrupt.

3.1.1 P = Presenter   M1 = Man 1   W1 = Woman 1   NR = News Reporter   PH = Phineas Harper

P: In business, as in life, things can and do go wrong. Imagine this situation: you are responsible for a major construction project that, after years of planning and careful project management, appears to fail in front of the world's media. A Project Manager's worst nightmare. In the case of London's Millennium Bridge, it was a nightmare come true.

The Millennium Bridge hit the headlines for all the worst reasons. As people walked across the bridge, it started to move from side to side.

M1: Bit surprised by the degree of sway.

W1: I feel very seasick, yes. But it's not too much further and we can get off the other end.

NR: The architects say that as a suspension bridge it was always intended to move, although not quite as much as it has been over the last few days.

P: What was making the bridge wobble? Was it safe? It wasn't a big movement, but people could feel it and were worried about the safety of the bridge.

PH: The Millennium Bridge opened in the year 2000, on the millennium, but that was actually slightly behind schedule and slightly over-budget, but in a project of that complexity, that's not so unusual. What was unusual; was that when people started to walk across the bridge, it began to sway, quite dramatically, from side to side.

P: The engineers were sure that the bridge was safe, but the team closed the bridge while they investigated the problem.

PH: One of the central parts of a project manager's job is risk management, so that's anticipating all the things that could possibly go wrong, and having a plan in place to reduce those risks. And in the case of the Millennium Bridge, they just didn't see the wobble coming at all.

P: While engineers investigated the mysterious wobble, the project managers also had a busy time.

PH: After a setback like this, the project manager's highest priority is to manage all the different specialist teams who are working on the bridge, but also to facilitate good communication between those teams. Together, they're going to have to come up with a new plan of what to do, which is going to involve setting new budgets, coming up with new schedules and agreeing new milestones; but the most important thing, immediately, is to figure out what the problem was and to find a solution.

P: The investigation was complicated and took a long time. The engineers found that the cause of the problem was the way people's bodies reacted to the very small movement of the bridge. The bridge's slight movement caused people to walk differently, and the change in their walking made the bridge move more. Engineers came up with the solution of attaching additional parts to the bridge to stop the movement. The work resulted in even greater budget and schedule over-runs.

PH: I don't think it's fair to blame the project managers on the Millennium Bridge for the wobble, because although we've known that lightweight bridges are prone to lateral motion, that phenomenon of thousands of people synchronising their steps had never been seen before. So, it's not the kind of risk you can just predict easily. However, from now on, you can be sure that at the top of every project manager's risk register, 'bridge wobble' will appear.

P: Two years after the initial problems, the bridge finally reopened, and it remains a popular London attraction. It has not suffered from any further severe movement. Despite that, it is still known in popular culture as the 'Wobbly Bridge'.

3.3.1 D = Daniel B = Beata C = Clarice

D: The thing is, I'm going to be really busy on Jessica's new project for the next few weeks. So I need Beata to do the day-to-day work on the Diabsensor.
I'm sure she'll be able to stand her ground and deal with the various issues. But, if she does have problems, I'm still the project manager, and she knows that my door is always open – apart from when I'm having my lunch break. That's my time.

B: Daniel mentioned that he would like me to speak to Clarice about the new requirements. I'm sure I can handle it. I've worked with sub-suppliers and clients on many other projects. And Daniel is always close by, in case I need him.

D: Clarice. Good to see you. This is Beata. She'll be taking over from me as your main contact on the Diabsensor. As you know, Clarice is our main sub-supplier on the project. Her company will be sending us almost all the components. She's almost as vital to the project as I am.

C: No one could be as vital as you, Dan. Very pleased to meet you, Beata.

B: Likewise. I'm looking forward to working with you.

D: I have a meeting room booked. Shall we … ? So, that's the tech side covered. There's just the details of the shipment deadlines to sort out. We need to make some changes. Beata, I'm already late for another meeting. Can you bring Clarice up to speed?

B: No problem, leave it with me.

D: Great.

B: He's so busy today. Well, we all are.

C: It looks that way.

B: Anyway as Daniel said, I think there is a problem with one of our shipment dates … Here we are. April 17th. That's when the delivery is supposed to leave your factory, isn't it?

C: Yes. Four weeks from now.

B: And the container will arrive on the 28th of May?

C: That's the plan.

B: The trouble is that one of our deadlines has been moved forward so we need at least some of the components by the 10th of May. I should have the details here … ah. Yes. These ones. The new schedule would mean we need at least one shipment early, probably by air.

C: Hmmm. Difficult. That will put a real strain on the budget. We planned to ship everything by sea. It was going to be part of a consignment for the UK.

B: There's no flexibility, I'm afraid. We really need the components earlier. Two weeks earlier, in fact.

C: OK. I understand your position. I think we can do it. Just let me recalculate the budget. There'll be additional costs.

B: But … is that really our responsibility? The original shipment was due in by the 9th of May. You changed it to the 28th.

C: That was all cleared with Daniel. Arrangements have been made. If we had known otherwise, we would have shipped earlier.

3.3.2 B = Beata C = Clarice

B: But things have changed now. You need to meet this new deadline. I'm afraid I can't compromise on this.

C: So there's no flexibility at all? How about a few days later?

B: I'm afraid I'm just not that flexible. My hands are tied. We need that shipment by the 10th.

C: Alright. Let's be clear here. You now need me to get these components to the UK by the 10th, and I have to cover all the costs myself?

B: Exactly, yes.

C: Seriously, Beata – there's nothing you can do here? No flexibility? Fine. Leave it with me. I'll call the factory in Shenzhen and get back to you.

B: Excellent. Thank you.
I got what I wanted, which is good. And she knows that I am the boss, which is also good. I don't think I'm going to have too many problems with Clarice in the future.

3.3.3 B = Beata C = Clarice

B: Yes, I know that Daniel cleared the existing schedule, but it doesn't change anything. We still need the shipment by the 10th. As I said earlier, I have no room for manoeuvre on this.

C: It's a pity we don't have another container leaving this week. We could have sent them straightaway. As I say, they're ready to go.

B: So it seems to me we have two problems here. I need the components to arrive by the 10th. You need to be able to cover additional costs. How about this? I could speak to one of our other suppliers. We have another container leaving China this week. Maybe they'll have some space?

C: That could work. We're talking two cubic metres, maximum.

B: Let me make some calls.

C: I'll see if we can get the components down to the docks in time. Pretty sure we can. Do you know where the container is right now?

B: Probably still in the factory.

C: Where's that?

B: I couldn't point it out on a map … but I know it's in Guangzhou. That's near Shenzhen, right? Looks like this could be a win for both of us.

C: A big win. And all before lunchtime, too.

B: I'm very happy with how that meeting went. I got what I wanted, and I think that listening to Clarice and trying to solve her problem, made our working relationship stronger. That will help me in the future.

3.3.4

We all have times when people tell us what to do. We all have times when we need to tell other people what to do. In the clip we see two ways of doing this.
In Option A, we see how Beata chooses to use her authority to get the job done – she's in charge and she knows that Clarice will do what she wants.
In Option B, we see Beata and Clarice working together to find a solution to the problem. So here she also achieves what she wants, but the outcome seems to be better for Clarice. I think in this option their relationship improves, too.
Of course, every situation is different, and it is impossible to say what always works best. But there is an English proverb which might help: 'to put yourself in the other person's shoes'. How would _you_ feel if someone didn't treat you in the way that you treated them? Would you still respect them and work hard for them? This is a question every person in authority has to think about.

4.1.1 P = Presenter ST = Susanne Taylor
BL = Betty Liu LM = Lawrence Maltz

P: Whilst markets may be global, not all products are universal. Multinationals need to analyse their target territories, adjust their marketing strategy and adapt their products to meet local preferences. China is a vast country with a rich elite and the world's largest middle class. This makes it a highly attractive market to multinational companies. There's a strong appetite for Western goods and brands. Chinese consumers have their own preferences. Therefore, product customisation is an important consideration for selling into China. This can affect both high-end luxury goods as well as mass-market consumer brands.
Cars are one example at the luxury end of the scale. Volvo launched a new high-end sedan in Shanghai. It is customised for the Chinese market. They have removed the front passenger seat to make more room in the back and added a host of luxury features. Why? Because wealthy Chinese have drivers and won't ever need the front passenger seat. They want more room in the back.
Jaguar adopted a similar approach for their new sedan. They didn't go as far as removing a seat, but they packed the rear with luxury features.

ST: The focus is on chauffeur-driven. There's a lot of chauffeur-driven cars within Hong Kong and mainland China. It's a very unique product that we think really appeals to premium customers who want a good experience in one of our cars.

P: But it's not just the richer consumers in China who are spending money on Western goods. China's huge middle class is a good opportunity for mass-market consumer brands.
But those global brands also have to adapt – even if only slightly.
For example, at the opening of Starbucks' flagship store in China, we could see that the Starbucks branding – known all over the world – was different. The words weren't there. This made it clearer for consumers used to the Chinese alphabet.
The rest of the world associates Starbucks with coffee. China, however, is the home of tea. So in China, Starbucks has adapted the brand to specialise in selling a range of premium teas, whilst still offering the same 'Starbucks experience' to consumers.

BL: Some of the teas that they're going to sell in China: black tea with ruby grapefruit and honey. And then there's a green tea with aloe … so you know that … that … continues to … um … reinforce that premium feel of Starbucks, right? That you're drinking something a little bit different.

P: And, of course, Starbucks also hopes to convert the Chinese to coffee.

LM: You know people say why … why … go to China, because they drink tea and not coffee? And I'm saying, what an opportunity. You know … We believe that the coffee consumption will continue to grow here, and we want to set a standard for that growth.

P: China will continue to grow as a market for multinational companies wishing to appeal to the middle class and the wealthy. And while the market continues to exist, so will novel adaptations of Western products in the Asian market.

4.3.1 A = Alex B = Beata

A: So, will it be your first time in Rio?

B: Yes, first time. I feel worried. But I know I shouldn't be. I don't really know why. I was in Japan for five years. I'm used to travelling.

A: Don't worry. You'll love Rio. I've been there twice. I guess you'll be meeting Mateo, right?

B: Mm.

A: Daniel's probably explained by now. Mateo is a nice guy but he can be very domineering. Likes the sound of his own voice. It's difficult to stay on track sometimes.

B: I'll bear that in mind. Here is my main worry, Alex. I think I'm well prepared. I bought a book about Brazil: history, customs and so on. But I have a feeling it's going to be really difficult. I'm only there a couple of days. Will that be enough time to get to know Mateo? What about the local market? Or how we can adapt the Diabsensor to its needs.

A: Seriously? Don't worry. You'll be fine. Just remember Mateo likes to multitask. Just go with the flow.

4.3.2 M = Mateo B = Beata

M: … on a vacation last year. Great memories. What about your family? Are your parents in the same field as you, the healthcare business?

B: Ah, no. Dad's a professor. Mum worked various jobs but she's basically retired now. Can we move to the Diabsensor?

M: Which university?

B: Excuse me?

M: Your father, the professor. Which university is he at?

B: Erm … Warsaw. The Chopin University of Music.

M: Ah, the Chopin University. That's not too far from the National Museum. I know Warsaw well. It's one of the world's great capital cities.

B: I'm very fond of the place, too. Anyway, the Diabsensor …

M: There will be plenty of time for that later. Remind me. What's the name of that really tall building in the middle of Warsaw? I went to a trade fair there once, many years ago.
Alô!
Tchau. Tchau. Obrigado novamente. Tchau.

B: Is this a good moment to start talking about the Diabsensor?

M: Relax. We'll come to that later. Back to the tall building. Do you know the one I mean?

B: The Palace of Culture and Science?

M: The Palace! That's it. That reminds me. I met Jessica Scott there for the first time. What was the event again? I think I still have a programme somewhere around here. Do you want to see it? Don't worry. We'll get to the Diabsensor in a moment.

B: Mateo, I really think we should get to the Diabsensor now. We don't have long to talk.

M: If you insist. Fine. I just thought you would be interested in the programme. That's all. Before I forget, tell me again why Daniel couldn't come.

B: Wow. We certainly have very different approaches. In the end Mateo seemed a little unhappy when I took control of the conversation. I tried again and again to bring him back to the Diabsensor. But he wanted to talk about other subjects. I see what Alex meant about multitasking.

4.3.3 M = Mateo B = Beata

M: … on a vacation last year. Great memories. What about your family? Are your parents in the same field as you, the healthcare business?

B: My parents?

M: Yes, are they in the healthcare business?

B: No, not at all. Mum had various jobs, but she's basically retired now and dad's a professor.

M: Oh yes? Whereabouts?

B: Warsaw. The Chopin University of Music. He's a bit of a musical mastermind.

M: Ah, the Chopin University. That's not too far from the National Museum.

B: You sound like you know Warsaw well.

M: I adore Warsaw. It's one of the world's great cities. I've been there twice. Remind me, what's the name of the really tall building in the middle of the city? I went to a trade fair there once. Many years ago. *Alô! OK. Tchau. Tchau. Obrigado novamente. Tchau.* Now, where were we?

B: I think you were talking about the Palace of Culture and Science?

M: The Palace! That's it. That reminds me. I met Jessica Scott there for the first time. What was the event again? I think I still have a programme somewhere around here. Want to see it?

B: Of course.

M: Great. And don't worry. We'll get to the Diabsensor in a moment.

B: He liked to talk a lot! But, as Alex said, it really was best to go with the flow. I didn't want to seem rude or uninterested even though I really wanted to discuss the Diabsensor. Mateo has a very different way of handling meetings to me and I had to respect that.

4.3.4

Mateo and Beata are different in terms of nationality, age, experience, status and personality. In this case Mateo seems very comfortable with the situation and is in control. He decides the topic of conversation. Beata can do little to change Mateo's more dominant style.

So, she has two choices. She can try to get Mateo to follow her agenda and talk about the Diabsensor, or she can simply go with the flow and see what happens.

If she tries to push her own agenda, she might save time, but she might also affect the business relationship. On the other hand, if she goes with the flow, she might build up the business relationship, but she could also end up losing control of the situation.

5.1.1 P = Presenter SD = Scott Drummond
M1 = Man 1 M2 = Man 2 MP = Mike Peng

P: These lunchtime diners in San Francisco are intrigued by a fully automated restaurant that looks more like a computer store with touch-screen ordering and freshly made meals, delivered in a box.

SD: Technology is allowing us to provide a product at an unprecedented speed, so the time-pressed consumer in the financial district really doesn't have the patience for the old ways of going out and buying food, interacting with somebody who might not hear your order correctly.
We've addressed that by creating a process that's incredibly fast, incredibly precise and ultimately gives the customer much more control about what they want for lunch.

P: I had to try it for myself. Much like any other touch-screen menu, it starts with the swipe of your credit card. You can customise the menu. The food here is all vegetarian. Once your order is placed, it's prepared at lightning speed by chefs working behind the scenes.
So here it is, that was less than two minutes, the food has been delivered, it says here tap twice, the door opens and here's lunch, with my name on it, my balsamic beet salad. Looks good.

M1: Usually we only have half an hour, 45 minutes for lunch, so it's nice to be able to come out during actual lunch hour and get a quick healthy lunch. This is the first time I've seen anything this automated and this high quality coming out of a machine. I've seen, you know, they have similar things in Amsterdam, but the quality of the food isn't half as good.

M2: I think that we're moving away from social interaction and this is just completely facilitating that. We didn't have to talk to anyone to get our, to get, uh, food made for us, which I don't necessarily think is the best thing, but it's certainly, um, I think the direction where we're all going.

SD: We've just taken the model and figured out how to interact with the customer differently, it's a completely different way of uh, assisting the customer in making the choices that are best for them.

P: Other restaurant chains have embraced touch-screen technology to replace humans. It's a trend in the business, fewer staff and a more automated approach to ordering food.

SD: What we're doing is changing the way that the workforce is contributing to the preparation of food. So instead of having, you know, a cashier, or five cashiers, um, we've created other opportunities for those, those workers, both in terms of being involved in the technology that's supporting the restaurant, um, having opportunities to interact with customers in a different and more personal way.
And in the process, not dissimilar to any innovation where technology comes in, changes the ball game, we believe that other jobs and other types of jobs will be created, they just won't be minimum-wage traditional restaurant jobs.

MP: Well, a lot of what we do is bring our clients out here to be inspired by, sort of, either new technologies or new services, new platforms, and so we had heard about Eatsa, and so we wanted to drop by and, kind of, experience it ourselves.

P: But in Japan you have similar restaurants to this, don't you?

MP: Yeah, there's a lot of vending machine-type restaurants, so meaning, like, you would order your food via vending machine and you get a ticket and you hand the ticket over and you get your meal automatically, but nothing as, sort of, designed, I think, as this and so I think that's why we wanted to experience the sort of, there's so many different magical moments uh that are just, kind of, uh, really fun.
And so once they introduce the app and you can order it and just go pick up your food, I think that's really gonna disrupt the current food business today.

5.3.1

I'm so glad that's over. Mateo wasn't focused at all … lots of questions about my family, non-stop talk about his trip to Warsaw. I suppose it was all good experience though.
I'll be talking to Daniel soon. But what should I tell him? If I go into detail on all the difficulties … he might think that I can't handle things. I think I'll just give him an overview. If he wants to know more … well, I'll just play that by ear.
OK. Let's do this. Sightseeing later.

5.3.2 D = Daniel B = Beata C = Clarice

D: So, Beata … tell us about your meeting with Mateo. Then you can go and enjoy some sunshine. You've earned it.

B: Well, he talked a lot about the colour of the product. His team carried out some market research last month … interviewed patients, healthcare professionals, pharmacists …

C: Wait, wait, wait. Did you say pharmacists?

B: Yes. They did some focus groups … sent out a really detailed questionnaire …

C: And *that's* what he asked them about? The colour? Seriously? What's wrong with the colour? Why did they spend so much time on this?

B: Sorry. I didn't really have a chance to ask.

C: You didn't?

D: Mateo can be a little domineering, Clarice. Have you ever met him?

C: No, no I haven't. Sorry. Please go on, Beata.

B: Well … according to their focus group results – I have them here if you want to see them – people prefer the darker shade of ….

D: Beata, … what does Mateo want us to change, exactly?

B: The colour of the Diabsensor. But I told Mateo I'd get back to him. I hope that was OK.

D: Of course. You did the right thing. Clarice, what do you think? Can we change the colour?

C: I'm sorry, no. It's really not possible at this stage of the production schedule.

D: Right. I thought so. Anyway, Beata, tell us about the rest of the discussion.

B: There's possibly some problem with storage, but we can come to that later. And … ah, yes, the packaging. There's a problem with the design.

D: What do you mean, a problem with the design of the packaging?

B: Mateo doesn't think it's very practical.

D: So, what does he want exactly? Does he want us to change the design?

B: Well … yes.

D: Are you sure?

B: Erm … yeah … I guess so …

D: Next he'll be asking for a whole new product altogether. Clarice? Is it possible to change the packaging design?

C: Maybe. I'll have to check with our product manager, but at this stage … it's a long shot.
D: It's a very long shot, I know. How long will it take for you to confirm this?
C: I'm not sure. We're closed tomorrow for a public holiday.
D: Can you get back to us by Monday?
C: Monday? Yes, no problem.
D: Beata, do you have any other news for us?
B: Um, no … That went well. I wasn't totally sure Daniel wanted to know all the little details … but I'd rather he knew everything.
Anyway. Sightseeing time!

5.3.3 D = Daniel B = Beata C = Clarice
D: So, Beata, over to you. Tell us about your meeting with Mateo. And once you're done, you can go and enjoy some sunshine.
B: Of course. There's not much to tell really. Mateo wants to change the colour of the product to a darker shade of blue.
D: The colour of the Diabsensor itself or the packaging?
B: The colour of the Diabsensor. I told him I'd get back to him. I hope that was OK.
D: Of course. Clarice?
C: I'm sorry, it's not possible at this stage of the production schedule.
D: Yes, I thought so. So, tell us about the rest of the discussion.
B: There's possibly some problem with storage, but we can come to that later. And … um, yes … they wanted to change the design of the packaging, but I told them that wasn't possible. That's about it, I think.
D: Really? Nothing else? Mateo must not have been in a talkative mood. For the first time in his life …
B: Yes. That's everything.
That went well. There was no point in boring them with all the little details – we would have been here all day. And if Daniel wanted to know more information, he would've asked more questions. Anyway. Time to join the tourists!

5.3.4
This clip is about managing information. In both options, Beata talks about the same meeting but, as we see, the information that comes across is quite different. There's a lot of detail in option A. In Option B, some things are left out. We can see how important it is for all participants to ask the right sorts of questions to get the information they need. A meeting is productive when it ends with everyone knowing what actions are required.
In Option A, Clarice and Daniel ask a lot of questions. They agree on one action point for Clarice: she needs to check if changing the design is possible. Beata mentions the storage problem, but it is not discussed.
In Option B, Clarice and Daniel don't ask as many questions about packaging and colour because Beata gives them all the information at the beginning. The meeting in Option B is shorter but key information is still communicated.

6.1.1 P = Presenter PN = Paul Neal
P: Safety is an important issue for all businesses. Companies must ensure that their operations are safe not only for their own employees but also for the public. Safety procedures are often regulated by law.
O'Donovan is a waste disposal company in London. I went along to find out how they manage safety across their operations.
Tell me who you are and what O'Donovan does.
PN: My name is Paul Neal. I'm the Logistics Supervisor here at O'Donovan Waste. O'Donovan Waste is a skip company where we collect waste from around London and recycle it.

P: The company's trucks operate on busy roads. Safety procedures that include measures for protecting the public are a priority for the company.
PN: We identified at an early stage there were too many cyclists being killed on London's roads, so we try to do as much as we can to reduce that. We initiated a programme where we tried to get the vehicle lower, so the driver can actually see more around the cab. And what we did was we fitted side guards to the vehicles just to see how low we could actually get them before they hit the ground.
P: And I also understand that you've fitted cameras and electronic sensors to all your vehicles.
PN: That's right. We have spent up to a quarter of a million pounds fitting these cameras and a system to the vehicle which tells us back at the head office how the vehicle is actually being driven. If we have any problems on the road, we can review the footage that the cameras take. They are 360 degrees, so we can see what's happening in front, to the rear and to the sides.
P: At O'Donovan's recycling centre, workers handle a wide variety of waste materials that do pose a risk of injury. Paul is responsible for maintaining a safe working environment for staff. This begins with suitable protective clothing for everyone.
How do you make sure your staff are safe both on and off site?
PN: Everyone is issued with the correct clothing to work in these environments. Also every couple of months at our head office in Tottenham we hold training programmes.
P: Tell me more about the personal safety equipment that your staff have to wear.
PN: Well, it starts from the top with the hard hat. We wear a hard hat. Firstly, anything could fall on top of your head, but what we find more often is, as people are walking around, they could hit something with their head. High-visibility clothing. With movement of vehicles we want everyone to know where everyone is. We have cut-resistant gloves. The employees are sometimes handling sharp debris. Also a mask. In the shed it can be quite dusty, so we have a mask to protect the breathing. Also steel toe-cap boots, just in case anything drops on the foot.
P: What happens if there is an accident on one of the O'Donovan sites?
PN: Well, unfortunately, accidents do occur, and if they do, we have trained staff on site, first aiders – that's the first port of call. After that, once the injured party is OK, we'll record everything. We have an accident book which we fill in and then, after that, we would try to learn what happened exactly and how we can go forward to make sure this doesn't happen again.
P: How much does all this investment in safety actually cost your business?
PN: Well, as a company, we don't see it as a cost, we see it more as an asset. We understand that by becoming a safer company, it's going to benefit us in the long run.
P: Paul, thank you very much for your time.
PN: My pleasure.
P: Nice to meet you.
There's no doubt that the safety culture at O'Donovan Waste Disposal is strong. They don't see it just as an issue of compliance with regulation, but as a core part of what they do and who they are.

6.3.1
I've got a really tough meeting with Mateo tomorrow. How will he react? Your guess is as good as mine.
I'm finding him more and more difficult to work with. He doesn't want to follow our regulations on storage procedures. So I'm going to have to

negotiate with him and … I'm not sure 'negotiation' and 'Mateo' go together well. Here's the big question: can I keep things professional and positive with Mateo while also *insisting* he accepts our storage regulations? We can't compromise on safety. But if I mess this up, that might make a bad impression with Daniel.

6.3.2 M = Mateo B = Beata
M: Let me get this straight. The Diabsensor needs storing at around five degrees Celsius?
B: Yes. It must be refrigerated, otherwise it's unsafe.
M: Sorry, but I disagree. Our storage team say there's no problem storing it at room temperature.
B: That may be the case, but …
M: Beata, I like you. You're good at what you do. I just don't think you quite understand – regulations are different here in Brazil.
B: I understand. Really. Nonetheless, perhaps we can talk about …
M: You don't have to worry about all those EU rules. We have our own safety regulations and we are very strict about them. We can store this product, no problem. Would you like to see the certificates?
B: We really appreciate all the work you're doing. But unfortunately …
M: I've told you, Beata. The plan is to launch the Diabsensor as soon as possible. Do you have any idea how much pressure that puts me under? We carried out a successful campaign at our diabetes clinic last week. My team has received all the necessary training. Look, I can assure you – we're all excited about this new product. It's going to change lives.
B: It's great that you've already done so much to promote the product. I'm sure Daniel is going to really appreciate this.
M: So am I. *Very* sure. Daniel and I have always worked very well together. I'll even speak to him myself and explain the situation. How does that sound?
B: Sounds good. I'll get him to call you.
Not the outcome I wanted … but at least Mateo seemed pleased. He'd rather speak to Daniel than me, that's pretty clear. I was able to keep things professional … even if I'm starting to think Mateo doesn't respect me. At all.

6.3.3 M = Mateo B = Beata
M: Let me get this straight. The Diabsensor needs storing at around five degrees Celsius?
B: Yes. It must be refrigerated, otherwise it's unsafe.
M: Sorry, but I disagree. Our storage team say there's no problem storing it at room temperature.
B: As I explained, Mateo … it's a question of safety. The product must be refrigerated. If we store it at room temperature, we can no longer guarantee that it *will* be safe.
M: Beata, I like you. You're good at what you do. I just don't think you quite understand – regulations are different here in Brazil.
B: I can assure you …
M: You don't need to worry about all those EU rules. We have our own safety regulations and we are very strict about them. We can store this product, no problem.
B: Yes, but unfortunately …
M: We are under a lot of pressure. Some of us more than most, perhaps.
B: Please. If I could just finish my point …
M: The plan is to launch the Diabsensor as soon as possible. My team has received all the necessary training. Look, I can assure you – we're all excited about this new product. It's going to change lives.
B: And *I* can assure *you* … the product needs to be refrigerated. I want you to understand, Mateo. *This* is a question of patient safety.

M: And, as I said earlier, I disagree. Storage is not a problem. We have the capacity, the staffing. Everything is in place. No cause for concern.
B: I understand that this is difficult for you. And you've already done so much to help promote the product. But my position is clear. We can't go ahead with the delivery unless the necessary storage measures are in place.
M: Fine. Let's see what Daniel has to say, shall we?
B: I have no doubt that Daniel will say the same thing. I'm sure we want the same outcome, Mateo. But either you find a compromise, or I can't approve the delivery.
M: You're being difficult, Beata. I don't like it. To be frank … I'm not sure I can work with you. OK. I'm going to speak to Daniel. You've left me no other choice.
B: I'm sorry you feel that way. I'm not comfortable agreeing to the delivery without the correct storage measures in place. And if you want to speak to Daniel, fine. I'll ask him to call you. Well … he's not happy. And neither am I. Still, what can I do? We can't compromise on safety. And I know for a fact Daniel is going to say the same thing. I just hope he's not annoyed with the way I handled this.

6.3.4

Beata uses quite different approaches with Mateo in this clip. In Option A, she focuses on maintaining a good professional relationship. She wants to avoid arguing with him, and succeeds. Mateo is still able to dominate the conversation and by the end, he thinks he has what he wants.

In Option B, she's more forceful and shows more confidence in her communication style. Her voice is slightly lower and she uses pauses to indicate important information. Her body language shows she's feeling much more confident and this gives the impression of more authority.

My suggestion is: if we need to explain rules and requirements, then we'll be more successful if we try to build or maintain a good professional relationship with the other person. One way to do this is to show we understand the other person's situation. But we still need to maintain our authority.

7.1.1 P = Presenter SC = Siobhán Creaton
C = Customer A = Agent LN = Lisa Francesca Nand
OM = Oscar Munoz BA = British Airways employee
P: In the early days of air travel, flying was an elite experience. All passengers got VIP treatment. Today, everyone flies. The airline industry gives passengers a choice of different levels of customer service. You can choose between classes and carriers offering a premium service – where they handle all your bags, you get a big seat and lots of personal attention – or you can go for a low-cost service. There are plenty of them: take AirAsia, Jetstar, Peach, for example. They just get you there cheaply.
Ryanair is a pioneer of low-cost, 'no-frills' flight. With flights often costing as little as the price of a good dinner, you're going to queue, and if you don't like that, you can pay for priority boarding and any other extras.
Journalist Siobhán Creaton has written about the airline and its CEO, Michael O'Leary.
SC: They offer you a cheap flight, it brings you from A to B, it gets you there safely and usually on time. That's his definition of customer service. He's always made it clear that they're not going to put you up in a hotel if your flight is delayed, that that's not part of the package.
P: The 'no-frills' model is popular worldwide. But it has a problem. There's a good chance customers will get angry when something goes wrong. Low-cost airline, Easyjet, approaches the challenge of dissatisfied passengers with training sessions

in assertiveness and interpersonal skills. These Easyjet trainees are roleplaying typical customer service problems.
C: Right, I've got … my husband's on his way. So if you could just check us in, that'd be great.
A: Where he actually is he? Is he parking the car or … ?
C: He's parking the car, yeah, he'll be … I don't know how long he is going to be …
A: I can't physically check him in without actually seeing him; well, passport-wise I have seen him. I have got to make sure he is, you know, is the same person. Yours is OK, you're fine.
C: Yeah, I know but I can't travel without him. We're going on holiday.
A: I'm sorry but I can't actually check you and your husband in without actually seeing your husband.
P: When confronting upset customers, employees are trained to use body language but not raise their voice.
C: He handled me perfectly, he brought … I was … I could have been quite anxious or angry and he brought me right down. So, James was fantastic.
LN: In the premium service segment, companies add on those little extras, those exclusive features that they feel help them justify asking a higher price tag. Each of the airlines in this segment work really hard to try and find that distinctive customer service experience so they can then charge more for it.
P: United Airlines, for example, works hard to attract business-class and first-class passengers with features like no queue to check in. The company likes to speak up about developing its customer service.
OM: We spent thousands of hours, thousands of hours, meeting with not only customers but with employees and doing a lot of extensive research … and as you might expect, the VIP treatment, the food, all of those things came into place. But interesting, our research showed that a good night's sleep was by far the most important.
P: Flag carrier British Airways distinguishes its high-price, first-class service not just in practical ways like priority baggage, but also through an elaborate ritual on board: afternoon tea.
BA: A lot of our customers from around the world will book a British Airways ticket … um … for the afternoon tea … because they like the Britishness of us.
LN: It's typical of a premium approach to customer service that businesses want to make people feel important and to focus on those things. So for the airlines, for example, it's providing things like a nice business lounge for them to relax in; it's providing them with a comfortable bed to sleep on when they're in the air. For a business like banking, it's something completely different, like increased levels of flexibility, but it all boils down to the same business issue: you can charge more if you make people feel better cared for.

7.3.1 D = Daniel B = Beata M = Mateo
D: This must be a let-down after all that gourmet coffee at the hotel in Rio.
B: I wish!
D: So take me through the main issues. How can I put Mateo's mind at ease?
B: He won't follow our recommendations and refrigerate the sensors. I was very clear: if there's no safe storage, there's no guarantee he'll get the product. He didn't like that. He kept saying I was overcautious.
D: And that's how you left it?
B: Pretty much, yes.
D: Strange. I wonder if something else is going on. Does he have other possible suppliers, perhaps? Or does he have budget issues?
B: There's one thing I did notice. All of the refrigerators were really full at Mateo's facility. Maybe he just had a big delivery.

D: Or maybe they have a shortage of refrigerators and no money to buy new ones? Only one way to find out.
M: Hello?
D: Hi, Mateo. It's Daniel. How are things?
M: Daniel, nice to hear from you. All good here, thank you.
D: Likewise. Anyway, Beata has filled me in on all of the details. It seems to me that we've got almost everything we need, except for one or two small things. I just want to hear your side of things before we have our meeting next week. I just want to make sure everything is OK for the contract signing.
M: Everything is fine, overall. But those small things you mention … Maybe some of them aren't so small after all.
D: Go on. By the way, just so you know, Beata is in the room with me. You're on speakerphone.
B: Hi, Mateo.
M: Beata, how are you?
B: Fine, thanks.
D: So, shall we get started?

7.3.2 M = Mateo D = Daniel B = Beata
M: It's nothing personal but Beata is new, so maybe there are some things that she doesn't understand. My experts assure me that there is no problem storing the sensor at room temperature, whereas Beata insists that it must be stored at five degrees.
D: Of course. Let's get back to that in a moment if we may. What about all the other issues? Delivery dates, colour, quantities, price?
M: All fine. The colour isn't right for me but I understand nothing can be done at this stage. As for everything else … Well … Storage is the only issue, really. I tried and tried to explain to Beata: things are different here in Brazil. And it goes without saying, really, no guarantee – no sale.
D: Absolutely. You've made that very clear.
M: I hope so. I'm not happy, Daniel. I'm not happy at all.
D: Mateo, may I ask a direct question?
M: Daniel, you know me. No need to ask.
D: What's your refrigaration capacity at the moment? Do you have enough storage space?
M: I'll be honest. Storage space is a problem here. But that doesn't really matter. The issue is whether or not we have to refrigerate the Diabsensors. And believe me – we don't.
D: OK, look, don't worry Mateo. I'm sure we'll come up with a solution. Let me do some calculations and speak to my people. And when you come over to Manchester next week , we'll talk some more and I'm confident we'll come up with a solution. How does that sound?
M: That sounds good. Just one thing, though.
D: Yes?
M: Please make sure it's not raining.
D: I'll see if I can schedule some sunshine. No promises, though. Speak to you soon.
M: Bye, my friend.
D: What's wrong?
B: It sounded like you agreed with Mateo. That you think I don't know what I am doing.
D: What? No, no. You're completely in the right. I wanted to give Mateo the impression that I was neutral, just to see what he would say. It's a tactic, that's all. Don't worry, I'm 100 percent on your side.

7.3.3 M = Mateo D = Daniel B = Beata
M: It's nothing personal but Beata is new, so maybe there are some things she doesn't understand. My experts tell me that there is no problem storing the sensor at room temperature, whereas Beata insists that it must be stored at 5 degrees. I tried and tried to explain to Beata: things are different here in Brazil.
D: Well, I have to say that she's right, I'm afraid. Five degrees is the required temperature.

M: So Beata said. And I'll tell you exactly what I told her. No. We just don't see the need.

D: Yes, she told me about that. OK, Mateo, let's get back to that in a minute. What about all the other issues? Delivery dates, colour, quantities, price?

M: All fine. The colour isn't right for me, but I understand nothing can be done at this stage. According to Beata, at least.

D: Yes, Beata is correct about that.

M: Fine, no big deal. The only other thing is this storage nonsense. Beata says she can't guarantee us the product if we store it at room temperature. And it goes without saying, really: no guarantee – no sale.

D: Hmm. Yes, I have to say Beata is absolutely right on this. But please understand I see your point. Your positions are both very clear.

M: I'm not happy Daniel. And neither are my diabetes teams.

D: Yes, I understand that. Beata told me about your teams. Mateo, may I ask a direct question?

M: You can always be direct with me, Daniel. You know that.

D: What's your refrigeration capacity at the moment? Do you have enough storage space?

M: I'll be honest. Storage space is a problem here, but that doesn't really matter. The issue is whether or not we have to refrigerate the Diabsensors. And believe me: we don't!

D: OK, look, don't worry Mateo. I'm sure we'll come up with a solution. Let me do some calculations and speak to my people. I'll go through all the details again with Beata, too. And when you come over to Manchester next week I'm confident we'll come up with a solution. How does that sound?

M: Perfect. See you next week. And please a little less rain this time.

D: I'll see what our Sunshine Department can do. Bye.

B: Thanks for supporting me.

D: No problem. You're completely in the right. And I wanted Mateo to know that.

7.3.4

As we see in this clip, the customer is not always right. Daniel has to find a way to make Mateo understand that the sensor cannot be stored at room temperature.

This type of situation can be very difficult to deal with.

As we also see in the clip, there are different approaches. In Option A, we see Daniel simply listening and not making any comments. Basically the idea is to appear neutral and gather information. Mateo has no idea if Daniel agrees with Beata. In Option B, Daniel also listens, but shows clearly that he agrees with Beata, and will support her. In this way, Daniel shows that there is a red line which cannot be crossed.

8.1.1 P = Presenter CC = Professor Cary Cooper
MB = Mike Brogan   E1 = employee 1
E2 = employee 2   E3 = employee 3
E4 = employee 4   E5 = employee 5

P: In the last thirty years digital technology has transformed the way we communicate in the workplace. A British company, Procure Plus, is tearing up the communications rule book. Let's see their story.

This is Mike Brogan. He and his team rely on digital technology for business. But Mike worries about their dependence on email to communicate with each other. And he's also concerned that his team spends too long working online after hours.

E1: Do I check my emails outside of work hours? Yes. Do I do it while I'm on holiday? Yes. Do I do it at the weekend? Yes. And I think that, worse than that, I tend to use the evening to try and catch up on emails. But because everybody else is doing that, it's a bit of a negative because people keep replying.

P: Professor Cary Cooper reckons this dependence could be harming the business's productivity. But, he has a plan.

CC: We have to find a better balance. Not only for our health, and the health of our families, and our relationships outside. But, actually, for the productivity and performance of our businesses.

MB: We're here today actually to conduct an experiment and we're very fortunate to have Cary Cooper here, Psychologist from Lancaster University, who's going to tell you a little bit more about what we're doing today.

CC: Thanks, Mike. We have a number of rules. From noon today, all internal emails will be banned for the rest of the week. So, you'll have to communicate eyeball to eyeball, face to face with all your colleagues. No texts, calls, emails, anything at all to do with work after hours. This should be a fun week, let's try to get our life back. We're currently the servant to the technology. We have to take over and become the master, and if we do that properly, then I think we'll get the benefits of better work–life balance, more team building, a better culture in the organisation, much more of a buzz and better morale.

P: So, for the next five days internal emails are banned, and there's a curfew on working outside of the office.

E2: I don't quite know how I am going to get all my work done between the normal working hours and not using the email or phone before work or after work because I am naughty at doing both.

P: High noon. The last email is sent and the new regime begins. We'll catch up on these gadget junkies later in the week.

MB: Last night, when I got home, I certainly felt a little bit bored at first. But then I started to feel more and more relaxed because I had nothing to think about, I suppose.

E1: I'm still a bit concerned about not replying to some emails last night, but I'll get over it.

P: The professor behind it all is back to see how they've got on.

CC: Well, the week's over and I just want to really thank you for getting involved in this. We've suspended technology a bit, haven't we? We've tried to control technology. We have become the masters rather than the slaves of it.

So, Mike. The week is up. How have you found it?

MB: There's a buzz about the place. Now we're seeing people moving about. There's a hum around the office that wasn't there before.

CC: It's kind of a balance, isn't it? Between the need for technology and working more humanly with the people you're working with.

P: But it's not just Mike who's excited about the changes.

E3: There's been a good atmosphere this week. People have talked to each other more.

E4: Actually, I've come in on a couple of days and had no emails. No new emails!

E5: It has really helped me get to know my colleagues a lot more.

CC: All the technology interference – the emails within the business – I think has overloaded people and actually reducing that has produced, I think, really positive results, in this work environment.

P: So that experiment suggests that when it comes to communication, less is sometimes more. Perhaps, especially, where technology is involved.

8.3.1 D = Daniel B = Beata M = Mateo

D: Feeling optimistic?

B: Yes, actually. I think we've got the perfect solution for Mateo. It's a win-win.

D: Me too. Just don't get too technical. We need to focus on the benefits. I really want to close this deal today.

B: I'll try to keep things simple.

M: Hello, everybody. It's like a cinema in here. Any popcorn?

D: We're all out of popcorn, I'm afraid. Welcome, Mateo. Really good to have you here in Manchester.

M: It's good to be here. And it's not even raining this time.

D: Well, I can't take credit for that, much as I'd like to. So, shall we get started? We've come up with some ideas that will hopefully solve the refrigeration problem we discussed, or at least put us on the right track.

M: Excellent.

D: I'd first like to review where we are, just to make sure that we're all on the same page, so to speak. Then we'll discuss outstanding issues. Hope that's OK? I've put a summary on these slides.

8.3.2 D = Daniel M = Mateo B = Beata

D: So that just about sums it up. We've agreed on the delivery dates, quantities, colour …

M: Yes, yes. That only leaves the same point as before. The refrigeration issue. It's still outstanding.

D: I think we may have a way around that problem. As I understand it, your, erm, local rules do not require the sensors to be refrigerated. But we feel that we simply can't guarantee the performance of the product without that refrigeration. Does that sum up the situation as you see it?

M: Exactly.

D: Beata has an idea. Beata.

B: Thanks, Daniel. So, I was doing some research into the packaging options. At the moment we plan to send you the sensors in insulated containers that keep the sensors below five degrees during transport. Now, these containers will keep the temperature stable for the journey to Brazil, but once they are opened the sensors need to go into a refrigerator.

M: Beata, I've told you countless times …

B: Hear me out. I've found a supplier that produces portable refrigeration units. These can be connected to an exterior power source at a reasonable price. So in other words these containers are more than insulated coolers. They can also be connected to a power supply. Then they act as refrigerators.

M: So what you mean is that I don't need to put the sensors into refrigerators? They already come in refrigerators?

B: Correct.

M: But if we use these portable refrigerators won't the cost go up? Let me tell you: refrigerators are not cheap.

D: True. And yes, the containers are a little more expensive, however we are prepared to cover that extra cost providing you buy enough sensors. We are confident that you will be happy with the product and will continue buying from us.

B: In return we would need you to provide the power supply when the containers arrive. You would need to plug the boxes into your power supply on arrival. And they don't use much energy, so I don't think this will be a problem for you. Here are the specifications.

M: This is a perfect solution. You're both geniuses. Move over, Einstein. To sum up, you provide the containers, and I provide the power supply. Great. Here's what I'll do. I'll take a longer look at the specifications and chat to my technical team, and if it is as you say it is, we will be able to go ahead.

D: You were a bit too heavy on the technical details, Beata.

B: Oh, I'm sorry.

D: Don't worry. I think he actually appreciated it in the end. Great work.

8.3.3 D = Daniel M = Mateo B = Beata

D: So that just about sums it up. We've agreed on the delivery dates, quantities, colour …

M: Yes, that only leaves the same point as before. The refrigeration issue. It's still outstanding.

D: Right, it is. But I think we may have a way around that problem. As I understand it, your, erm, local rules don't require the sensors to be refrigerated. But we just can't guarantee the performance of the product without refrigeration. Does that sum up the situation as you see it?

M: Absolutely.

D: OK. Well, Beata has an idea I think you might be interested in. Beata.

B: Thanks, Daniel. Mateo, I think you're really going to like this solution. Not to mention the hidden benefits it provides. I was doing some research into the packaging options and I figured out that we can change the type of package we use. As you know, the plan right now is to use insulated containers to keep the sensors cool, but you would need to put the sensors into a refrigerator after the journey …

M: Beata, we've been through this over and over …

B: … which is why we have a new package now. One which also acts as a refrigerator. After they arrive, you simply plug in the containers into your power supply and the sensors remain cooled.

M: So what you mean is that I don't need to put the sensors into refrigerators? They already come in refrigerators?

B: Yes.

M: But if we use these portable refrigerators, won't the cost go up? If there is one thing I know about refrigerators, it's that they're expensive.

D: That's true. And yes, the containers are a little more expensive, but this supplier that Beata found is using quite interesting technology to keep the costs low. We are prepared to cover the extra cost providing you buy enough sensors. We are confident you will be happy with the product and will continue buying from us.

B: In return we would need you to provide the power supply when the containers arrive. I think your diabetes teams will be very happy.

D: And there's another benefit, too. Once the sensors have been used you end up with empty refrigeration units, which you can use for other things. You know, like keeping your drinks nice and cold.

M: If you keep my drinks cool, you're guaranteed to keep me happy. Great solution, my friends. To sum up, you provide the containers, and I provide the power supply. Let me speak to my technical team, and if it is as you say it is, we will be able to go ahead.

Do you have any information about how much power we would need?

B: Right here.

M: Thank you. Excellent. Excellent.

D: Nice work. Light on the tech stuff. Just like I asked.

B: We make a good team.

D: We certainly do.

8.3.4

One key skill to end a negotiation is to summarise what has happened so far, so that everybody understands what still needs to be done. Daniel does this very well.

Daniel also has to persuade Mateo that he has a good solution.

The refrigeration problem has not yet been sorted out. In this clip, we see two possible ways of doing this.

In Option A, Beata presents a technical solution, which she explains in some detail. In Option B, she focuses less on the technical aspects and more on the benefits. As we see, both these approaches work.

As always, what we decide to do depends on lots of factors – the issues, the personalities involved, the relationships and so on. At the end of the day, the skill is in finding ways to communicate well with your business partner.

1.01

A: Hello, caller …

B: Hello?

A: Yes, hi. Welcome to the show. What can I help you with today?

B: Hi, Jenny. I'm a recent graduate – I have a good degree. The problem is, I'm finding it hard to get a job interview. I mean, forget getting a job … I can't even get an interview.

A: OK …

B: I'm using social media – a professional-networking website – and I have a few contacts in the industry I want to work in …

A: That sounds good so far … using these sites is a great idea.

B: But honestly, I don't think there's anything on my profile that's special. I mean – I use all the right words – I'm creative, I'm good at problem-solving, I'm hard-working …

A: … but everyone says that.

B: Exactly. Everyone says employers want those things, so everyone uses the same description of themselves! So my question is: How can I make myself stand out from the crowd on social media?

A: That's a great question, caller, and I'm here to help. So first, why not try deleting everything you've written about yourself?

B: Delete everything?

A: Yep. And after that, why don't you take your description of yourself – creative, good at problem-solving and so on, and for each word, think of an example from your own experience that *shows* who you are?

B: Er … OK, like …

A: You said you're creative. How about telling me about something creative that you've done?

B: Sure, OK. Er … when I did my degree, I created a website for one of my projects. I designed it and took the photographs for it and everything.

A: That's great! So you really should put that on your social media profile – you designed and built a website. What's next? Did you say you're good at problem solving?

B: Yeah …

A: So how can you show me that?

B: Problem solving?

A: Right.

B: Well, this isn't related to school or work, but I do a lot of hiking and camping. A few times, I've had serious issues with weather or broken equipment, and I've had to figure out what to do.

A: OK, you could consider putting something about that on your profile. Explain your love of the outdoors and how you deal with the challenges in your hiking and camping.

B: I've never thought of putting that on my profile …

A: Well, you ought to think outside the box – and you need to *show* employers who you are instead of just *saying* who you are.

B: Yeah, I understand – I get it. That's really helpful. Thank you so much.

A: No problem. Good luck with your new profile and with getting some job interviews!

B: Thanks!

1.02

A: Hello, caller …

B: Hello?

A: Yes, hi. Welcome to the show. What can I help you with today?

B: Hi, Jenny. We spoke a few weeks ago …

A: OK …

B: And I just wanted to let you know … I still have a problem.

A: Really? So can you remind me – what was your problem?

B: My professional networking profile – it wasn't working.

A: Oh, sure, OK, I remember. So … my advice wasn't useful?

B: Well, not exactly. I mean it *was* useful … Maybe a bit *too* useful.

A: Ha, ha – OK, I see. So what's the problem now?

B: Too many choices! I followed your advice, and soon after, when I applied for six jobs, I got four interviews.

A: Well, congratulations!

B: And after four interviews, I got two job offers. And my problem now is that I can't decide which job to take.

A: OK, well, why don't you tell me about the two jobs?

B: Basically, one looks very interesting but not very well paid. The other, honestly, is probably a bit boring, but the money is good.

A: And you're a recent graduate, right?

B: Yes, that's right.

A: And you're single – no kids?

B: Yep, that's me.

A: OK, I think you should follow your heart. Why not try asking yourself which is more important: money or excitement?

B: That's the problem, Jenny – I really can't decide! University cost a lot of money, and I want to pay back my loans. That will take a lot longer with a low-paying job.

A: Yes, I see what you mean. OK, well, let me ask you a few more questions. What …

1.03

My first piece of advice is, be prepared. Find out which companies will be attending the careers event, choose five or six that might be interested in your profile and research them online. Visit their careers pages and find out which ones are hiring or offering internship programmes.

Update your CV and make several copies. Then, prepare an 'elevator pitch', or brief introduction – let's say 30 seconds – to talk about yourself: who you are, what you do and your past experiences. Be prepared to explain how your skills can be useful to their company. Also, think of questions to ask such as: What is the training programme for new recruits? What do you look for in a candidate? On the day of the careers event, make sure you dress as you would for an interview – look professional. Choose your company, then network, don't interview; your aim is not to get a job interview immediately – in fact this rarely happens. Instead, introduce yourself, shake hands and make good eye contact. First impressions are important, so speak clearly and confidently and demonstrate your ability to interact professionally. Recruiters are looking for people who are adaptable and resourceful, but also ambitious and passionate. Be honest. If you don't know something, say you don't know, but show the recruiter you can learn and learn quickly. Most importantly, don't forget to get the recruiter's contact details so you can follow up afterwards.

After the event, email the recruiters or company reps you met and thank them for their time. Remind them of the conversation you had and repeat your interest in their company. Send an updated CV if necessary. Ideally, you should do this within five days after the event.

1.04

1

E = Ella R = Recruiter

E: Hi, I'm Ella, I'd like to ask you a few questions, if possible.

R: Yes, of course. How can I help you today?

E: I heard you were taking on new recruits. Can I give you my CV?

R: Yes, of course. Which department are you interested in, Ella?

E: Oh, anything in marketing, I don't really mind. I've just always wanted to work in the tourism industry. I have a degree in marketing and I enjoy travelling.

R: Well, OK, that's a good start.

E: Can I take a brochure? I'd like to learn more about what you do.

R: Sure. Here you are. And here's my card. If you have any questions, I'd be happy to answer them.

E: That's great. Thanks for your help. Sorry, what was your name?

R: Ben Richardson. I'm the Assistant Recruitment Manager.

2

R = Recruiter   J = Jamie

R: Good morning. How are you enjoying the fair?

J: I've only just arrived to be honest, but there are a lot of very interesting companies present though. Sorry, could I just ask you a few questions about Travelogue?

R: Yes, of course. Have a seat. What's your name? I'm Ben Richardson and I'm the Assistant Recruitment Manager.

J: My name's Jamie, Jamie Mitchell.

R: Good to meet you, Jamie. So, what can I do for you?

J: I've just graduated from the University of Manchester with a marketing degree, specialising in tourism. I know you're busy, but I'd like to talk to you about my skills. I think they might be useful to your company.

R: Congratulations on getting your degree.

J: Thank you. I understand you're looking for Junior Marketing Associates.

R: We are, Jamie, that's right. What kind of practical experience do you have?

J: Well, I did my internship with a team that developed a marketing plan to promote UK tourism for a small village in Spain.

R: That sounds interesting. Can you tell me more about that?

J: It was for a small village in the south of the country. As I said, we created this marketing plan and then presented it to the local tourist board and it was adopted.

R: I see, wonderful. It sounds impressive. As you probably know we do a lot of work in Italy.

J: Oh, really? I speak a little Italian.

R: OK, that might be useful. Do you have a CV?

J: Sorry, I just gave away my last one, but I've got a business card. There's a link on there to the village website that I helped create.

R: Thank you very much. And here's my card.

J: I'd like to know more about the work you do in Italy. Can you put me in touch with the person in charge of your marketing projects? I'd like to ask them some questions if possible.

R: If you send me an email, I'll do that.

J: Can I take a brochure?

R: Here you are. It's been nice talking to you. Enjoy the rest of the event.

J: Thank you for your time, Ben. I really appreciate it.

2.01

Message 1

Hello, this is a message for Emma Newman in HR. My name's Mark Thomas, T-H-O-M-A-S and I'm calling about the logistics position you interviewed me for last Thursday. I'd like to discuss the financial package in more detail if possible. Could you call me back please on my mobile – that's 0044-7623-911-129. That's 0044-7623-911-129. I'm available until 4 p.m. today. If not, then you can send me an email so we can we fix a time to speak. I look forward to hearing from you. Thanks. Goodbye.

Message 2

Hi, it's Carla again. Erm, I hope I've got the right number. Erm, my message got cut off last time so I'm calling you back just in case. Er, erm, yeah, I've got wall-to-wall meetings all afternoon and then I have to leave early so erm I don't really have time to send an email, but the internet was down yesterday, anyway, so, er. Anyway, erm, I'm super busy as you can imagine. I wanted to speak to you about the candidates we interviewed last week for the logistics job. Er, what did you think? Not bad, erm…

Message 3

Good morning. This is Zhanna Petrovna in Logistics. Could you ask Emma to call me back? We have a bit of a problem with the references for one of the shortlisted candidates. If she can call me back on extension 4385. It's pretty urgent now, so I'll expect her call by the end of the day.

2.03

Message 4

Good morning. I want to leave a message for Emma Newman. This is Daniella Rossi, R-O-S-S-I, returning her call. Emma asked me to contact her to discuss the terms of my new consultant contract. I'm available to talk until 2 p.m. today but then I'm in meetings all afternoon. In case she doesn't have my mobile number, I'm on 07654 322 187. Otherwise, maybe she can leave a message with my assistant, Elliot Barber. Elliot is on extension 5283, that's 5-2-8-3. Sorry, can she also re-send a copy of my new contract? I can't open the document. I hope to hear from you soon. Many thanks.

2.04

A = Alice M = Matthew S = Stanley

A: Morning, Matthew. I'd like you to meet Stanley Dongoran, our Indonesian business partner, who's helping us set up the factory in Indonesia.

M: Hi Stanley, nice to meet you.

S: Nice to meet you, too.

A: So, Stanley what do we need to do now?

S: Well, the first thing is to get the licence from the Indonesian Investment Board. I've already submitted everything for that and it'll be ready next week.

M: That's great, so we'll be able to visit Indonesia then?

S: Yes, I think next month would be a good time to go.

A: What will we have to do first when we get there?

S: We'll need to open a bank account and then we've got to think about the factory – those are the priorities.

M: You mean we need to find one or the land for one?

S: The land. I've found a couple of suitable locations and we're going to visit them to make a final decision. Then we can arrange all the documents we need to register the business premises. All these things take time but we can get the process started.

M: How long exactly?

S: Here's the time schedule for each element.

A: Thanks.

S: Then we've got to organise all the other permissions we need. That's all on the schedule, too.

M: Right. Are we going to interview some local people for jobs while we're there?

S: I've found three great candidates to be the Site Manager for you to interview. We're going to meet them and have formal interviews so you can choose someone.

A: Thanks. Matthew, can you organise the flights and accommodation for the trip tomorrow?

M: Of course.

Ext2.01

N = Nikolay A = Aiko G = Genna P = Philip S = Sam

N: Good morning, everyone! We're going to discuss what we need to do about the problems we had last week.

A: Well, I think we should look for new suppliers. Our current supplier is always late and deliveries have been incomplete.

N: That's true, but their materials are excellent quality.

P: Yes, but we can't afford to lose any more production time because we don't have supplies.

N: OK, Aiko, can you look for alternative suppliers and give us the details at next week's meeting?

A: Sure. I'll get onto it straight after this meeting.

P: We also need to employ more factory staff. We can't produce the quantities on time even when we have the supplies. Two people left last month and we haven't replaced them, have we, Genna?

G: That's true. Nobody asked me to replace them. You said you thought you could manage.

N: I think you'd better advertise for new staff this week and ideally have some candidates ready to interview sometime next week. What about Wednesday?

G: Certainly.

P: I'm sorry, but even if we have the staff and the supplies, we've got problems with the equipment, which keeps breaking down. We really need to buy some new equipment. Is that possible?

N: It might be. Philip, can you let Aiko know by tomorrow what you want?

P: Absolutely. That'd be great.

N: Now, I understand we've had a lot of complaints from customers this month. We need to do something about that quickly or we'll lose customers. Sam, can you write a report for me about the problems and your strategy for dealing with it? I'd like it by Thursday this week if possible.

S: Yes, of course. I'll get onto it immediately.

2.05

K = Kenzo S = Susan

K: We need to discuss how we're going to keep everyone informed about the potential takeover of the company by Bines plc. Firstly, I think we should send a letter to all employees about the situation guaranteeing that no jobs will be lost if Bines takes over.

S: Why don't you meet the staff and explain it face to face first? I think they'd appreciate that.

K: Yes, but not yet. Email all staff inviting them to a meeting on Friday 15th in the staff room. I'll tell them then.

S: I'll email them straight after this meeting.

K: We can send them a letter with all the details after we've told them face to face.

S: OK. Good idea. And what about our customers? We don't want them to hear about this from the newspapers. Shouldn't we let them know that it's business as usual?

K: Yes, I agree. We can do that after we've signed the contract on Wednesday 20th. How do you think they'll respond?

S: I think they'll be concerned about quality. Bines are not known for their quality and customer service, as we are.

K: They'll still get the best customer service we've always offered and we'll make sure the quality doesn't suffer. Bines don't want us to lose that.

S: Do you think it would be better to speak to our biggest customers individually?

K: I think that'd be a good idea, actually – before we announce it to the world.

S: Exactly. So we won't send out a press release until we've spoken to our biggest customers then.

K: Exactly.

3.01

China's Grand Canal, which connects the cities of Beijing and Hangzhou is 1,700 kilometres long. It's the longest artificial waterway in the world, and an important shipping route through the years. But what's more amazing than the length of the canal is its age. Work on the project began in the fifth century BC – more than 2,500 years ago. There was never a plan or budget for the whole project. A series of Chinese governments built and extended the canal in sections over a period of 1,700 years, finally finishing it in the 1280s. When they were working the hardest on the project, five million men and women were involved in the construction – mostly labourers, but also engineers. Today, only the section between the cities of Hangzhou and Jining– about 500 kilometres – is open for shipping. It is about 100 metres wide at its narrowest point. In some places, the canal is less than a metre deep. The Suez Canal in Egypt connects the Mediterranean Sea and the Red Sea. Work started in 1859. They thought the project would take six years, but they finished later than planned, in 1869 – four years behind schedule. At one point five million people worked on the project – mostly labourers, but also engineers, accountants and project managers. Some sources say that at least 30,000 people were working on the canal at all times during its construction. The project ran 1,900 percent over budget. The total cost was $100 million. But it is still one of the most important shipping routes in the world. With a length of about 190 kilometres, the canal makes the journey between the North Atlantic and the Indian Ocean much shorter than going around Africa. It reduces the trip by 7,000 kilometres, making the journey less difficult and time-consuming. At its shallowest point, the canal is about twelve metres deep and fifty-five metres wide.

The Panama Canal, in Central America, connects the Atlantic and Pacific Oceans. In 1881, a team from France started work on the project after seeing the success of the Suez Canal. However, the Panama team had to work a lot harder than the Suez team. Construction in the jungles of Panama wasn't as straightforward as digging in Egypt's dry, sandy desert. In fact the digging itself was the least challenging part of the job. Dealing with the heavy rains made work impossible at times. The team missed target after target, soon falling behind schedule. They finally gave up in 1889, when they ran out of money. Fifteen years later, an American team took over the project. Work on the canal began again in 1904. It took 75,000 workers ten years to build the seventy-seven-kilometre canal – four years longer than the original estimate of six years. The team included engineers, specialised machine operators and of course labourers. Finally, in August 1914, the first ship passed through the canal. Amazingly, although the canal cost $375 million to build, the project came in $23 million under budget. At its narrowest point, the canal is about thirty-three metres wide and twelve metres deep.

3.02

1 It's the longest artificial waterway in the world.

2 But what's more amazing than the length of the canal is its age.

3 When they were working the hardest on the project, five million men and women were involved in the construction.

4 They finished later than planned.

5 It is still one of the most important shipping routes in the world.

6 The canal makes the journey between the North Atlantic and the Indian Ocean much shorter than going around Africa.

7 It reduces the trip by 7,000 kilometres, making the journey less difficult and time-consuming.

8 The Panama team had to work a lot harder than the Suez team.

9 Construction in the jungles of Panama wasn't as straightforward as digging in Egypt's dry, sandy desert.

10 In fact the digging itself was the least challenging part of the job.

3.03

Bid A

We can start the installation two weeks from now, on February twentieth. It will take our two technicians five days, but you can continue working in the office the whole time, so it's convenient. Our price doesn't include product support – we can provide a separate bid for that. But we do guarantee the hardware and the installation for three years. We can do the job for 13,000 euros.

Bid B

We can do the job next week, on February the thirteenth. We can send ten technicians and finish the job in one day, but you'll need to leave the office completely empty for us, so we can work. The price includes full product support and training, if you need it. This also includes the hardware manufacturer's standard one-year guarantee. It will be 17,000 euros for everything.

Bid C

We need to order the hardware from our supplier, and it will take three weeks to deliver. That means I can start the job one month from today – on the sixth of March. I'll do the installation myself, over three weekends – so it will take three weeks to finish, but you won't see me. It won't interrupt your work at all. I'm happy to give full product support, and I guarantee the entire installation for two years. The whole package is 11,000 euros.

3.04
Part 1

Welcome to our first stand-up meeting. No sitting down. The idea is that these meetings will be over very fast, not more than fifteen minutes, and the aim is to bring us all up to date about what is going on in the team. This is very important. It is for all of us, not just for management.

From today these take place every morning at 9 a.m. This is a new type of meeting for most of us, so I will just explain what we plan to do.

It's very simple. I will start by throwing this ball to a person. The person with the ball then gives the rest of us three pieces of information. One: What they did yesterday. Two: What they plan for today. Three: Any problems or impediments that they see. That's it. No discussion. They then throw the ball to another person, who answers the same three questions. We go on until everyone has spoken. After the meeting I will then follow up and speak to individuals about any action items. Any questions? No? Good. OK. Let's start with Jack. Catch!

3.05
Part 2

J = Jack S = Sal T = Tom TL = team leader

J: OK. Yesterday I worked on the new contract for the China project. Today I have a meeting with the lawyers to clarify some of the questions I have. So the draft contract is in progress, and I expect to complete it today. The only impediment I see is time – the lawyers say they can only give me one hour, and it may not be enough.

S: Hi, everybody. So ... I had a meeting with a sub-supplier in the morning, where we agreed some new deadlines. We followed up the meeting with a nice lunch. And then in the afternoon I went to the dentist. Today my plan is to finish writing a summary of yesterday's meeting, and then I'll be briefing the production team leader. I don't see any impediments at the moment.

T: OK, I'm planning to work on the designs for the new logo for the rest of today. Oh sorry ... Yesterday I spent most of the day discussing ideas for the new logo ... with different departments. That was difficult because I didn't have any fixed appointments with anybody so it was really a matter of luck. ... So today, as I said, I'll be working on the designs and then I'll be discussing them with the people I missed yesterday. Hopefully. If they are available. Oh, I nearly forgot. Yesterday I also met with one of the new designers who will be working on this project until the end. Thank you.

TL: Thank you, everybody. That's great. My turn now. I've been working on the schedule for the factory shut down in November. Nothing to report. I'll be spending most of today working on the plans and I hope to finish them this afternoon. I'll then be discussing them with the boss before they go public, so I won't be answering any questions at this stage.

3.06
Part 3

B = boss TL = team leader

B: How are we doing with the redrafting of the China contract?

TL: Jack is handling that. He's meeting with the lawyers today, and is hoping to finish the draft today, too.

B: That's good. What about Sal's meeting with the sub-suppliers yesterday? I saw her in the canteen. What's happening with the deadlines?

TL: Well, they did agree some new deadlines, but I haven't seen them yet. I'm sure they'll be OK.

B: And where are we with the logo?

TL: Tom's working hard on that. He's going round the departments getting feedback, and he's meeting with the designers. It's all in hand.

B: Can you bring me up to date on the programme for today?

TL: Well, let's see, Jack is doing the contract, Sal is writing up yesterday's meeting and doing some briefings, and Tom is working on the logos. I'll be focusing on the new schedule and the factory shut down.

B: Ah, yes. What's the latest on the new schedule? Let's see ... Can you give me an update on the plans?

TL: Yes, I can do that now, if you like.

B: Fine. When will you be able to bring me up to speed on the factory shut down?

TL: I should be in a position to do that this afternoon. Can I come round your office, say four-ish?

B: Sounds good. Thanks.

4.01
Part 1

OK, so what I want to do today is focus on ways of building consensus. Building consensus is all about finding what the group wants to do, not what each individual wants to do. It's about group needs, not individual needs. Sometimes we need to meet halfway, to find the middle ground. And sometimes we will be persuaded that one way is best. We will do some practice activities later on, but first I want to remind everybody of two basic principles we all need to follow. First, if we want to build consensus, we must make sure that everybody is involved in the conversation. Everybody must have the chance to speak. And second, everybody's opinion is of equal weight and is to be respected. No one in the group is more important than anyone else. OK? Got it? Good, so now here's what we are going to do.

4.02
Part 2

**M = Manager J = Jose T = Tanya S = Sam
D = Dorothy**

M: So the first thing we are going to do is decide as a group how we want to proceed. We have three options. We can stay as one large group, we can break into smaller groups, or we can work in pairs. Any thoughts? Remember, everybody must be involved in the discussion, and everybody's opinion is to be respected. Yes, Jose? What do you think?

J: So I think we should stay as one big group. There are not so many of us, and it will be easy for everyone to be heard.

T: I'm afraid I disagree. It will be much better in smaller groups. That way everyone gets much more talking time.

S: I agree with Tanya. Much better. With a big group one or two people always dominate.

D: Yes, I agree, too. We can be much more efficient if we work in small groups.

J: Well, I don't think my idea is that bad. I agree that in a big group one or two people could dominate, but that is easy to fix. We use talking sticks.

S: What are talking sticks?

J: Each person has two sticks. This gives them the right to talk twice. Each time they say something they must give up a stick. When they have no more sticks they cannot talk. That way everyone has the same chance.

S: Actually, that's not a bad idea. But we will need more than two sticks.

J: That was just an example. Of course we need to decide how many sticks to use.

D: So we need to find consensus about the number of sticks before we can even start a real discussion?

M: That's a good point. Yes, we need to decide on the process before we can move to a discussion. So nobody is interested in working in pairs? Good, OK. So we're already narrowing down the options

and moving towards consensus. Not everybody has spoken, so I would like to hear what the rest of us have to say. Sandrine?

5.01
Kendra

Good morning. Today, I want to introduce you to the new ZX3 Hot-Seat. The ZX3 Hot-Seat is a portable, heated seat. It's designed for sitting outside, especially in cold weather, either in the park or at a music or sports event.

So first, let me talk you through the product specifications. As you can see from the slide, the ZX3 seat is made of memory foam that automatically moulds to your body shape and is designed to be extremely comfortable. It has a removable, washable cover made of a water-resistant nylon mesh that comes in a choice of three colours – red, blue and green.

The ZX3 Hot-Seat measures 940 by 480 mm, and weighs just 1,050 g. As you can see, it comes with retractable arms to provide maximum comfort. Each arm measures 300 by 125 mm, weighs 45 g, is made of lightweight plastic and comes in black or grey. As well as two USB ports, the ZX3 also has an optional plastic container used for holding hot or cold drinks. Finally, the heavy-duty rubber handles and padded straps are designed to make transportation easier ...

Paolo

So you've heard Kendra telling you about the features of the ZX3 Hot-Seat. It's a great product, but what's in it for your customers?

How many football fans in the audience today? Quite a few. You must agree nothing beats watching your favourite team play at the stadium. But when it's cold and wet, wouldn't you rather be in the warmth and comfort of your living room? Well, the ZX3 Hot-Seat is the solution. For example, its heated seat means you can combine the excitement of the stadium with the comfort of home. For added comfort, there are optional arm-rests which allow you to sit back and relax as you watch the game, while the plastic cup-holder lets you enjoy your favourite drink at the same time. The Hot-Seat has a washable cover so it's easier to clean, plus the lightweight seat with handles and straps make it easier to carry.

Kendra mentioned the Hot-Seat has two USB ports, so you can recharge your mobile devices if you need to. In today's instant world, we know how important this will be, especially for younger customers. This also lets you post pictures on social media of those all-important goals, as they happen.

6.01
Jenn

Security is a big issue in the hospitality business although it can be very different depending on the hotel category. I mean, some low-cost hotels these days don't even have an in-room safe for people to keep their valuables in, and I think that's crazy. I work in a five-star hotel and guests need to use their room key card in the lifts to get to their floor. You just touch your room key card to the pad and the lift automatically selects your floor. You also need the room key card to get from your floor back down to the lobby. I think it's becoming quite standard in newer city hotels. Not everyone likes it. Some guests complain it's annoying when they want to visit another floor. Of course, you don't have to take the lift. You can get access to other floors by the stairs, but it's like setting your house alarm or locking your doors. It's not going to make it completely impossible for someone to commit a crime, but it's an extra barrier.

Paul

You know I've never thought about it before, but security is very relaxed in the university building where I work. Students and staff are walking in and out all day long and anyone can just walk in off the street. There's only ever one receptionist on duty and she has to answer the phones, deal with queries and work on the computer, so she can't possibly keep an eye on everyone who comes and goes. And whenever she needs to go somewhere or take a break, the reception area is completely unattended. There are signs on the walls in all the classrooms warning students to keep their valuables with them, and lecturers have to remember to lock the staffroom door, but it's not ideal and we occasionally have had problems with theft and vandalism. There aren't even CCTV cameras in the corridors.

Aisha

I've worked in a multinational IT company for almost ten years now. We need to leave our mobile phones with the guard on reception and he puts them into a locker and you mustn't bring in any pen drives or any type of USB storage devices to the office. In the past you didn't need to wear your photo ID, but now your badge must be visible on you at all times. If a manager or the security guard catches you without it, they'll say something. And you need it for everything. You see, it has a chip with radio frequency identification which you have to use for checking into and out of the building, and it opens doors based on your access to certain areas. And you have to use it to print or scan anything as well.

6.03

Part 1

A = Alex T = Tony

A: I've told you several times already about the cleaning problem on the factory floor, Tony.

T: Yes, you have, and I've told you – several times – that the ZX390 needs repairing. We had another leak yesterday. As far as I'm concerned, I've followed procedure. I reported the fault on the machine. It's over to you now.

A: I appreciate it's difficult for you, Tony, and thank you for telling us about the leak. However, it's important that your apprentices clean up as they work. The management team are worried this is a real hazard.

T: It *is* a hazard. But I'm sorry, this is *not* my responsibility. My apprentices don't have the time to clean. And what happens if someone slips and falls? We need a full-time cleaner. He only comes in the evening and that's often too late.

A: Tony, as you know we're a small business. We just can't afford a full-time cleaner.

T: I understand what you're saying, Alex, but what's the solution? We need to repair the ZX390. I reported the problem ten days ago.

A: Yes, but to repair the 390 we will have to stop production. This is impossible – we need to meet our deadline for the Japanese order.

T: I know that, but it's also important that we fix it as quickly as possible.

A: I totally agree. I can see it from both sides.

6.04

Part 2

T = Tony A = Alex

T: So how do we proceed?

A: I think we need to come to a compromise so that we can complete the Japanese order.

T: OK. So, what's your solution?

A: Well, my suggestion is to supply your team with slip-resistant footwear. That will help prevent accidents.

T: Uh-huh, sounds like a good idea. But what about repairing the machine?

A: Well, as we both agreed, we will lose time if we stop production. So, let's complete this order first and I'll request an engineer to fix the leak. Can I just check you're happy with this idea before I speak to the management team?

T: Yes, that's fine with me.

A: And then let's review this situation at the end of the week.

T: Sure, why not?

A: Great. I'll put that in an email, just to summarise what we've agreed.

7.01

1

R1 = Recorded message 1 D = David

A = Angela K = Kabir

R1: Welcome to Noderphone. This call may be recorded and monitored for training purposes. All our agents are busy right now, please hold. All our agents are busy right now. You can also visit the Noderphone.com website for customer service information.

D: Good afternoon, my name is David. May I have your name, please?

A: Yes, it's Angela Parsons.

D: How can I help you, Angela?

A: My internet connection isn't working.

D: Is the account in your name?

A: Yes, it is.

D: Can I just ask for some further identification? Can you give me the phone number for this account, Angela?

A: Yes, it's 0208 892 2149.

D: Thank you, Angela. I'll put you through to our customer service agents. Can I ask before you go, do you have any mobile phone numbers you'd like to add to your account? There is a special offer right now.

A: No thank you, David. I only have one mobile and it's already on this account.

D: OK, just transferring you now.

R1: All our agents are busy right now, please hold.

K: Hello, Angela, my name is Kabir, how can I help you?

A: I just told your colleague, my internet isn't working.

K: I see. Have you tried switching off the router and turning it on again, Angela?

A: I'm sorry, I can't hear you very well. Could you speak up, please?

K: Yes, of course. Have you tried switching off the wifi router and turning it on again?

A: Yes, I've done all that. The lights don't come on as usual though.

K: OK, I'll re-boot it from here. This will take a few seconds. I'll just put you on hold …

K: Hello Angela, can you tell me if the lights start to come on on the router?

A: Yes, something's happening. They've started coming on. There's a yellow light, and now two blue on the left, oh, and another yellow one on the right.

K: Are you in front of your computer?

A: Yes, I'm just trying to get into my email. Yes, it's working now.

K: Is there anything else I can assist you with this afternoon, Angela?

A: No, that's fine, thanks.

K: Have a nice afternoon.

2

R2 = Recorded message 2 A = Angela J = Judith

R2: Welcome to Noderphone. This call may be recorded and monitored for training purposes. Please say the phone number about which you have an issue. If it is the phone from which you are calling, say 'It's this phone.'

A: It's this phone.

R2: How can I help you today?

A: I have a query about my mobile phone bill.

R2: I'm sorry, I don't understand. For internet services, press one; for television services, press two; for … press seven; for technical support, press eight; or please hold to speak to an agent.

J: Good morning, this is Judith speaking. Can I have your name, please?

A: At last! Yes, it's Angela Parsons. It's taken me fifteen minutes just to speak to a real person.

J: I'm sorry for the long delay – we're receiving lots of calls today. How can I help you, Angela?

A: I want to query my mobile phone bill for last month. It's ninety-three euros thirty-eight cents. That's more than three times what I normally pay.

J: Can I just ask your date of birth for verification purposes?

A: Yes, it's 23rd June 1988.

J: Thank you, Angela. I'm just looking at your bill on the screen. Yes, I see you were in Andorra and there was a roaming charge of forty-six eighty-seven.

A: What? A roaming charge? Why?

J: Andorra isn't a European Union country. It falls into our Rest of the World, Zone 2.

A: But … I don't remember using the phone's data, I used the hotel's wifi connection and I only called my mum a couple of times. Look, could you possibly reduce the charge?

J: I'm sorry, we can't do that, Angela. We always recommend contacting customer services to check roaming charges abroad before you travel. Next time don't forget to do that. You can also find the information on our website.

A: Well, I'll certainly remember to look for a cheaper operator as soon as I can.

J: Can I help you with anything else today?

A: Yes, could I speak to your supervisor, please?

J: I'm afraid she'll give you the same information.

A: Well, I still want to speak to her anyway.

J: OK, I'm just transferring you now.

7.04

We all have good ideas. They come to us when we're reading or listening to music, in conversation with friends, or alone with our thoughts. But most of the time, they just disappear. I think there are many reasons for this. We may simply forget. We may be afraid of being laughed at. But I think mostly it's because we don't have a system for capturing them.

So I want to hear your ideas about how we can generate more ideas, and how we can share them with each other. But it's not enough just to have good ideas. What I want to do in this session is to brainstorm ways we can capture those ideas to make sure we don't lose them. Yes, we need to be creative, to experiment, to innovate, to explore, to imagine. But we also need to think about how we put our creativity into practice. So in your groups, in thirty minutes, I'd like you to come up with a list of ideas – not only for how to generate great ideas, but also how not to lose them.

7.05

Speaker 1

We think the first thing we need to do is to make lists. So we should brainstorm as many ideas as possible, and write them all down. Quantity not quality is the key. We can decide what we want to keep later.

Speaker 2

We think that the big problem is those ideas which come to us when we are not expecting them. How do we record them? We suggest everyone needs to get into the habit of carrying a small notebook. Another way is to use the recorders on our smartphones. The thing is, it's got to be easy, otherwise we won't do it.

Speaker 3

Our team would like to push the idea of mind mapping. Basically, starting with a word or phrase, and then simply writing down all the ideas that come from that phrase. So it's a bit like brainstorming, which the first group mentioned. But then we need to connect the ideas so that we end up with things that are related to each other.

Speaker 4

We like the idea of using different viewpoints to generate ideas. So everyone takes on a different role to normal, a different personality, and then tries to think like that person might think. For example, if you are thinking about ideas for improving customer service, you could take on the role of a customer, or one of the suppliers.

Speaker 5

Our team came up with the idea of visualisation, or of using pictures to record our creativity. So not just writing down the idea in normal words, but drawing a picture or a diagram which summarises the idea. Doing this helps to think the idea through.

Speaker 6
We like the devil's advocate approach. Basically every time someone comes up with an idea or an innovation we take the opposite view and question everything about the idea. The risk is that we make people upset or angry, but what we want to do is make sure that we really think through the issues, instead of just accepting them. It helps prevent group thinking.

8.01
Part 1
Nowadays we all have too many tasks. Everything seems urgent, and nobody has time to wait. But part of the secret of success is not to get distracted, not to react to everything that comes to your desk, but instead to prioritise. Setting priorities is very easy to do. First, you make a list of the tasks that you need to do. Second, you compare these tasks and decide which ones are important and which ones are urgent. These are not the same thing. Important tasks have to be done because they matter to your business; urgent tasks have to be done now, even if they are not important.
In his book *The 7 Habits of Highly Effective People*, Stephen Covey describes a time-management matrix which helps us to visualise the relationship between important and urgent. Imagine a square divided into four quadrants. In the top left quadrant we put the tasks which are important and urgent. The top left quadrant is for high-priority tasks. In the top right quadrant we put important tasks which are not urgent. In the bottom left quadrant we put tasks which are urgent but not important. And in the bottom right quadrant we put the tasks which are neither important nor urgent. Bottom right are very low priority, and will probably never get done.

8.02
Part 2
So let's go through your list of tasks. I see you have numbered them. Good! Task one is not that urgent, and not that important. Don't waste your time on it. Task two is quite important, but not really that urgent. Put it in your schedule. Task three is really urgent. It is also of utmost importance. Make it your number one priority. Task four is not important, but extremely urgent. Do it today if you have time. Task five is really low priority. It's a bit of a distraction, to be honest. Put it at the bottom of your list of things to do. Do it when you have time. Task six is extremely urgent and important. Give it a high priority, please. Task seven has no priority whatsoever. It's information only. You can put it off for a while.

8.03
Part 3
One last tip. I have already said that part of the secret of success is not to get distracted. But that's only part of the secret. The other part of the secret, the real tip, is discipline. Don't put things off. No excuses. Once you have identified your tasks, just get on with them.

BW1.01
**JN = JobNow representative   M = Maria
A = Agata   T = Taro**
1 Maria
JN: Tell me a bit about yourself, Maria.
M: I'm forty-two years old, and I've been a doctor for about fifteen years, managing my own clinic. I feel very tired – exhausted – all the time. I think I want a completely new career. I'm considering going back to university for another degree, but I don't like the idea of being the oldest person on the course.
2 Agata
JN: Hi, Agata. Could you give me a little background information about yourself?
A: I'm twenty-two and in my final year of studying economics at university. I'd like to find a job in the finance sector, but I've never had any kind of paid job. I play football and volunteer at a hospital, but those are not related to finance.

3 Taro
JN: Thanks for coming in, Taro. Could you give me a quick summary of what you're hoping for?
T: I'm thirty-two. I've worked for ten years writing travel magazine articles as a freelance writer. I've seen the world, but I haven't made very much money. I want to continue writing, but in a secure job in a company.

BW2.01
M = Melanie   F = Franco   T = Toni
M: OK. Shall I start? I looked at the graphite mining industry.
F: Why that one in particular, Melanie?
M: Well, although we've used graphite in things like pencils for years, there's a very exciting new material called graphene that can be made from graphite. I think there could be some good investment opportunities with companies using graphene.
T: I read an article about it recently. Apparently, it's the new super material. But, what is *graphite* exactly? And where do you find it?
M: OK, here's the science bit. It's a metallic mineral made of carbon but there's so much more to it than just pencils, and, even better, there's lots of it all over the world!
F: Really? Is there enough to meet demand?
M: It looks like it. I think it's a great area to invest in. Graphene's 200 times stronger than steel and very lightweight and flexible. It's definitely the material of the future. And, because it conducts heat and electricity much faster than anything else, we find it in the touchscreens on our phones and tablets.
T: What about sports equipment?
M: That too. It's great for things like racing bikes and tennis rackets. And of course it's also fantastic for electric car batteries because it's much safer than anything else.
F: It sounds like a miracle material.
M: Yeah, it does, doesn't it? And I haven't even told you about other potential uses.
T: Really? Like what?
M: It could upload data at one terabit per second or charge your phone in just five minutes.
T: Wow, that would be useful!
M: And you could even use it to clear up nuclear waste, so it'd be good for the environment, too. That's why I think we should invest in the graphite mining industry.

BW2.02
T = Toni   M = Melanie   F = Franco
T: I looked at the tourism industry and the main thing to report is that tourism's very big business especially in some areas where it's expanding fast.
M: What, like package holidays?
T: That's not the only growth area. I've looked at online travel providers, cruise companies, hotel chains and mega-resorts, all of which could be good investments.
M: What's a mega-resort?
T: It's where companies develop all the hotels, villas, entertainment facilities, restaurants, etc. on one site so guests have everything they want in one place. You know, things like swimming pools, villas, a spa, sports facilities, a golf course.
F: I went to one in the Caribbean last year. It was amazing.
T: They are great. But I think we should invest in the cruise industry. More people than ever are going on cruises and profits are high. In fact several companies are building enormous new cruise ships, which are like mega-resorts on the ocean. That's the industry we should be putting our money into.

BW2.03
M = Melanie   F = Franco   T = Toni
M: OK, what about you, Franco? Where do you think our money should go?
F: Definitely the food industry. I know it's an industry with tight margins, but everyone has to eat, don't they?

T: That's true.
F: And people are buying more snacks than ever before because they don't have time to sit down and eat proper meals, so companies are now focusing on healthy snacks. That's what we should focus on because companies new to the industry are doing extremely well and making big profits.
M: So you think the healthy snack market is a good bet?
F: Yes. Everyone's health-conscious these days and looking for more *free-from* products, you know, snacks without sugar, salt, fat, gluten, milk, etc.
M: It's true. I'm always checking the packaging to see what's in a product. I love those healthy breakfast bars. They save me a lot of time in the morning.
F: Exactly. They're ideal for today's busy working person so it won't surprise you to know then that they're flying off shelves around the world. Growth in the healthy snack market is the largest in the food industry. And it's the smaller companies that are beating the big multinationals in the healthy fruit and vegetable-based snack market. That's the kind of thing we want to invest in.

BW2.04
Welcome to this month's investment club podcast which today is aimed at new members. I'm going to tell you about the things you should know about a company before you invest in it.
Investment always involves taking a risk. Therefore you have to make sure the risk is as small as possible and that means doing some research. For example what is the company history? Finding out as much company information as possible is vital for assessing risk. Find out who set the company up and when. Naturally, most investors want to look at the financial performance first. You will need to study the figures from the past three years at least. You do this by checking the financial reports. Looking at these allows you to see what the company is worth, the trend in sales and revenues and where the strengths and weaknesses of the company are. Although the financials are very important, don't forget to look at the management team running the company as, ultimately, they're key to a company's success. You want to find out as much as possible about their experience and skills as well as those of the employees. Ask yourself, is the leadership of the company effective and able to make the best use of the skills of employees?
So you've looked at what exists now, but what about the future? You need to know what the company's future plans are. How are they going to move the company forward and how risky do you think their plans are?
These days another important thing to consider is how environmentally friendly a company is, and what their social responsibilities are. For example, do they help local communities?

BW3.01
L = Lily   C = Carlos
L: OK, Carlos, sorry, but this has to be really quick. I have to leave for the airport in five minutes, so let's do this as quickly as possible.
C: Sure, sure.
L: Item one on the agenda is the 'Save the date' invitations. Are they ready to go?
C: Yes, they are. The email is ready, it's approved by Casa Paradiso – we just need to send it.
L: OK, then let's do that tomorrow.
C: Great. No problem. Tomorrow is fine. I'll take care of that.
L: Item two – the contract with Lana Gabler-Jones. Has that been signed yet?
C: No, it hasn't. Her agent – her name is Constance – says she's very busy.
L: We need to use her name to promote the event. We wanted that contract signed a month ago – July first.
C: I know. We're working on it.

L: Well, we need it today, so just get it done. Can you do it today?
C: Well, I can try. I can try. I'll email her agent straightaway.
L: OK, great. Now, item three. What's this about an engineer?
C: We talked about having an engineer explain how the wind turbines work. I've talked to a couple of people …
L: Listen, I don't think … I mean, an engineer? Sorry, but I'm not convinced. I think we need to focus on the fabulous hotel, and not on the engineering of the wind turbines. Can we just forget about that?
C: Yeah, sure. I mean, you're right. It's probably just a waste of time. We can cut that.
L: Now, the food order. Where is that?
C: We don't need to order the food until a couple of weeks before the event – so mid-September.
L: OK. But we've chosen the catering company, right?
C: Right. It's called Sam's Catering Company.
L: OK, then let's say we'll do the food order on September fifteenth.
C: September fifteenth? OK. No problem. I'll ask Sarah to place the order.
L: Anything else?
C: No, I think that's it.
L: OK, thanks, Carlos.
C: Yeah, thank you, Lily.

BW4.01

I = Interviewer   G = Greg
I: As more and more smaller companies go global thanks to the rise of e-commerce and social media, the supply chain is more important than ever. Today I'm talking to Greg Marshall, Supply Chain Management Consultant. Welcome, Greg.
G: Thanks, Pritti. Good to be here.
I: What are the key factors that businesses moving into a global market need to be aware of?
G: Well, you really need to have an effective and efficient supply chain that you can rely upon.
I: How do you get that?
G: First of all, it's important to keep costs to a minimum when you are competing in a global market. If the supply chain is too long and outside of your control, you'll end up dealing with delays and other problems along the chain. You have to make sure that you can offer the best customer service at the best price so your supply chain has to be able to support not only existing local customers but also the new customers in other countries as well as in your own.
I: How important is it to understand the culture of the countries you are supplying or selling to?
G: Of course it's important and, if you are targeting a specific market, then the more you know about that market, the better. However, for smaller businesses, going global often happens without a planned strategy.
I: What do you mean by that exactly?
G: Well, a customer from another country makes enquiries and then places an order and suddenly the small business has taken the first steps to going global. But it can be a very steep learning curve because you haven't exported before or done any homework on that particular country.

BW4.02

I = Interviewer   G = Greg
I: So what things do you need to consider?
G: For example, cost of increased production, distribution costs – that is, how are you going to transport the items to the customer – payment terms, currency, methods and the amount of stock you can keep as online orders come in quickly and customers expect their goods as fast as possible. And of course there are the different trading laws for each country and specific documentation required.
I: So, a small business could suddenly find themselves in a very different kind of business set-up when they start exporting?

G: Exactly. And the one thing that mustn't suffer during all the expansion is the product quality or you'll have a scandal on your hands. Do you remember the scandal in the UK when it was discovered that some food products had horse meat in them? Or the terrible scandal of tumble driers catching fire and burning down kitchens and houses? There are so many parts of the supply chain that could go wrong.
I: So are you saying that not everyone should go global?
G: Not at all. It's the way to succeed if you can learn fast and get organised. Many home businesses have become global phenomena. Did you know that some of the biggest companies in the world, including Google, Apple, Microsoft and Amazon, all started in a garage?
I: No, that's amazing!
G: So what I'm saying is that it doesn't matter where you start, it's where you go and how you get there that's important.

BW4.03

I = Interviewer   G = Greg
I: So, if you were a small business owner moving into the global market, how would the business change?
G: Well, let's look at a simple supply chain model first. That'll explain it best. Let's imagine a company that makes organic apple juice. It started when Walter, a student, was experimenting in his kitchen. His supplier was a local farmer who let Walter have the apples for free if he collected them. Walter created the product in his kitchen and started selling it to his friends and neighbours, so he was the manufacturer and the retailer all in one. Already you've got the beginnings of a supply chain – local farmer gives apples to Walter who makes the juice in his kitchen and then sells it to customers; in this case his friends and neighbours. However, Walter's customer base is slowly expanding and then a local shop wants to sell his product but the order is too big for him to do alone in his kitchen. Suddenly his supply chain is changing. Because he can't get all the apples he needs from the local farmer, he has to look for new suppliers, who don't give him the apples for free, which of courses pushes the price up. Then he finds he hasn't got the time to produce the quantities ordered himself so he has to find a company to produce his juices, and he's no longer the manufacturer. Then he's got to stock the products, so he has to find a warehouse and organise distribution. Now he has become a wholesaler because he sells to the shops at a wholesale price, but he's still a retailer when he sells directly to consumers online. So you can see how complicated it could get if you don't plan properly.

BW5.01

R = Researcher   F1 = Female 1   F2 = Female 2
M1 = Male 1   M2 = Male 2
R: I'd like to thank you all again for taking the time to help us out with our market research. We think smart fabric is going to be the next big thing in fashion, but we need your help to get it right. So, you've all been given a T-shirt to try out – everyone had a chance to wear it, at least for a few hours? OK, you've all filled out some written feedback as well, but I'd really love to hear what you thought. So … who will start?
F1: The shirt looks absolutely amazing.
M1: Totally. My girlfriend couldn't believe it – how cool it was.
F2: That's completely true, but was I the only one who … I thought it felt like – like plastic on my skin, but kind of rough …
M2: I think that's the big disappointment. After about two hours, I had to take it off. It was actually really uncomfortable.
F1: You're right. And it smells strange, too …
F1: But, … so … I'm a keen cyclist – I go everywhere by bike. My shirt had the lighting-up option. A couple of times, I put it on over another T-shirt,

and I wore it cycling. So I think this could be a great piece of safety equipment, maybe – if it were brighter? It's good for being seen!
M1: Right, right – good for safety, but just really uncomfortable – it feels kind of horrible to touch it – and it smells really weird.
R: Right, OK. So what I hear is that nobody really wants to wear this next to their body.
F2: The other thing – what's the washing like? You told us *not* to wash the T-shirt.
M2: I wondered the same thing. Are there special washing instructions?
R: Yes, it definitely can't just go in the wash with other clothes.
F1: That's a huge problem. A T-shirt, especially, needs to be easy to wash.
M1: It's so cool, the fabric, but you want to do something with it where you don't need to wash it.
F2: Right. I'm thinking … I don't know, curtains?
M2: Curtains are a great idea. Or wallpaper?
F1: Yeah – you could change the colour of your wallpaper without changing the wallpaper. That would be so cool.
M1: Or back to the idea of clothing – could this be a good material for road workers to wear – like on a safety jacket? It would make them easy to see.
F2: And you could even have words, right? Like 'slow down' on the back of a safety jacket.
R: OK, yes, those are some great ideas. I'd like to just go back to …

BW5.02

M = Man   W = Woman
M: It's obvious that the smart fabric has great potential – we just need to figure out the marketing mix.
W: OK, so the products we have on the list so far: cycling safety wear, road-worker safety wear, curtains, wallpaper. So two basic categories – safety clothing and home decoration.
M: Right. So let's look at cycling safety wear first. The product would be …
W: To begin with, it would be a cycling safety vest. This would work because it wouldn't be worn next to the skin, and because it makes great use of the smart fabric.
M: Right, OK. So it would be practical – it lights up, so it's safe – but also we could bring fashion to it, too, right?
W: Exactly. At the moment, there isn't a safety vest for cycling that's also fashionable. In the market, *safe* and *fashionable* are two very different ideas. So we could bring those together in a great new product.
M: OK, great. So who wants to buy that?
W: Well, I think this one probably isn't for serious racing cyclists, or sports cyclists – they don't usually wear safety gear like that. But people who cycle to work – commuters – who in fact are often very serious about cycling, they're out in traffic every day – they're probably the target market.
M: OK, agreed – at least to begin with. So that means we probably don't want to promote it in serious cycling magazines, but maybe we do want to push it in … I don't know, lifestyle magazines – travel, women's magazines, men's magazines … ?
W: Yeah, OK. And probably online. Social media …
M: Definitely, if we're selling online – which of course we will. But what about bike shops?
W: Distribution is expensive – shipping is getting more expensive all the time. That's a big consideration. But I think if people actually see the product in a bike shop, they'll want one.
M: That's true. So that's an obvious placement, but also a big opportunity for promotion. So what about price?
W: It won't be easy. The smart fabric isn't cheap to produce, but a cycle safety vest isn't really a premium product.
M: Well, the usual bright orange and bright green ones aren't, but we're selling something special here. The basic ones are about five euros, and some of the nicer ones are about twenty euros. Our cost, per vest, at least at first, will be about twenty-two euros, so we're looking at a retail price of over forty euros.

W: Forty euros …
M: I know. It's high. But then … if we price it as a premium product – a fashion safety vest …
W: … we might place it in some of the more expensive department stores, not just cycle shops.
M: I like that idea! And who knows, if the vests are popular, we might develop a whole range of cycling products.

BW6.01

M = Man   W = Woman
M: Why do you have to do risk assessment for offices?
W: We do it to make sure that the work environment is safe for the employees and any visitors. In fact, in most countries you have to do it – it's the law.
M: So how does it work?
W: Firstly, you have to identify any significant hazards in the office and also who is at risk: employees, visitors, cleaners, etc.
M: What kind of things can be dangerous?
W: Well, things like wires and cords that trail across the floor, and carpet that doesn't fit properly or is torn, both of which could trip people up. Erm, dangerous machines that don't have guards on them, for example. You don't want to have any accidents.
M: Is that all you're looking at?
W: Oh, not at all. Then there are things like the heat or the noise in the workspace. Is it too hot or too cold or noisy for people to work safely and comfortably?
M: I hadn't thought of that. But I suppose if you're too hot or cold, you can't work effectively because it can make you feel ill.
W: Exactly.
M: Would you also look at things like lighting?
W: Yes, you can't expect people to work in places where there's inadequate lighting because it could damage their eyesight.
M: What about office furniture? Is it important to have good chairs for example?
W: Oh, absolutely. One of the most common causes of staff being off sick is backache, so it's a good idea to ensure that the seating is good for their posture.
M: So, once we've identified these risks, what happens next?
W: Then you need to evaluate the risks involved and put procedures in place to limit the risks and …

BW7.01

This morning I'm going to talk about dealing with unhappy customers and how to turn a bad situation around. When things go wrong, many people's first reaction is to be very angry and demand that it be dealt with immediately. So whether the complaint is on social media, the phone or in an email, act as quickly as you can to resolve the situation. However, don't go making offers without checking the facts as that can be almost as bad as not resolving it. Customers like to know that a company cares about them.
With social media and emails, respond immediately by apologising and indicating that you are looking into the complaint and will contact the person as soon as you can. But then don't fall into the trap of taking too long. It's important to treat each complaint as a priority. If necessary, imagine that if you do not solve the problem, you could lose your job. That's a good way to focus your mind. Then get back to the customer with a solution as quickly as you can. And if you can give a customer a little more than they expect, they are likely to become your most loyal customer.
Many employees in customer service are dependent on the manager to give them permission to solve problems. All customer-facing staff should be able to solve as many complaints as possible without referring back to someone who may not be available at the time. This is where a comprehensive company policy and good training can be invaluable. These can help to ensure that similar problems don't occur again. A company must create a culture of good service and respect for the customer. It should keep accurate records of every communication between the company and the customer for each complaint so that everyone knows what's happened or is happening and can use this information to either improve a service or make sure something similar doesn't happen again.
BW8.01
Speaker 1
I'm based in Durban, in South Africa, but I sometimes visit our production facility in Vietnam, near Hanoi. On my first visit there, I was introduced to the top management of our subsidiary soon after I arrived. My visit wasn't very long, and we had some important business to discuss. I expected to meet people, have a short conversation, then get down to business. On the first day, we went to the factory in the afternoon, and I had a tour. That was interesting, but not very useful to me. Then we went out for dinner. I expected this to be a business dinner, but my hosts never mentioned work, and whenever I tried to go onto that topic, they changed the subject quickly. We finally discussed business on the second day. The whole experience really confused me. It was only later that I learnt about how important it is in Vietnamese business culture to get to know people first, before talking business. Also, apparently it's OK to talk business at lunch, but almost never at dinner. Now that I understand, it makes a lot of sense. I like it, actually. I guess they think we South Africans are probably too direct!

Speaker 2
I completely understand that the management needs to know what the sales team is up to – what we're doing. The business depends on our performance. But a few months ago, they asked us to write a weekly report of our sales activities. Before that, it was a monthly report, which I liked. But a weekly report – it's too much, a real pain. I really need to focus on selling. And do the managers really want to read a weekly report from sales reps all over the world? Don't they have more important things to do? I would understand if the sales team were failing, but we aren't failing. The last couple of years have been outstanding for the business. This is a case of too much communication – too much paperwork.

BW8.02

I've scheduled a meeting with one of our biggest clients in France next Monday. China is going to supply the model for the meeting just in time, but it's stressful. If something goes wrong with the shipping, I'll have big problems. We don't have to work this way! Why didn't Mr Lau send the design model back to manufacturing as soon as he realised there was a problem? Why did he have to ask what I wanted? Why couldn't he just *do something* instead of waiting for orders from me? It doesn't make sense to me – not at all.

BW8.03

When I received the design model of the HM-02, I knew the problem was serious. However, Frederik works in Head Office in Denmark, and he's above me in the company. It's really important for employees to respect their superiors and to include them in making important decisions, so I could never have returned the design model for the correction without first asking Frederik. Teamwork is extremely important in business. It's why we are successful as a company. Also, I knew we could supply the model just in time, so there wasn't going to be a big problem.

P5.02

1   the best rest'rant in town
2   while they're deliv'ring the food
3   I've seen something sim'lar in Amsterdam
4   only because it's necess'ry

P7.02

1
A: Why don't you take a few days off work?
B: I can't <u>afford</u> to take a few days off work.
2
A: Why don't you phone customer services?
B: I <u>hate</u> phoning customer services.
3
A: Maybe it's better not to join the project?
B: I've already a<u>greed</u> to join the project.

- **adjective** (*adj.*) Headwords for adjectives followed by information in square brackets, e.g. [only before a noun] and [not before a noun], show any restrictions on where they can be used.
- **noun** (*n.*) The codes [C] and [U] show whether a noun, or a particular sense of a noun, is countable (*a customer, two customers*) or uncountable (*assistance, branding*).
- **verb** (*v.*) The forms of irregular verbs are given after the headword. The codes [I] (intransitive) and [T] (transitive) show whether a verb, or a particular sense of a verb, has or does not have an object. Phrasal verbs (*phr. v.*) are shown after the verb they are related to.
- Some entries show information on words that are related to the headword. Adverbs (*adv.*) are often shown in this way after adjectives.
- **region labels** The codes *AmE* and *BrE* show whether a word or sense of a word is used only in American or British English.

account for *phr. v.* to form a particular amount or part of something

action *v.* [T] to do a specific thing that needs to be done, especially after discussing it

action point (*also* **action item**) *n.* [C] something that you decide must be done, especially after a meeting or after studying something carefully

adapt *v.* **1** [I, T] to gradually change your behaviour and attitudes in order to be successful in a new situation
2 [T] to change something to make it suitable for a different purpose

adaptable *adj.* able to change in order to be successful in new and different situations

adaptability *n.* [U] the ability to change in order to be successful in new and different situations

adaptation *n.* [U] the process of changing to become suitable for a new situation

advanced *adj.* using the most modern ideas, equipment, and methods

advertise *v.* [I, T] to tell people publicly about a product or service in order to persuade them to buy it

advertisement *n.* [C] a picture, piece of film or piece of writing that is used to tell people publicly about a product or service in order to persuade them to buy it

after hours happening after the normal hours of opening for a business, financial market, etc.

agency *n.* [C] a business that provides a particular service for people or organisations

agenda *n.* [C] a list of the subjects to be discussed at a meeting

agent *n.* [C] a person who represents or speaks for a company

ambition 1 [C] a strong desire to achieve something
2 [U] determination to be successful, rich, powerful, etc.

ambitious *adj.* determined to be successful, rich, powerful, etc.

analyse *v.* [T] to examine or think about something carefully, in order to understand it

analyst *n.* [C] someone who is a specialist in a particular subject, market, industry, etc. and examines information relating to it in order to give their views about what will happen or should be done

anticipate *v.* [T] to expect that something will happen and be ready for it

appeal[1] *n.* [U] a quality that makes people like something or someone

appeal[2] *v.* [I] if someone or something appeals to you, they seem attractive and interesting

appealing *adj.* attractive or interesting

applicant *n.* [C] someone who applies for a job, usually by writing a letter or filling in a form

appoint *v.* [T] to choose someone for a job or position

approach *n.* [C] a method of doing something or dealing with a problem

aspirational *adj.* something that is aspirational is wanted by people because they connect it with wealth or success

assess *v.* [I, T] to make a judgement about a person or situation after considering all the information

assist *v.* [I, T] to help someone to do something

assistance *n.* [U] help or support

attribute *n.* [C] a quality that someone has, especially one that is good or useful

auction *n.* [C] a meeting where land, buildings, paintings, etc. are sold to the person who offers the most money for them

authentic *adj.* showing your real character, beliefs and attitudes, and not pretending to be a different kind of person

authenticity *n.* [U] the quality of showing your real character, beliefs and attitudes, and not pretending to be a different kind of person

authority *n.* [U] the power that a person or organisation has because of their official or legal position

automated *adj.* using computers and machines to do a job, rather than people

automotive *adj.* [only before a noun] relating to cars or the car industry

background *n.* [C, U] the situation or past events that explain why something happens in the way that it does

benefit *n.* [C] a good effect or advantage that something has, for example a product or service

bid *n.* [C] an offer to do work or provide services for a fixed price, in competition with other offers

biometrics *n.* [U] technology that uses measurements of people's eyes, face, fingerprints, etc. in order to recognise who they are

body language *n.* [U] changes in your body position and movements that show what you are feeling or thinking

brainstorm *v.* [I, T] to have a discussion or meeting with other people to suggest a lot of ideas for an activity or for solving a problem

brand *n.* [C] a name given to a product by a company so that the product can easily be recognised by its name or its design
global brand *n.* [C] a product name that is known by people all around the world, because the product is sold in most countries

branding *n.* [U] the practice of giving a product or a group of products a name and then advertising the product so that the name becomes well-known

brochure *n.* [C] a thin book giving information or advertising something

budget *n.* [C] a detailed plan made by an organisation or a government of how much it will receive as income over a particular period of time, and how much it will spend, what it will spend the money on, etc.

business model *n.* [C] a plan for how a business should be run in order to succeed and make money, for example what its products are and how they are produced, how they are sent out to customers, etc.

candidate *n.* [C] someone who is being considered for a job

can-do *adj.* **can-do attitude** the opinion or feeling that you can solve problems and achieve the things you want to do, even when this is difficult

capture *v.* [T] to succeed in writing down or describing an idea, situation or feeling, using words or pictures

career *n.* [C] a job or profession that you have been trained for and intend to do for your working life
career ladder *n.* [singular] the series of jobs or positions that someone can have during their career, with each job being more important or responsible than the one before
careers advice (*also* **career advice** *AmE*) *n.* [U] advice about which is the best type of job for you
careers event *n.* [C] *BrE* an event that many employers go to, where you can get information about their business or industry and meet many business people

catch up *phr. v.* to do what needs to be done because you have not been able to do it until now

CCTV *n.* [U] (**closed circuit television**) a system of cameras placed in public buildings or in the street, used to help prevent crime or catch criminals

CEO *n.* [C] (**Chief Executive Officer**) the manager with the most authority in the normal, everyday management of a company. The job of CEO is sometimes combined with other jobs, such as that of president.

CFO *n.* [C] (**Chief Financial Officer**) the finance manager with the most authority in a company

chain *n.* [C] a number of shops, hotels, cinemas, etc. owned or managed by the same company or person

classic *adj.* attractive in a simple traditional way

client *n.* [C] someone who buys goods or a service from a seller

climate change *n.* [U] a permanent change in the Earth's weather conditions

close a deal/sale/contract etc. to reach the point in a deal, sale, etc. where everyone involved agrees to it

commission *n.* [C, U] an amount of money paid to someone according to the value of goods, shares, bonds, etc. they have sold

compensation *n.* [U] an amount paid to someone because they have been harmed in some way or hurt

compete *v.* [I] to try to get people to buy your company or country's goods or services rather than those available from another company or country

competition *n.* [U] a situation in which businesses are trying to be more successful than others by selling more goods and services and making more profit

competitor *n.* [C] a person, product, company, country, etc. that is competing with another

complaint *n.* [C, U] a written or spoken statement by someone complaining about something

compulsory *adj.* something that is compulsory must be done because it is the law or because someone in authority orders you to

concept *n.* [C] an idea for a product or service

confidence *n.* [U] the belief that you have the ability to do things well or deal with situations successfully

confident *adj.* sure that you have the ability to do things well or deal with situations successfully

consensus *n.* [singular, U] agreement among a group of people

consulting firm *n.* [C] a company that gives advice and training in a particular area to people in other companies

consumable *adj.* consumable goods are intended to be used and then replaced

consume *v.* [T] to use time, energy, goods, etc.

consumer *n.* [C] a person who buys goods, products and services for their own use, not for business use or to resell

consumption *n.* [U] **1** the amount of goods, services, energy or natural materials used in a particular period of time
2 the act of buying and using products

contract *n.* [C] a formal, written agreement between two or more people or groups which says what each must do for the other, or must not do

cost *n.* **1 costs** [plural] the money that a business or an individual must regularly spend
2 [C, U] the amount of money that you have to pay in order to buy, do, or produce something

craftsman *n.* [C] a skilled worker, especially a man, in a job that involves making things with your hands

critical thinking *n.* [U] the process of thinking very carefully about something and making judgments about what is good, bad, true, or will work well

custom *adj.* custom products or services are specially designed and made for a particular person

customer *n.* [C] a person or organisation that buys goods or services from a shop or company
customer base *n.* [C usually singular] all the people who buy or use a particular product
customer service *n.* [U] **1** when an organisation helps its customers by answering their questions and listening to their complaints, giving them advice on using a particular product or service, providing a good quality product, etc.
2 (*also* **Customer Services**) the department in a large organisation that deals with questions and complaints from its customers, gives advice on using the product or service it provides, etc.

customer-facing *adj.* dealing directly with customers

customisable (*also* **customizable**) *adj.* able to be changed in order to be suitable for a particular customer, task, object, or situation

customisation (*also* **customization**) *n.* [U] the process of specially designing and building a product or service for a particular person or organisation, so that the product or service is different from that used by other people

customise (*also* **customize**) *v.* [T usually passive] to design, build, etc. a product or service specially for a particular person or organisation, so that the product or service is different from that used by other people, making it different from other things of the same kind

customised *adj.* designed, built, etc. specially for a particular person, task etc., so that a product or service is different from that used by other people

cutting-edge *adj.* relating to using the newest and most advanced ideas, methods, equipment, etc.

CV *n.* [C] (**curriculum vitae**) a short written document that lists your education and previous jobs, which you send to employers when you are looking for a job (= **résumé** *AmE*)

deal with *phr. v.* to take the necessary action, especially in order to solve a problem

debriefing *n.* [C, U] the process of asking someone questions about a job they have just done or an experience they have just had, in order to gather information

delegate *v.* [T] to choose someone to do a particular job, or to be a representative of a group, organisation, etc.

delivery *n.* [C, U] the act of bringing goods, letters, etc. to a particular person or place, or the things that are brought
cash on delivery a payment system in which the customer pays for goods when they are delivered
delivery company *n.* [C] a company that delivers goods to customers
delivery date *n.* [C] the date that has been arranged for goods to be delivered

demand *n.* **1** [U] the total amount of a type of goods or services that people or companies buy in a particular period of time
2 [singular, U] the need or desire that people have for particular goods and services

department *n.* [C] one of the parts of a large organisation, such as a company or university, where people do a particular kind of work

dependability *n.* [U] the ability to be trusted to do what is needed or expected

dependable *adj.* able to be trusted to do what you need or expect

deposit *n.* [C] a small first payment that you make for a house, car, holiday, etc.

determination *n.* [U] the quality of trying to do something even when it is difficult

development *n.* [U] the process of planning and making new products or providing new services

devil's advocate *n.* [C] someone who pretends to disagree with you in order to have a good discussion about something

dispatch *v.* [T] to send something or someone to a place

disrupt *v.* [T] to start doing something in a new and more effective way that changes the way a type of business does things

distribution *n.* [U] the actions involved in supplying goods to shops and companies after they have been produced, for example moving, storing and selling the goods

diversify *v.* [I] if a company or economy diversifies, it increases the range of goods or services it produces

domestic *adj.* relating to the country you live in, rather than abroad

downside *n.* [C] the negative part or disadvantage of something

draft *n.* [C] a document or piece of writing that has to be checked and possibly changed, and so is not yet in its finished form

e-commerce *n.* [U] (**electronic commerce**) the practice of buying and selling goods and services over the internet

effective *adj.* working well and producing the result or effect that was intended

efficient *adj.* working well without wasting time, money or energy

elite *n.* [C usually singular] a group of people who have a lot of power and influence because they have money, knowledge or special skills

emission *n.* [C usually plural] a gas or other substance that is sent into the air

empathetic *adj.* showing an ability to understand other people's feelings

empathise (*also* **empathize**) *v.* [I] to be able to understand someone else's feelings, problems, etc., especially because you have had similar experiences

empathy *n.* [U] the ability to understand other people's feelings and problems

employment *n.* [U] the condition of having a paid job

enclose *v.* [T] to put something in an envelope with a letter

endorse *v.* [T] if a famous person endorses a product or service, they say in an advertisement that they use and like it

enthusiasm *n.* [U] a strong feeling of interest and enjoyment about something and wanting to be involved in it

enthusiastic *adj.* feeling or showing a lot of interest and excitement about something

equipment *n.* [U] the tools, machines, etc. that you need to do a particular job or activity

e-shop *n.* [C] a shop that sells its goods from a website on the internet

evaluate *v.* [T] to carefully consider something to see how good, useful or valuable it is

exclusive *adj.* exclusive places, organisations, clothes, etc. are so expensive that not many people can afford to use or buy them

executive *n.* [C] someone who has an important job as a manager in a company or business

expand *v.* [I, T] **1** to become larger in size, amount or number, or to make something larger in size, amount or number
2 if an economy, industry or business activity expands, it gets bigger or more successful

export *n.* [U] the sale of goods to other countries

face *v.* [T] to have a difficult problem or situation that is going to affect you and that you must deal with

facilities *n.* [plural] buildings or equipment that are provided for a particular use

factor *n.* [C] one of many things that influence or cause a situation

feature *n.* [C] a part of something that is important, interesting or useful

feedback *n.* [U] advice, criticism, etc. about how successful or useful something is

finance *n.* [U] the management of money by countries, organisations and people

financial *adj.* [usually before noun] relating to money or the management of money

firm *n.* [C] a company or business, especially one which is quite small

flexibility *n.* [U] the ability to change or be changed easily to suit a different situation

flexible *adj.* a person, plan, etc. that is flexible can change or be changed easily to suit any new situation

focus *v.* [I, T] to give special attention to one particular person or thing, or to make people do this

focus group *n.* [C] a small group of people that a company asks questions in order to find out what they think of their products, advertising, etc.

follow something ↔ **up** *phr. v.* [T] to do something to make sure that earlier actions have been successful or effective

fossil fuel *n.* [C, U] a fuel such as coal or oil that is produced by the gradual decaying of animals or plants over millions of years

freelance *adj.* working independently for different companies rather than being employed by one particular company

freelancer *n.* [C] someone who works independently for different companies rather than being employed by one particular company

funds *n.* [plural] money that an organisation needs or has

generate *v.* [T] to create, produce or cause something, especially something new

global *adj.* **1** relating to doing business all over the world
2 go global if a company or industry goes global, it starts doing business all over the world
global player a company that produces or sells a product or service worldwide, especially a company that is a leader in that type of business

globally *adv.* in a way that affects or includes the whole world

global warming *n.* [U] a general increase in world temperatures caused by increased amounts of carbon dioxide around the Earth

go with the flow to agree that you will do the thing that most people want to do

goal *n.* [C] something that you hope to achieve in the future

goods *n.* [plural] things that are produced in order to be sold

grow *v.* (*past tense* **grew**; *past participle* **grown**) **1** [I] to increase in amount, size or degree
2 [T] to make a business or part of a business bigger and more successful

growth *n.* [singular, U] an increase in the value of goods or services produced and sold by a business or a country

guarantee *n.* [C] a formal written promise to repair or replace a product, if it has a fault, within a specific period of time after you buy it

handle *v.* [T] to deal with something

handling *n.* [U] the way in which someone does a job or deals with a situation, problem or person

hazard *n.* [C] something that may be dangerous, or cause accidents or problems

head *n.* [C] the leader or person in charge of a group, organisation or part of an organisation

head office *n.* [C, U] the main office of a company

headquarters *n.* [plural] the main office or main building of an organisation

health and safety *n.* [U] the activity of protecting employees from illness or injury at work

high-end *adj.* high-end products are the most expensive ones in a particular market or range

high-visibility (*also* **high-vis** *informal*) *adj.* high-visibility clothing is made out of brightly coloured cloth and has stripes on it that reflect light, so that people wearing the clothing can be easily seen

hire *v.* [T] to employ a person or an organisation for a short time to do a particular job for you

hi-tech (*also* **high-tech**) *adj.* high-tech equipment, activities, etc. involve or use advanced technology (*opposite* **low-tech**)

honest *adj.* someone who is honest always tells the truth and does not cheat or steal

honesty *n.* [U] the quality of being honest

HR (*also* **human resources**) *n.* [plural] the department in an organisation that deals with employing, training and helping employees

ID badge *n.* [C] something you carry or wear to show who you are and that you work for a particular company or are allowed to be in a particular place. The badge usually has your name and a photograph.

identification *n.* [U] when you recognize something or discover exactly what it is

identify *v.* [T] to recognize something or discover exactly what it is, what its nature or origin is, etc.

implement *v.* [T] to take action or make changes that you have officially decided should happen

import-export *adj.* relating to a person or company that both buys goods to bring into a country and sells goods from one country to another

income *n.* [C, U] money that you earn from your job or that you receive from investments

in-company *adj.* done within an organisation (=**in-house**)

independence *n.* [U] the freedom and ability to make your own decisions in life, without having to ask other people for permission, help or money

independent *adj.* confident and able to do things by yourself in your own way, without needing help or advice from other people

induction *n.* [C, U] the introduction and training of someone into a new job

industrialised (*also* **industrialized**) *adj.* having a lot of factories, industrial companies, etc.

industry *n.* **1** [C] businesses that produce a particular type of thing or provide a particular service
2 [U] the large-scale production of goods or of substances, such as coal and steel

innovation *n.* **1** [U] the introduction of new ideas or methods
2 [C] a new idea, method or invention

innovative *adj.* an innovative product, method, process, etc. is new, different and better than those that existed before

integrity *n.* [U] the quality of being honest and strong about what you believe to be right

intern *n.* [C] someone, especially a student, who works for a short time in a particular job in order to gain experience

internal *adj.* within a company or organisation, rather than outside it

invest *v.* [I, T] to buy shares, bonds, property, etc. in order to make a profit

investigate *v.* [I, T] to try to find out the truth about something such as a crime, accident, or scientific problem

investigation *n.* [U] the act of investigating something

investment *n.* [C] **1** the money that is put into a business to try to make it more successful and profitable
2 something you buy, such as shares, bonds or property, in order to make a profit

investor *n.* [C] a person or organisation that invests money in order to make a profit

invoice *n.* [C] a document sent by a seller to a customer with details of goods or services that have been provided, their price and the payment date

job fair *n.* [C] a large event where people looking for jobs and companies looking for employees can meet

job seeker (*also* **jobseeker**) *n.* [C] someone who is looking for a job

labourer (*also* **laborer** *AmE*) *n.* [C] someone whose job involves a lot of heavy physical work

large-scale *adj.* [only before noun] using or involving a lot of people, effort, money or supplies

launch *n.* [C] an occasion at which a new product is shown or made available for sale or use for the first time

leader *n.* [C] the person who directs or controls a team, organisation, country, etc.

listing *n.* [C] an entry on an official list

logo *n.* [C] a design or way of writing its name that a company or organisation uses as its official sign on its products, advertising, etc.

low-cost *adj.* not costing a lot of money

low-tech *adj.* not using the most modern machines or methods in business or factories (*opposite* **hi-tech**)

loyal *adj.* if customers are loyal to a particular product, they continue to buy it and do not change to other products

loyalty card *n.* [C] a card given by a shop or company that gives regular customers lower prices, money back on goods, etc.

luxury *adj.* relating to goods that are expensive and not really necessary, but are pleasing and enjoyable

manageable *adj.* easy to control or deal with

management *n.* [singular, U] the people who are in charge of a company or organisation

manufacturer *n.* [C] a company that makes large quantities of goods, usually in factories

manufacturing *n.* [U] the process or business of producing goods in factories

market *n.* **1** [C] a particular country or area where a company sells its goods or where a particular type of goods is sold
2 [singular] the number of people who want to buy something, or the type of people who want to buy it
  domestic market *n.* [C] the country you live in or where a company is based, seen as a place where goods or services can be sold
  export market *n.* [C] a foreign country to which goods and services from a particular country are sold
  financial market *n.* [C] the activity of buying and selling stocks, bonds, currencies, etc., or the places or businesses that do this

  global market *n.* [singular] the markets for goods and services around the world, considered as one large market
  international market *n.* [singular] the markets for goods and services in many different countries around the world
  market demand *n.* [C] demand for a particular type of goods or services from a particular group of buyers
  market research *n.* [U] a business activity that involves collecting information about what goods people in a particular area buy, why they buy them, etc.

marketing *n.* [U] the activity of deciding how to advertise a product, what price to charge for it, etc.

marketing mix *n.* [C usually singular] all the different actions that are done by a company to try to sell their products, which usually include having the right product for the market, giving it the right price, selling it to the right shops and customers, and advertising the product well

marketplace *n.* [C] a place, area or website where you can buy or sell things

mass market *n.* [singular] very many ordinary people, considered as a group, to whom goods are sold

mass-market *adj.* [only before noun] designed for sale to as wide a range of people as possible

mass production *n.* [U] the process of making products in large numbers by machines, so that they can be produced cheaply

middle class *n.* [singular] the social class that includes people who are educated and work in professional jobs, for example teachers or managers

middle-class *adj.* typical of people who are educated and work in professional jobs

milestone *n.* [C] a stage in the development or progress of something

mind mapping *n.* [U] the process of creating a mind map (=a picture of how different facts or ideas relate to each other, that usually has the main subject in the middle, and facts or ideas that relate to the subject are around it and have lines connecting them to the main subject or to each other)

minutes *n.* [plural] an official written record of what is said and decided at a meeting

monitor *v.* [T] to carefully watch and check a situation in order to see how it changes or progresses over a period of time

motivated *adj.* very keen to do something or achieve something, especially because you find it interesting or exciting

motivation *n.* [U] willingness to do something without needing to be told or forced to do it

multinational *n.* [C] a large company that has offices, factories and business activities in many different countries

multitask *v.* [I] to do several things at the same time

narrow something ↔ **down** *phr. v.* to reduce the number of things that you can choose from

negotiation *n.* [C usually plural, U] official discussions between groups who are trying to reach an agreement

negotiator *n.* [C] someone who takes part in official discussions, especially in business or politics, in order to try and reach an agreement

network *v.* [I] to meet with people involved in the same kind of work, in order to share information, help each other, etc.

networking site *n.* [C] a website on which you can connect with other people who do the same type of work, in order to find jobs or employees, share information, etc.

no-frills *adj.* a no-frills product or service includes only basic features and is not of the highest possible quality

onsite, on-site *adj.* at a particular place of work or at a place where something is being built, rather than away from it

open-plan *adj.* an open-plan office, school, etc. does not have walls dividing it into separate rooms

operate *v.* [T] **1** to use and control a machine or equipment
2 if a person or organisation operates a business, system, etc., they manage it and make it work

order *n.* **do/make something to order** to produce something especially for a particular customer

outcome *n.* [C] the final result of a process, meeting, discussion, etc. (=**result**)

output *n.* [C, U] the amount of goods or work produced by a person, machine, factory, etc.

outstanding *adj.* not solved, done or dealt with

overload *n.* [C, U] the fact of having more work, information, etc. than can be dealt with

overloaded *adj.* having more work, information, etc. than you can deal with

partner *n.* [C] someone who starts a new business with someone else by investing in it

passion *n.* **1** [C, U] a very strong belief or feeling about something
2 [C] a very strong liking for something

passionate *adj.* **1** someone who has a passionate belief believes something very strongly
2 if you are passionate about something, you like it a lot

perform *v.* [T] to do work, carry out a duty, task, etc.

performance *n.* **1** [C,U] the degree to which a company, investment, financial market, etc. is profitable
2 [U] the way that someone does their job, and how well they do it

personalisation (*also* **personalization**) *n.* [U] the process of designing or changing something so that it is suitable for a particular person

place *v.* [T] **place a product** to decide which people are the most likely customers for a product, and where the best places to sell that product are likely to be

plant *n.* [C] a factory and all of its equipment

policy *n.* [C] a course of action that has been officially agreed and chosen by a political party, business or other organisation

popular culture *n.* [U] the ideas, art, music, films, products, etc. in a particular society that are familiar to and popular with most ordinary people in that society

position *n.* [C] *formal* a job

precaution *n.* [C] something done to prevent something unpleasant or dangerous happening

predict *v.* [T] to say that something will happen, before it happens

prefer *v.* [T] to like someone or something more than someone or something else, so that you would choose it if you could

preferable *adj.* better or more suitable

preference *n.* [C, U] the state of liking something more than something else, or something you like more than another thing

premises *n.* [plural] the buildings and land used by a shop, business, hotel, etc.

premium *adj.* premium products, goods, etc. are of higher quality than usual

prevention *n.* [U] the process of stopping something bad from happening

price *v.* [T] to decide the price of something that is for sale

price range *n.* [C] the limits within which a price can vary

pricing *n.* [U] the act of deciding the price of something that you sell, and comparing that price to the price of similar things that your competitors sell or to other things that you sell

primary *adj.* relating to a type of industry that produces raw materials (=a substance that is used to make a product), for example metals or oil

prioritise (*also* **prioritize**) *v.* [I, T] to put several tasks, problems, etc. in order of importance, so that the most important ones are done first

priority *n.* [C] the thing that is more important than anything else, and that needs attention first

procedure *n.* [C, U] a way of doing something, especially the correct or usual way

process *n.* [C] a series of actions taken to perform a particular task or achieve a particular result

produce *v.* [T] to make, write, etc. something to be bought, used, or enjoyed by people

product *n.* **1** [C] something useful and intended to be sold that comes from nature or is made in a factory
2 [C] a service
product design *n.* [U] the work of planning and making a new product, including how it works, what it looks like, etc.
product support *n.* [U] help that a company gives to people or businesses that buy its product

production *n.* [U] the process of making or growing things to be sold as products, usually in large quantities

productive *adj.* producing or achieving a lot

productivity *n.* [U] the speed at which goods are produced, and the amount produced in relation to the work, time, and money needed to produce them

profession *n.* [C] a job that needs a high level of education and training

professionally *adv.* in a way that shows high standards and is suitable for a workplace

profile *n.* [C] a short description of someone or something, giving the most important details about them
online profile *n.* [C] a profile of yourself that you put on a social media site

profit *n.* [C, U] money that you gain from selling something or from doing business in a particular period of time, after taking away costs

profitable *adj.* producing a profit

project management *n.* [U] the process of planning how a particular piece of work will be done and organising all the people and tasks to do it

project manager *n.* [C] the person whose job it is to plan how a particular piece of work will be done and organise all the people and tasks to do it

promote *v.* [T] to try hard to sell a product or service by advertising it widely, reducing its price, etc.

promotion *n.* [C] an activity such as special advertisements or free gifts intended to help sell a product or service

protective *adj.* used or intended to protect people from danger or harm

prototype *n.* [C] the first form that a newly designed product, car, machine, etc. has, that is used to test the design before it is made in large numbers

provider *n.* [C] an organisation that provides goods or services

public relations (*also* **PR**) *n.* [U] the work of persuading people to have a good opinion of an organisation, company, etc.

purchase *n.* [C] something that has been bought

put something **off** *phr. v.* to delay doing something or to arrange to do something at a later time or date

qualification *n.* [C, usually plural] an examination that you have passed at school, university or in your profession

quality *n.* **1** [C] something such as courage or intelligence that someone may have as part of their character
2 [U] used to talk about how good or bad something is
quality assurance *n.* [U] the practice of checking the quality of goods or services that a company sells, so that the standard continues to be good

range *n.* [C] **1** (*also* **product range**) a set of similar products made by a particular company or available in a particular shop
2 the limits within which a price, amount, quantity, age, etc. can vary

rapport *n.* [singular, U] friendly agreement, communication and understanding between people

raw material *n.* [C] a substance that is used to make a product

recommend *v.* [T] to advise someone to do something, especially because you have special knowledge of a situation or subject

recommendation *n.* [C, U] official advice given to someone about what to do

recruit *v.* [I, T] to find new people to work for an organisation, do a job, etc.

recruiter *n.* [C] someone who tries to find new employees for a company

recruitment *n.* [U] the process or the business of finding new people to work for a company

recruitment agency (*also* **recruitment firm**) a business that works for organisations to find people for jobs when the organizations need them

regulation *n.* [C] an official rule or order
rules and regulations all the rules that a person or business must follow when doing something

reliable *adj.* someone or something that is reliable can be trusted or depended on

relocate *v.* [I, T] if a company or worker relocates or is relocated, they move to a different place

renewable *adj.* renewable materials, sources of energy, etc. will continue to exist or will grow again and are therefore never used up

request¹ *n.* [C] a polite or formal demand for something

request² *v.* [T] to ask for something in a polite or formal way

require *v.* [T] to need something

reschedule *v.* [T] to arrange a new time or date for a meeting or event

research and development (*also* **R &D**) *n.* [U] the part of a business concerned with studying new ideas and planning new products

resourceful *adj.* good at finding ways of dealing with practical problems

resourcefulness *n.* [U] the ability to find good ways of dealing with practical problems

retail *n.* [U] the sale of goods to customers for their own use, rather than to shops, etc.

retailer *n.* [C] a business that sells goods to members of the public, rather than to shops, etc.

revenue (*also* **revenues** *plural*) *n.* [C] money that a business or organisation receives over a period of time, especially from selling goods or services

risk *n.* [C] the possibility that something may be lost, harmed or damaged, or that something bad, unpleasant or dangerous may happen
risk assessment *n.* [C, U] an examination of the possible risks involved in doing something, so that organisations can decide whether something is worth doing and how they can reduce the risks
risk management *n.* [U] the process of deciding what things are likely to be a risk, and deciding how to deal with them to avoid problems
risk register *n.* [C] a list of all the possible things that could go wrong on a project and how likely the risk is to happen, often with a possible solution listed as well

role *n.* [C] the way in which someone or something is involved in an activity or situation, and how much influence they have on it

safety *n.* [U] the state of being safe from danger or harm
safety clothing *n.* [U] special clothes that you wear to protect you in dangerous situations
safety equipment *n.* [U] tools, machines, clothing, etc. that have special features that help protect you in dangerous situations

salary *n.* [C, U] money that you receive as payment from the organisation you work for, usually paid to you every month

satisfaction *n.* **1** [C, U] a feeling of happiness or pleasure because you have achieved something or got what you wanted
2 [U] when you get money or an apology from someone who has treated you badly or unfairly

satisfied *adj.* feeling that something is as good as it should be, or that something has happened in the way that you want

satisfy *v.* [T] **1** to make someone feel pleased by doing what they want
2 if you satisfy someone's needs, demands etc, you provide what they need or want

scenario *n.* [C] a way in which a situation could possibly develop

schedule *n.* [C] a plan of what someone is going to do and when they are going to do it

secondary *adj.* relating to a type of industry that is involved in making products from raw materials (=basic materials used to make goods)

sector *n.* [C] all the organisations or companies in a particular area of activity, industry, etc.
economic sector *n.* [C] an area of business activity or industry
primary sector *n.* [singular] the companies or organisations that are involved in producing raw materials (=basic materials used to make goods), for example metals or oil

secondary sector *n.* [singular] the companies or organisations that are involved in making products from raw materials (=basic materials used to make goods)
tertiary sector (*also* **service sector**) *n.* [singular] the companies or organisations that are involved in services, such as the transportation of goods, banking, tourism, etc.

security *n.* [U] actions to keep someone or something safe from being damaged, stolen, etc.
security door *n.* [C] a door that is made to be very strong or has a lock that only particular people can open
security system *n.* [C] a system of cameras, alarms, etc. to provide security
security tag *n.* [C] a special piece of plastic or paper that makes an alarm sound if the item it is attached to is stolen from a shop

segment *n.* [C] the products or services in a particular part of the market

selling point *n.* [C] a feature of a product that makes it sell well

sense *n.* [U] **make good/bad business sense** to be the sensible or not sensible thing to do for your business

service *n.* [C] a particular type of help or work that is provided by a business to customers or by a government to people, but not one that involves producing goods
service sector *n.* [singular] the companies or organisations that are involved in services, such as the transportation of goods, banking, tourism, etc.
commercial services *n.* [plural] the companies or organisations involved in transporting people or goods in order to earn money, or that sell you a service in return for payment
financial services *n.* [plural] the business activity of giving advice about investments and selling investments to people and organisations
private services *n.* [plural] services to customers that are provided by businesses in return for payment
public services *n.* [plural] services, such as police and healthcare, that are provided by the government of a country

set *v.* [T] to decide that something should happen on a particular date, cost a particular amount, be done in a particular way, etc.

setback *n.* [C] a problem that delays or prevents progress, or makes things worse than they were

sharing economy *n.* [singular] a system in which people earn money by allowing other people to use their house, car, etc. in return for payment

ship *v.* [T] to send goods somewhere by ship, plane, truck, etc.

shipment *n.* [C] a load of goods sent by sea, road, train or air

shipping *n.* [U] the delivery of goods, especially by ship

short-list *v.* [T] to put someone on a list of the most suitable people for a job, chosen from all the people who were first considered

skill *n.* [C, U] an ability to do something well, especially because you have learned and practised it, or the particular thing you can do well
communication skills *n.* [plural] the ability to express yourself in a way that other people will understand, including the words you use and the way you behave when you are speaking
IT skills *n.* [plural] the ability to use a computer and different types of software
life skill *n.* [C usually plural] something that you should be able to do in order to deal with situations and problems that happen in everyday life, for example being able to cook or to talk to people politely
outdoor skill *n.* [C usually plural] a skill that you can use when you are outside and doing something such as camping or walking in the countryside
transferable skill *n.* [C usually plural] an ability to do something that can be used in many different situations, especially one that helps you do a job for which you have not been formally trained

sofapreneur *n.* [C] someone who starts a new business or service that they run from their own home

sofapreneurship *n.* [U] the practice of starting a new business or service from your own home

solar panel *n.* [C] a piece of equipment, usually kept on a roof, that collects and uses the sun's energy to heat water or make electricity

special *adj.* not ordinary or usual, but different in some way and often better or more important

specialisation *n.* [C, U] the practice of limiting your interests or activities to one particular subject

specialise *v.* [I] to limit all or most of your study, business, etc. to a particular subject or activity

specialist *adj.* someone who knows a lot about a particular subject, or is very skilled at it

specification *n.* [C usually plural] a detailed description of how something should be designed or made

staff *n.* [U] the people who work for an organisation or business

stage *n.* [C] one of the parts which something such as a process is divided into

stand your ground to refuse to change your mind about something, even though people are opposing you

standard[1] *adj.* regular and usual in shape, size, quality, etc.

standard[2] *n.* [C] a size, shape, quality, etc. that is usual or accepted, and that can be used to measure or judge something similar

standardisation *n.* [U] the process of making all the things of one particular type the same as each other

standardise *v.* [T] to make all the things of one particular type the same as each other

statistic *n.* [C usually plural] a number that represent a fact or measurement

stay on track to continue to work in a way that makes you likely to achieve the result you want

stock *n.* [C, U] a supply of goods, kept for sale by a shop or other retailer
out of stock not available for sale

stock market *n.* [C usually singular] **1** the business of buying and selling stocks and shares
2 the place where stocks and shares are bought and sold (=**stock exchange**)

strategy *n.* [C] a plan or series of plans for achieving an aim

subsidiary *n.* (*plural* **subsidiaries**) [C] a company that is at least half-owned by another company

sub-supplier *n.* [C] a company that provides a particular type of product to a supplier

sum (something) **up** *phr. v.* to use only a few words to describe something or give the main information from a report, speech, etc.

supplier *n.* [C] a company that provides a particular type of product

supply chain *n.* [C] the series of organisations that are involved in passing products from manufacturers to the public

system *n.* [C] an arrangement or organisation of ideas, methods or ways of working

swipe *v.* [T] to pull a plastic card through a machine that can read the electronic information on it

target[1] *v.* [T] to aim products, something you are doing, etc. at a particular group of people

target[2] *adj.* **target market/customer/group** the group of people that a product, service, idea, etc. is aimed at

target[3] *n.* [C] something that you are trying to achieve, such as a total, an amount, or a time

tax *n.* [C] an amount of money that you must pay to the government according to your income, property, goods, etc., that is used to pay for public services
tax deduction *n.* [C] a part of someone's income that is not taxed, for example because it comes from a particular source, was used for a particular reason, or because they have children

team player *n.* [C] someone who works well as a member of a team, especially in business

technique *n.* [C] a special way of doing something

term *n.* [C] one of the statements of what must be done or is true in an agreement, contract or other legal document
payment terms *n.* [plural] the conditions of a sales agreement that relate to how the customer will pay, and especially how much time is allowed for payment
terms and conditions *n.* [plural] all of the things that must be done as stated in a contract or agreement. If they are not done, the contract or agreement will end.

territory *n.* [C] an area in a town, country, etc. that someone is responsible for as part of their job, especially someone whose job is to sell products

tertiary *adj.* relating to the types of industry that are involved in services, such as the transportation of goods, banking, tourism, etc.

test *v.* [T] to find out what people think about a product, by asking questions about it or by allowing them to use it for a short time

tester *n.* [C] a person or piece of equipment that uses something for a short time to make sure it works properly

testing *n.* [U] the process of checking something to see if it works, if it is suitable, etc.

textile *n.* [C] any type of woven cloth that is made in large quantities

think outside the box to think of new, different or unusual ways of doing something, especially in business

top-of-the-range *adj.* a product that is top-of-the-range is the best and most expensive made by a particular company or available in a particular shop

tour operator *n.* [C] a person or company that organises and provides travel, hotels, visits to places, etc. as their business

trade *n.* [U] the activity of buying, selling or exchanging goods within a country or between countries

trading *n.* [U] the activity of operating as a business and buying and selling goods and services

trainee *n.* [C] someone who is being trained for a job

training [singular, U] the process of teaching or being taught the skills for a particular job or activity

treatment *n.* [U] a particular way of behaving towards someone or of dealing with them

trend *n.* [C] the general way in which a particular situation is changing or developing

unique *adj.* being the only one of its kind

update[1] *v.* [T] to tell someone the most recent information about a situation

update[2] *n.* [C] the most recent information about a situation

user-friendly *adj.* easy to use or operate

vacancy *n.* (*plural* **vacancies**) [C] a job that is available for someone to start doing

value *n.* [C, U] **(good/excellent etc.) value for money** if something is value for money, it is not too expensive and it is of good quality or you get a large amount

visualisation (*also* **visualization**) *n.* [U] the process of forming a picture of something or someone in your mind

volunteer *n.* [C] someone who does a job willingly without being paid
volunteer work *n.* [C] work that you do as a volunteer

wages *n.* [plural] money that someone earns according to the number of hours, days or weeks that they work, especially money that is paid each week

warehouse *n.* [C] a large building used for storing goods in large quantities

wholesaler *n.* [C] a person or company that sells goods in large quantities to businesses, rather than to the general public